NEGRO POLITICS

Negro Politics

THE
SEARCH
FOR
LEADERSHIP

By James Q. Wilson

THE FREE PRESS, *New York*
COLLIER-MACMILLAN LIMITED, *London*

To Roberta

Copyright © 1960 by The Free Press, a Corporation

Printed in the United States of America

Collier-Macmillan Canada, Ltd., Toronto, Ontario

Library of Congress Catalog Card Number: 60-10906

FIRST FREE PRESS PAPERBACK EDITION, 1965

Third printing January 1969

Preface to the Paperback Edition

Any book on Negroes, particularly on their politics, ought to be published in a loose-leaf binder so that it can be corrected and updated on a monthly basis. When the research for this book was done in 1958–1959, many of those interviewed agreed—indeed, many proclaimed—that the most important thing to know about Negro leaders in Chicago was that there weren't any. This was an exaggeration, of course—no one denied the reality of the Dawson political organization, or of the Urban League, or of the NAACP. But with few exceptions, the Negroes with whom I spoke were preoccupied with what they took to be the absence or weakness of Negro leadership in Chicago. The mood of the city, and thus of the book, was that little was changing and little was being attempted.

No one needs to be told that today (May, 1965) there are many vigorous Negro leaders, at least nationally. Events are moving swiftly and a great deal is being attempted. Birmingham, Selma, and Little Rock have become household words. Congress has passed three civil rights acts. Organizations that scarcely existed in 1958—the Southern Christian Leadership Conference, the Student Non-Violent Coordinating Committee—have come to occupy the center of the stage and organizations which did exist (such as CORE) have begun to play a new role. A Negro leader almost unknown in 1958—Malcolm X—rose to prominence, became the symbol of black nationalism, and was assassinated. A young senator became President and was murdered under circumstances which, for a few incredulous hours, led millions to assume—erroneously—that his assassin was a white segregationist. A Southerner became President by succession and was then elected in his own right after a campaign in which civil rights was one of the most important issues.

All these events—and many more—touched Chicago and the

other cities on which this book reports. Chicago today is not quite the same as it was seven years ago. A few of the changes are worth mentioning. (Not all changes are mentioned here and the reader should not assume that things not mentioned have remained the same.)

First, race is a public issue in a way it never was before. Newspapers and television, city council and school board debates, business and civic association meetings resound with an explicit discussion of concrete race issues which once would have been alluded to obliquely, if at all.

Second, certain institutions have become involved in race relations to an extent no one could have foreseen in 1958. Most particularly, the churches—by direct action as well as by conferences—have begun to play a significant role.

Third, certain issues have come to a head. Charges of *de facto* school segregation were made long before 1958; by 1965, however, the issue had intensified to the point where it was perhaps the single most important political controversy in the city. One man—Superintendent of Schools Benjamin Willis—became for Negroes the symbol of white resistance to their demands. The existence of a dramatic, named "enemy" seemed to add strength and unity to the Negro efforts. Demonstrations, picketing, and school boycotts became common weapons in a deepening crisis.

Fourth, new forms of mass organization are visible. Negroes in the Woodlawn section of the South Side began to participate in a power-oriented civic association (The Woodlawn Organization), initially to challenge urban renewal plans associated with the land policies of the University of Chicago and ultimately to challenge city hall on a variety of issues.

Finally, the limits to the influence of the Democratic machine can be seen more clearly. Richard J. Daley continues to preside with great skill over an organization which has brought ward leaders, Democratic voters, and State Street businessmen into a coalition. Some issues—such as a major police scandal—were handled effectively; other issues, however—particularly Negro demands on the public schools—have threatened to tear the organization asunder. The inability (or willingness) of the machine to handle the school crisis suggests that two groups on which the machine depends—lower-income whites and lower-income Negroes—may be so passionately at odds on this issue that no way can be found to reconcile them.

Furthermore, as the Negro community continues to grow in size and as many (but not all) Negroes continue to rise in income and education, the reach of the Dawson Negro organization falters. The old core South Side wards—the 2nd, the 3rd, the 20th—continue to deliver massive pluralities for the organization ticket, but farther South, in Wards 8 and 17, where more and more middle-class Negroes are found, the organization is barely holding its own. In the 1964 Democratic primary, Congressman Dawson was challenged by another Negro backed by civil rights groups. Although the challenger lost two-to-one in the district as a whole, he carried the middle-class Negro precincts of Ward 8 and elsewhere.

Taking all this into account, the reader might assume that this book is now an historical study, analyzing the politics of a bygone era. This, for better or worse, is not the case. Dramatic as some changes have been, the major dimensions of the political system have remained the same. The constraints of party organization, the division of leaders, differences in goals and tactics, and the maintenance needs of civic associations continue to operate. Although the "Negro revolution" of 1963–1964 profoundly affected the mood, the tempo, and the tone of race relations in Chicago, that "revolution" was a *national* phenomenon which may have stimulated an increase in the pressure on local institutions but which did not fundamentally change those institutions, particularly in the North. The organization of Richard Daley and William Dawson may have faltered, but it has hardly collapsed. Its very existence some militants regard as an outrage, but they have been unable to either defeat it or devise a constructive alternative. The twofold challenge it now faces is perhaps more serious than any with which it had to deal in the past: Can the ward leaders and precinct captains find the terms on which whites and Negroes will continue to support a common slate of candidates? Can (or will) the organization find ways to absorb or co-opt the newer, more militant aspirants for influence in the Negro community? Despite the great events of the last seven years, no answer is yet possible to either question.

James Q. Wilson

Cambridge, Mass., 1965

Acknowledgments

MANY people have been of great help in this study. Most of them cannot be thanked by name, as their anonymity was one of the conditions of their co-operation. They know who they are, they will see themselves in this work, and I only hope they will receive it kindly. Not all of them will agree with what I have said. Whatever controversy this book provokes can, I believe, be of value to all men concerned with the grave problem of race relations.

Others who were not informants improved this study by their advice and help and can be thanked personally. Foremost among these are Professor Edward C. Banfield and Dr. Peter B. Clark. To both I owe a great debt for encouragement, criticism, suggestions, and questions. The impress of both men is on almost every page, and it is only in the conventional and narrowest sense that I can absolve them of responsibility for the final product.

Others have read the manuscript in whole or in part, and it has benefited substantially from their advice. These include Professors Grant McConnell, Charles M. Hardin, Norton E. Long, Charles Adrian, Edward A. Shils, Wallace B. Sayre, and Robert A. Dahl.

I wish to express my appreciation to the University of Chicago and to its Social Science Research Committee for financial assistance.

To my wife, I am indebted for help beyond statement or measure.

Contents

NEGRO POLITICS

Chapter I

Introduction

THIS is a study of a phenomenon which many people believe does not exist. Anyone wishing to examine Negro
leadership in a city such as Chicago will be met at the outset
with the assertion, particularly from intellectual Negroes, that
"there is no Negro leadership." At the same time, the person
who makes this comment will very likely be himself a member
of the NAACP (National Association for the Advancement of
Colored People) or the Urban League, or perhaps both; he will
be a member of one of the major political parties, probably the
Democratic; he will often be in a fraternity, an organization which
exists largely as a part of adult, rather than student, life; he
may well be a member of a social club, a church, one or more
organizations affiliated with the church, or a lodge; if he is a
worker, he will likely be a union member; if he is a businessman, he will probably belong to a chamber of commerce; and
it would not be unusual if he were a supporter of the YMCA,
a boys' club, a settlement house, a professional society, a neighborhood block club, or a conservation association. Each of these
organizations will almost inevitably be led, at least at the local
level, by a Negro. These men are, in some sense, Negro leaders.

What is meant, of course, is that there are no "good" Negro
leaders — leaders who are selflessly devoted to causes which
will benefit Negroes as a race and as a community.

One will also be told that Negroes are "unorganized." But
the simplest reckoning of the number of organizations in a Negro
community will immediately suggest that this comment, like the

3

one about leadership, cannot be taken at face value. In 1937, when Chicago had only 275,000 Negroes, an actual count revealed more than 4,000 formal associations among them.*[1] Today, when the Negro population is about three times as large, there seems to be little doubt that the number of organizations is also comparably greater. In comparison with white communities of equivalent size, there is some evidence that Negroes are organized to an even greater extent than whites.[2] Although Negroes, like whites, are more organized among middle-class than lower-class groups, on the whole, Negroes are fully as inclined to join associations as whites.[3] The Negro community, whatever else its problems, is not characterized by an inability to create and sustain at least some kinds of organizations. What the Negro critics who argue that the Negro is "unorganized" mean is that he is not organized as a community to seek ends of benefit to the community or the race as a whole. There can be little doubt that the great majority of Negro associations have purposes other than Negro protest or improvement, and that these associations consume much of the time and money of Negroes which, their critics argue, should be devoted to race ends. Periodically, attempts are made to alter this, either by starting a new organization which will be *the* organization for the betterment of Negroes and to which all Negroes can flock, regardless of their special interests, or by creating an "umbrella" organization which will "co-ordinate" the plethora of existing Negro associations into collective action for communal goals. Such organizations have not endured.

There are, nonetheless, leaders and organizations in Chicago which act as if the betterment of the Negro community were their goals. Civic issues are raised in the Negro community, or forced upon it, and Negroes step forward who attempt to deal with them. The Negro newspaper rarely lets a week pass without printing several stories in which Negroes are named as "civic leaders." Although the NAACP can rarely attract as many as fifty people to its meetings, there is keen—even fierce—competition for office, with alternative slates of candidates developing elaborate campaigns to insure election. Testimonial banquets at which Negro civic leaders are honored occur almost weekly.

*Notes are printed by chapter at the end of the book.

Plaques and awards for civic leadership are periodically distributed by innumerable groups in the Negro community. On the boards of such organizations as the Urban League are Negroes who busy themselves raising money, speaking at meetings, and discussing issues in committees. In some sense, civic activity is going on ceaselessly. Something is happening.

But although activity is evident, little seems to occur as a result of this activity. Provident Hospital, an all-Negro institution in Chicago which is filled to overflowing with Negroes seeking medical aid, has great difficulty in raising its budget, and must rely heavily on white charity. The Joint Negro Appeal, organized to help support welfare services in the Negro community, experiences great difficulty in raising $25,000 from a community of 750,000 people. The local branch of the NAACP has until recently been unable to create and sustain even a modest staff of workers to deal with the problems which that organization attempts to act on. The Urban League, which for about forty years has provided a variety of services to Negroes which no other agency offered, could not in a typical year in the recent past raise $10,000 from Negroes as their contribution to a budget which was fixed at between $80,000 and $90,000. Although perhaps 300 Negro lawyers live in Chicago, the NAACP can rarely find more than three or four who will assist in the work of providing legal defense for Negroes who are the victims of racial persecution. Despite the fact that Negroes number about one-fifth of the total population of Chicago, and have in their midst one of the most powerful and well-organized political machines in the United States, the larger race problems rarely receive legislative treatment or even discussion from governmental authorities. No effective fair employment practices act exists; medical services are largely segregated; and the housing market is based on strong racial barriers.

Faced with this situation, a deep sense of frustration, anger, and despair overcomes many thoughtful Negroes. Expressions of distrust, cynicism, and even hostility against other Negroes are not infrequently encountered. The extent to which there is widespread private criticism by Negroes of Negroes as a race is remarkable, and more and more this criticism is being made public. Ralph Ellison, in his novel, *Invisible Man,*[4] draws bitter portraits of a Negro college president, a minister, and a politician. The letters to the editor columns in the Negro newspapers have racial criticism as one of their principal themes. Public meetings of Negroes rarely are without hostile reference to those Negroes who have had the advantages of education, wealth, or position but who have not turned back to help other Negroes— who have, in Negro phraseology, become "dicty" or "silk-stocking."

Powerful constraints work against Negro influence in civic and political affairs—race prejudice, class differences, geographic concentration, and a weak economic position—but a thorough inquiry into the course of specific civic issues in which Negro interests are involved strongly suggests that these external or environmental constraints are not sufficient to explain the lack of Negro effectiveness in the public life of the community. Efforts by Negroes to deal with race relations in a northern city are not simply blocked by hostile forces, although powerful obstacles are undoubtedly raised. In part, Negro civic action is hampered by constraints inside the Negro community. Some of the important obstacles to civic action are products of the Negro's own community and way of life. Segregation may enforce, or even at some point in time create, the Negro community as it exists today, but within that community alternative modes of behavior are still possible. Segregation is a great determinant of Negro life in the city, but it is not an invariable determinant. Different responses to this single fact are possible and these different responses can be discovered. The Negro may live in a prison, as a Negro author wrote, but "the prison is vast, there is plenty of space."[5]

The classic and most widely accepted statement of the nature of race relations in America has been that of Gunnar Myrdal. To Myrdal, race relations are not a "Negro problem." There is no Negro problem in America. Rather, it is a "white man's problem." The white man has imposed a way of life on the Negro which is at variance with the "American creed" the white man himself espouses, and it is the responsibility of the white man to formulate a more adequate and morally correct treatment of the Negro.[6] This may correctly describe the ultimate cause of the race problem in America and accurately forecast the changes which must eventually occur if the problem is to be solved. However, the immediate problem is what can and should be done to deal with the situation as it exists today. Most thoughtful Negroes in the North long ago rejected the notion that the white man will gradually concede to them the rights they demand without effort on their part. A need is seen for vigorous Negro action to aid in the realization of these goals. In Chicago, such action has been manifestly lacking on the part of Negroes—more so, as will be suggested in later chapters, than in some other large northern cities. Whatever the ultimate cause of the race problem, the present question concerns what is being done about it today. The answer to this question indicates that in addition to the "white man's problem," there is also a "Negro problem." That problem is the difficulty in generating vigorous and prolonged civic action toward race goals. The civic life of a community—the raising, agitating, and disposing of issues—is carried on by civic leaders. Negro civic leaders in Chicago have not been able, by and large, to create and sustain a vigorous civic life. In some sense, Negro critics of their own leaders may be right: there may well be a scarcity of able and creative leadership.

If Negro civic action is truly less effective than it might be, it becomes important to know why. Many have explained all such shortcomings on the ground that the obstacles created by whites prevent the accomplishment of any more than is already being attempted. It will be argued here that the ghetto has a life and a logic of its own, apart from whatever whites might do to create and maintain the outer walls of it. It is the task of this study to explore the state of Negro civic and political leadership, assess its strength and effectiveness, and account for whatever weaknesses or conflicts might be found.

It must be said at the outset that no full explanation of the problems of Negro civic life can be given. We shall examine many aspects of that life, suggest some of the forces and constraints at work, but we cannot answer the most fundamental question: why is that life the way it is? Hopefully, in studying the problem and approaching, in tentative and uncertain steps, the elusive answer, some light will be thrown on the structure and processes of influence in a large Negro community. It will not be argued that everything to be discussed about Negroes is peculiar to them alone, or that the simple fact of being a Negro in some way creates difficulties for the attainment of civic ends that white leaders do not face. On the contrary, many of the problems of and constraints on Negro leaders are precisely those which confront any civic leader seeking to mobilize or to represent a community. In some cases (and in many of the more interesting cases), the fact of being a Negro accentuates and even exaggerates these problems for a variety of reasons. Being a Negro is not the sole factor which occasions perplexities for civic leaders, but neither is it an insignificant one. Some of these factors include the widely shared beliefs about the proper stance and goals of Negro leadership; the direction which the aspirations of the recently successful Negroes take; and the social distance which exists, because of the color line, between Negroes and whites who are concerned with the same issues. The Negro leader is judged by harsher standards than are white civic leaders, in part because more is believed to be at stake and in part because Negro leaders are conspicuous for having advantages that the rank-and-file lack. As will be indicated later, the process of diversification and stratification which would be normal in any community is resisted by Negro opinion; advantage is suspect, and achievement is publicly praised but privately deprecated.

Several levels of explanation for the pattern of Negro public life are possible. Perhaps the most fruitful would emerge from an intimate and prolonged inquiry into the ethos of Negro life in the city—a study which would illuminate the elemental forms of Negro organized life in somewhat the same manner that William Whyte explored the young Italo-American men in *Street Corner Society*. Another perspective might come from an investigation of the economic position of the Negro and the pattern of aspirations which sudden urban prosperity produces in people accustomed to great rural deprivation. Undoubtedly a cultural history of the American Negro could be written that would describe the kinds of values perpetuated in his culture, stemming from early family and plantation experience and responding to the different forms of society and personal relationships of the city. The northern Negro community could be viewed as a system of migration, in which rural in-migrants arrive, come to terms with the community in some fashion, and begin to move from the crowded "ports of entry" in the Negro areas of the city to the more desirable areas on the periphery—acquiring urban traits and leaving a rural imprint in return.

The purpose of this study is to examine Negro public life at the level of leadership as one of many possible levels of description. These leaders cannot be divorced from the community and culture which produced them; at the same time, they are a more or less identifiable group of men and women involved in a more or less common set of circumstances—civic issues and civic associations—which raises problems, creates opportunities, and poses threats that elicit interesting and informative reactions. They stand on the border between the white and the Negro world, and must interpret each world to the other. The bones of civic affairs and race relations are fleshed out with the thoughts and actions of these people. An inquiry into Negro civic life can usefully begin with Negro leaders, in whom one can see both the impact of the "white problem" and the constraints of the "Negro problem." The task before us is to describe the opportunities and problems of Negro leaders and analyze what they seek and the means they employ.

To accomplish this, the barriers to civic betterment which are raised and maintained by the white community must be described insofar as they are relevant to Negro leadership and politics. Chicago will be placed in a context of several large northern cities, both politically (in Chapter II) and civically (in Chapter V). These brief surveys will suggest that, although Chicago presents as many or more barriers to Negro integration as do other cities, the size or strength of those barriers is not a sufficient explanation for the state of Negro civic and political activity. In some cities the obstacles are fewer but Negro civic leadership is weaker than in Chicago, and in other cities the obstacles are greater but the civic action is more vigorous. The bulk of the book, then, will concern the factors conditioning Negro public life internal to the Negro community, and for this purpose, Chicago will be the focus of the study.

In singling out Chicago for detailed analysis, there is inevitably the risk that it will appear to be more fragmented and complex, with more problems and conflicts, than other cities examined in less detail and with greater perspective in time and distance. It is believed that this problem does not vitiate the most important comparisons drawn between Chicago and other cities, but the *caveat* should be borne in mind nonetheless.

We shall not begin with definitions, as the leaders selected for research in Chicago were not chosen by the application to the Negro community of a single concept of leadership. Rather, a list was compiled which started with those Negroes who were reputed to be civic leaders as indicated by newspaper accounts and the roster of officers of various Negro voluntary associations and political organizations. The list was built up by adding to it names of Negroes who were participating in specific civic issues in some capacity, as well as Negroes who were named by other Negro leaders as being leaders in some sense. A list of 105 names was prepared. The haphazard manner in which it was compiled appears to have presented no serious problems, for by the end of the process, closure was, for all practical purposes, reached — the continued examination of civic issues and the further questioning of Negro leaders as to the identity of other leaders failed to produce more than one or two names which were not already on the list.

In all cases, the leaders selected were those who could be described as *civic* leaders — that is, leaders who acted as if the interests of the race or the community were their goals. Excluded were the officers of benevolent and fraternal associations except when such men were active with relation to some issue or participated in voluntary associations which were involved in community affairs. The list of 105 names can be divided into two broad categories: *lay leaders* and *professional leaders*. The lay leaders were those who volunteered for civic work as activity separate from their normal employment. They may have volunteered in hopes of .a reward, tangible or intangible; this is an empirical question which will be dealt with in the study. But whatever rewards they may have sought, it was not their regular means of livelihood. This group numbered 64, and included 19 businessmen, 11 lawyers, 10 ministers, 8 doctors, 8 labor leaders, 3 government employees, 3 housewives, and 2 teachers.

The second major group were the professional leaders. These were paid to act in a civic capacity or to take an interest in civic affairs. This group numbered 41, and included 21 politicians holding elective or appointive offices, 7 staff members of voluntary associations, 7 government bureaucrats working for agencies explicitly concerned with the field of race relations, and 6 journalists.

Of 105 on the list, 95 were interviewed at length. These interviews were loosely structured explorations of the issue-involvement of the respondent. No fixed interview schedule was employed; each interview was designed to elicit from the particular individual the activities and issues that most concerned him and in which he played some role. Each was asked, in various ways, to describe and explain his involvement or lack of involvement, his attitudes toward the issue, the goals he sought, the means he favored using, what in fact he had done about the issues, how he saw the other actors involved in the issue, what opinion he had about the ultimate resolution of the issue, what work he did in his organization, and so on. The interviews ran, in length, from forty-five minutes (in a few cases) to more than twenty hours (in one case). The average interview consumed about an hour and a half. In addition, interviews were held with white persons involved in these issues, as well as with other Negroes who were not in leadership positions. In each case, the responses of the interviewee were recorded in as nearly verbatim form as possible.

To orient the reader certain background information on the Negro respondents will be quickly given. Most were born in the South and came north to Chicago in the great wave of Negro migration that was occasioned by the first World War and the period of prosperity that followed it. Of those not born in the South, most were born elsewhere than in Chicago—mostly in other portions of the Middle West. Most were college educated, and many had professional or graduate-school education. The group as a whole was conspicuously part of the Negro middle and upper class, and partook of many of the attributes discussed in other analyses of social stratification among Negroes.[7] The income, education, and occupation of most of the Negro civic leaders qualifies them for this label, although exceptions can be readily found. Like other middle- and upper-class Negroes, Chicago Negro leaders show religious preferences different from those of the rank-and-file. Where the bulk of the Negro populace that is church-affiliated is Baptist, the Negro civic leaders interviewed were much more likely to be members of the Negro upper-class churches—Episcopalian, Presbyterian, Congregational, Lutheran, and Roman Catholic. These churches, to which only 10 per cent of the Negro populace belongs, claimed the majority of *lay* civic leaders. The Baptist denomination was largely represented by civic leaders who were ministers of that faith, plus some others—such as several politicians—who were also members. The Negro civic leader was often prominent as a deacon, trustee, or committee chairman of his church.

Each of the Negro Greek-letter fraternities has an active chapter in Chicago, and large numbers of Negro civic leaders were members. The extent of their affiliation varied from great activity—one man was cited as "Man of the Year" by his fraternity—to membership in name only. There are also several local social clubs for men, three or four of which are quite old and exclusive. Many Negro civic leaders were well-known members of these clubs.

An interesting and important fact is that the social distance which usually separates, in the white community, the lay civic leaders from the professional politicians is not so evident in the Negro community. In Chicago, the white businessmen who are active in civic affairs belong to clubs where few, if any, ward politicians are ever found. It is a major and newsworthy event when the Mayor addresses a meeting of one of the more exclusive of such clubs. Among Negroes, much greater social contact takes place between political and civic leaders. Many belong to the same clubs. The lavish winter formal dances of these clubs or fraternities often attract both civic leaders and politicians. This is not to say that the civic leaders and the politicians do not have divergent interests and styles of civic action; we do suggest that the wide separation between those formally influential (the politicians) and those informally influential (the civic leaders) which has occurred in most large American cities is much less in evidence in the Negro community. Civic life is largely within the province of a single class. This condition makes all the more remarkable the fact that in many situations Negro civic leaders and Negro politicians co-operate very little, and quite often are intensely antagonistic.

The Negro community has changed over the years, largely as a result of increasing prosperity, and these changes are reflected in the recruitment of civic leaders. The old occupational elites—the postal workers, the pullman porters, the undertakers—which formerly provided much of the civic leadership have to a great extent been replaced by persons of higher status—executives of Negro insurance companies, successful Negro real estate brokers, lawyers, doctors, and manufacturers. Even among the politicians, who in the lean years of the past were often drawn from the ranks of the uneducated and unemployed, there are growing numbers of young lawyers and professional men.

Another important factor is that, for the most part, the Negro leadership does not—cannot—live apart from the Negro masses. There are Negro "suburbs" in Chicago, but most Negro civic leaders and all Negro politicians live within the "Black Belt." There are pockets of upper-class dwelling units—the Lake Meadows apartment project, Kenwood, South Parkway—but they are tiny enclaves surrounded by the manifestly lower-income areas where most of the Negroes of Chicago live. For the Negro leader it is difficult to retreat physically from the life of the ghetto and contact with the Negro masses; they are everywhere about him, visible and numerous. With a few exceptions, escape from the ghetto can only be psychological, reinforced by a style of life which endeavors to exclude from the senses as much as possible the evidence of life in decaying neighborhoods. Even psychological escape is difficult and anxious when physical escape is almost impossible, and the resulting tensions are reflected in the often bitter comments of Negro leaders about the quality of the Negro masses which everywhere and in everything seem to follow and engulf them.

The Negro civic leaders were involved in a sizeable number of issues that were current during 1958-59 when this research was done. Those who hope to find a description of a Negro "power structure" in this study will be disappointed, however. Each issue brought forward a different set of leaders; each issue elicited a slightly different pattern of actions and fell into the province of different organizations. All that can be said with certainty about structure is that if one knows the nature of the issue, one can usually predict which group or what kind of group of Negroes will become involved. About seventeen civic issues were examined with varying degrees of thoroughness in the course of the study. They ranged from those in which Negroes were only tangentially in- volved to those which struck directly at the core of race relations in the city. The issues were almost evenly divided between those in which Negroes acted reflexively (i.e., responded to changes in the status quo proposed by white groups) and those in which Negroes acted assertively (i.e., proposed changes in the status quo.) Some issues concerned lofty principles of integration and equality; others related to the material well-being of Negroes; still others involved the business or personal interests of small groups of Negroes. They will not be described in historical terms as case studies; rather, the data gathered from an inquiry into their course will provide illustrations and evidence regarding kinds of attitudes and behavior evinced by Negro civic leaders in Chicago. For reference purposes, it might be useful to list the issues under six general categories:

A. *Housing*
   1. Proposed legislation to achieve "open occupancy" in the Chicago real estate market, freeing sales and rentals from racial discrimination
   2. Efforts to integrate public housing and to build public hous- ing in white neighborhoods
   3. Problems of Negro relocation from an urban renewal project
   4. Impact upon Negroes of an urban redevelopment project

B. *Police*
   1. Demands for protection against anti-Negro violence
   2. Complaints about alleged police maltreatment of Negroes
   3. Problems of vice in certain Negro neighborhoods
   4. Efforts of certain Negroes to have particular kinds of Negro taxicabs (the "jitneys") removed from streets in Negro neighborhoods

C. *Employment*
   1. Efforts to obtain passage of a state FEPC law
   2. Efforts to secure promotions for Negroes in the city police and fire departments
   3. A campaign to induce white banks to hire Negroes

D. *Education*

    1. A campaign to build a new vocational school in the Negro community

    2. Negro complaints of racial discrimination in public schools

E. *Medicine*

    1. Efforts to eliminate alleged racial discrimination in patient admissions and staff appointments in white private hospitals

    2. Charges that a plan to build a branch of the county hospital on the South Side involved an effort to give Negroes a segregated hospital

F. *Business*

    1. Efforts to form a conservation group to improve neighborhoods and property values in Negro areas

    2. Efforts to reduce alleged anti-Negro policies governing the sale of fire insurance in the Negro community

In analyzing the material which emerges from the history of these issues, the principal questions to be asked at every point are: what do the Negroes *want?* what *can* the Negroes do? what *do* the Negroes do? The answers to these questions will provide some measure of the character of civic affairs in the Negro community. We shall see that in almost every case there exists a "white problem"—anti-Negro attitudes, the exclusion of Negroes from positions of influence, threats of violence directed against Negroes, beliefs concerning the low standards prevailing among Negroes, refusal to deal with race relations, and so on. We shall also see a concomitant phenomenon inextricably bound up with it, a "Negro problem"—the difficulty in concerting action toward agreed goals with adequate support and some degree of persistence.

Any attempt to formulate conclusions on such matters must proceed in constant awareness of certain fundamental problems that affect research in Negro public life. First is the elementary but important problem of recognizing the steady tensions between Negroes *qua* Negroes and Negroes acting a variety of specific roles. In most cases, and for most purposes, the Negro politician acts as politicians do anywhere. Similarly, the Negro businessman is, in most of his activities, principally a businessman, and this, too, is a role with fairly stable expectations. Both the Negro

politician and the Negro businessman are, because they play
certain clear roles which are common and well understood, reasonably easy to describe and analyze. They are, nonetheless, *Negro*
politicians and *Negro* businessmen, and at some point it inevitably
becomes important.

The role of the lay civic leader, however, is much more ambiguous. As Clark has observed, one can do almost anything
that is loosely "public" and be called a "civic leader."[8] This is
true among Negroes as well as among whites, but the fact takes
on singular importance in the Negro community. Because the
role of "civic leader" is vague and ambiguous, the consequences
of being a Negro become much clearer. If the role does not define what one should do, race values will; the latter provide much
of the content which the former, by default, does not provide.
Here the implications of being a Negro are important and, because
these implications are so various and subtle, the problems of
describing Negro civic leaders becomes difficult. There is no
simple "civic leader" role which one can picture, and then apply
it to Negroes and their public lives; it is hard to describe the
former, because it is vague, and even harder to analyze the latter, because it is elusive.

A second problem reflects the bias of the observer. It is important to portray the immense complexity and diversity of public life in the Negro community—in part to provide a necessary
balance to those accounts which speak of a monolithic, undifferentiated "Negro community" or "Negro leaders," and in part
simply to provide an awareness of the great richness of detail
and texture which characterizes Negroes. But to focus on diversity leads, inevitably, to an emphasis on diversity, and this can
obscure or conceal the important strands of unity and purpose
which do exist. Negro end conflicts can be described, but only
a reading of the interview documents themselves can give an
appreciation of the extent to which there is a commonality of
interest and an evident concern about matters of importance to
the race and the community. An attempt is made to build an
argument about diversity, and this serves a certain purpose; that
purpose, however, should not be allowed to obscure all other
points of view. In particular, it should not be allowed to obliter-
ate the important point that no matter how different may be the

expression of values, issues, ends, or means, every Negro interviewed wishes to reduce the extent to which his color is held against him as a man. When read from this standpoint, the interview materials show a relatively high level of concern about race problems and a more or less acute feeling of the problems and obstacles that confront attempts at improvement.

The study is in three parts. The first three chapters comprise a description of the political organization of the Negro community. They begin with an overview of the impact of northern metropolitan political systems on Negro politics and proceed to a detailed examination of how in one of those communities, Chicago, Negroes function within that system. The second three chapters are a discussion of the organization of Negro civic life and Negro-white relations. Here we shall meet the groups and leaders who carry on community-serving enterprises. This section of the book begins with a summary of some of the important *external* determinants of Negro civic leadership (principally the pattern of segregation) found in several northern cities, and proceeds to an analysis of civic life in Chicago as it occurs within the limits imposed by these constraints. In the third section, the preceding descriptive material is cross-cut by an analysis of the principal dimensions of leadership: the ends leaders endeavor to serve and the conflicts among those ends, the means they adopt ("political styles"), and the functions different leaders serve (types of Negro leaders). The principal themes of this analysis are brought together in an additional chapter. Finally, summary observations are offered and some trends suggested.*

---

* The research on Chicago took place during 1958-59. Research in other northern cities (Detroit, Los Angeles, and New York) was conducted during the summer of 1959, and consisted of a number of interviews with selected civic and political leaders in each city. My analysis of the situation in each city was then circulated to the people interviewed, as well as to others, for comment. Although not all their suggestions have been adopted, each was given careful consideration.

Quoted material which appears without footnote citation in the following pages is taken from interview documents in the possession of the author.

PART ONE

THE ORGANIZATION OF
NEGRO POLITICAL LIFE

Chapter II

Negro Politics in the North

C HICAGO, Detroit, Los Angeles, and New York are important centers of Negro population. Although the proportion of Negroes living in these cities is not as high as elsewhere, in total numbers they are among the very largest.[*1] Political activity in these Negro communities is generally high. Three of the four cities have sent a Negro to the United States House of Representatives.[2] In two of the cities, the Negro political leader is a nationally known figure—William L. Dawson in Chicago and Adam Clayton Powell, Jr., in New York. In each city except Los

---

*1. The Negro population of these four cities, during the period 1955-1957 for which the last estimates are available, is approximately as follows:

City	Negro Population	Per Cent of City Total	Per Cent Increase, 1950-56
Chicago	631,750	18.0	22.1
Detroit	400,000	22.0	24.1
Los Angeles	254,595	11.3	32.8
New York	948,196	12.2	21.2

Sources: Chicago — Otis Dudley Duncan and Beverly Duncan, *The Negro Population of Chicago* (Chicago: University of Chicago Press, 1957), p. 29. The estimate is for 1955. *Detroit* — average of estimates supplied by the Human Relations Commission and Professor Albert Mayer of Wayne State University. *Los Angeles* — the figures are from the 1956 Special Census of Los Angeles. *New York* — the figures are from the 1956 Special Census of New York City (all five boroughs). The data, in each case, are for the *city* (not the Standard Metropolitan Area) and for *Negroes* (not non-whites). Other sources of estimates are Morton Grodzins, "Metropolitan Segregation," *Scientific American*, October, 1957, pp. 33-41, and R. Norgren et al, *Employing Negroes in American Industry* (New York: Industrial Relations Counsellors, Inc., 1959), p. 161.

21

Angeles at least one Negro sits on the City Council, and in
Chicago there are six. Each city sends at least one, and usually
more, Negroes to the state legislature. Negro judges sit on the
bench in each of the four cities. In every case except Los Angeles,
the Negro voters comprise one of the largest single ethnic groups
in the central city electorate and a group that is rapidly growing
both in absolute size and as a proportion of the total population.
This growth, accompanied by the retreat of whites from the periphery of Negro areas, means, among other things, that the size
of Negro political representation at all levels of government will
continue to grow. In just the four cities under consideration,
there are at least six Congressional districts in which substantial
numbers of Negroes already live and which are generally expected
to elect Negro politicians in the near future.

The growing number of Negroes in northern cities suggests
the increased possibility that Negro political power will become
a decisive factor in the quest for race goals. Political leadership,
based on this large electorate, might presumably be a potent force
for change. This chapter will discuss the general features of Negro
political leadership in several large northern cities as a prelude
to a more detailed analysis of Negro politics in Chicago. In these
chapters, we shall suggest that Negro political influence has not
grown in proportion to the numbers of Negro voters, that the
emerging Negro political leadership has thus far (in most cases)
not been an effective agent for social change, and that the reasons for this are to be found in the nature of political organization itself. The limitations on political influence are a product,
first, of the political system of the particular city, and second,
of the constraints imposed by the requirements for maintaining a political organization.

The Structure of Negro Politics

The most important single conclusion that emerges from a
survey of Negro politics in large northern cities is that, in all
cases, the structure and style of Negro politics reflect the politics of
the city as a whole. Politics for the Negro, as for other ethnic
groups before him, can be viewed as a set of "learned responses"
which he acquires from the distinctive political system of the city
in which he lives.

Negro politics cannot be understood apart from the city in which it is found. This suggests, happily, that by examining Negro politics on a comparative basis we are at the same time examining American city politics. It also implies that research on this topic must be much broader than the subject itself indicates. The student must cast a wide net; inquiry must begin with the city as a whole in order to understand fully the actions and problems of Negro politicians in that city. This point, obvious by itself, takes on added significance when one considers the nature of the organization and the means by which it induces workers and voters to contribute to it, the pattern of Negro registration and voting, and the relative strength and unity (or weakness and disunity) of the organization.

The Negro political organization is created and shaped by the political organization of the city. The existence of a Negro machine, as in Chicago, is dependent upon the existence of a white machine. Machine politics requires a centralization of leadership, a sizeable stock of tangible incentives with which to reward contributors, a large group of people in the city who would be attracted by the kinds of rewards a political machine can distribute, and (usually) a ward or district system of selecting party leaders, aldermen, and candidates for public office. The prior existence of a machine, operating under such conditions, means that the entry of Negroes into politics will take place under the forms and rules already established. Where various factors have weakened the city organization and produced a situation of factional rivalry and imperfect solidarity, the Negro political organization will be similarly gripped by internecine warfare and competing leaders. This is the case in Manhattan, where the city organization is weak—i.e., it cannot enforce its rules on its members or maintain an undisputed single leadership. There, the elements of machine politics have been decaying rapidly, and the results are evident in white and Negro areas. In Los Angeles and Detroit, where almost none of the elements of machine control exists, the politics of the city as a whole is characterized by *ad hoc* groupings which come into being in election years to elect good-government, economy-minded leaders whose appeal must be largely based on personality, issues, and newspaper influence. Negroes, where they can enter this kind of political system at all, are forced to do so on its own terms and with the limited resources at hand. No Negro "boss" can spring up where there is not already a white boss. When a strong civil service system, a mobile and prosperous electorate, and a long tradition of "public relations politics" exist as in Los Angeles, Negroes must play the game by the same rules and under the same conditions. In doing so, of course, they are placed at a profound disadvantage.

The most important modification of the statement that Negro politics in northern cities is a reflection of the politics of the cities as a whole is the general time lag in the entry of Negroes into positions of political influence.

Contributing to this lag is the operation of those same factors which have delayed the entry of other, earlier ethnic groups. Big city politics often takes the form of a succession of new arrivals each trying to scale the same ladder of political achievement by pressing those above them for "recognition." Resistance to Negroes is not, in part, different from the general resistance put up by (for example) the Irish political leadership of the big city to the demands for political recognition expressed by Poles, Italians, or Germans. Little is given without a struggle, even when the maintenance needs of the political organization as a whole would seem to require it. The personal interests of those who hold the higher positions inevitably tend to override the organizational interests of the machine which provides them with those positions. In the case of the Negro, however, this resistance is intensified by the frequent operation of personal prejudice and hostility. Negro entry into politics thus far has been less than proportional to their numbers, as expressed in the size of their contribution to the Democratic vote in city elections. Often, as in Chicago's 24th Ward, Los Angeles' 55th and 63rd Assembly Districts, and parts of New York's 13th Assembly District, Negroes can be the largest group in the political unit long before they manage to take control of the leadership of that unit.[3] This is true, again, because Negro voters—unless they are made the objects of really intense, well-led organizational campaigns—will not vote along strictly racial lines in a Negro-white contest, especially when it occurs at the bottom of the ticket in the seemingly unimportant race for ward committeeman or district leader.

In addition to political resistance stiffened by personal hostility and prejudice, another factor works to delay Negro entry into political organizations. Negroes—whose income and educational levels are almost always among the lowest in the city and whose rural background deprives them of sophistication in the ways of the city—are often hard to organize for political ends. Many of them doubt that politics offers any real opportunities. The difficulty in building a Negro organization *from outside the machine* which will then make a bid for recognition and power has been discovered many times in all four cities. This obstacle makes all the more remarkable the achievement of William Dawson of Chicago in rising to power in the 1930's from a powerless base. The aid of Mayor Edward Kelly, valuable as it may have been, was no guarantee of success—if only because of the large number of Negro rivals to Dawson whose factional fights could easily have paralyzed all attempts at coherent organization. In non-machine or weak-machine cities, the active intervention of another strong force which has a vested interest in mobilizing Negroes seems to be necessary to bring them into important political roles. In Detroit, this has been the function of the CIO. In Los Angeles, where no machine and no intervening organization exists, Negro political organization becomes an immensely difficult task.

The time lag characterizing Negro entry into northern politics has not been uniform in all cities. Negroes held important political offices in Chicago long before they did in New York, and Negroes emerged in New York before they were active in Los Angeles or Detroit. To account for these differences, three factors, in addition to the political organization of the city, appear to be important: (a) the rate of in-migration, (b) the density of the Negro area, and (c) the size of the basic political unit.

In Chicago, Negro entry occurred as early as 1915 when a Negro was elected to the City Council, and later (in 1920) another became a ward committeeman (the real center of political power in the Chicago wards). The powerful city machine was at that time firmly in the hands of the Republicans, and thus the Negro political leaders were at first Republicans. Their entry was partly a reflection of the need of the city organization to insure its strength in the Negro wards by co-opting Negro leaders, and it was partly a product of a bitter struggle by Negroes to gain "recognition" in politics against the opposition of established non-Negro leaders. The machine system in the Negro wards solidified as early as 1920, and by 1928 Negroes were able to elect a member of their own race to Congress.

The relatively early date by which Negroes were able to gain elective office in Chicago, as compared to other northern cities, can be explained by the fact that (a) the concentration of Negroes in one or a few all-Negro areas was, from the first, higher in Chicago and (b) the Chicago political system was based on a large number of relatively small wards usually drawn to conform to the racial, nationality, or religious character of the neighborhood. This demographic concentration in small political units facilitated the entry of Negroes into politics in Chicago, while relatively less concentrated Negro population centers in cities with large districts (or, in some cases, no districts at all) meant that Negro entry was greatly delayed. This was the case in New York, and to an even greater extent in Detroit and Los Angeles.

New York, with even more Negroes than Chicago, and with a political system somewhat comparable, did not have a Negro district leader in Tammany Hall until 1935, and it did not have a second until 1941. In part, this reflected the relatively larger size of New York districts as compared to Chicago wards. This size facilitated a process of gerrymandering that worked to exclude Negroes from important posts. Furthermore, New York districts have been, and still are, divided into halves or even thirds for leadership purposes in order to find compromises between the competing claims of various ethnic groups residing in the district. Thus, a district containing significant numbers of Negroes, Italians, and Jews would be split into three parts, and each part given to a Negro, an Italian, and a Jewish leader. In turn, the single vote which that district had in Tammany Hall would be split into three one-third votes. This often worked to weaken the influence of Negroes even after they had captured a leadership. For this and other reasons which will be taken up later, Negro influence in Tammany was less and increased more slowly than Negro influence in the Cook County Central Committee in Chicago. The first Negro Congressman from New York was not chosen until 1944, after redistricting had created a new Congressional District with a Negro majority. Other things being equal, Negro political strength in city organizations tends to be directly proportional to the size and density of the Negro population, and inversely proportional to the size of the basic political unit.

In Los Angeles, where the growth of the Negro population has been more recent (largely since World War II, rather than World War I as in the case of Chicago and New York), Negro entry into politics has really not occurred at all. The only Negro holding elective office is one member of the State Assembly. No Negroes are on the City Council, and no Negroes are in its Congressional delegation. Los Angeles politics are largely nonpartisan. There are no wards, and no ward leaders. City Councilmen are elected from large heterogeneous districts which must, by law, be reapportioned every four years. Considerable pains have been taken to insure that such redistricting will operate to exclude Negroes from the Council. Civil service is strong in Los Angeles, and there are few material incentives with which to construct a political organization. There is no city-wide organization with a need to attract all segments of the population to support a complete slate of candidates, and hence no group which would have a vested interest in constructing a "balanced ticket" and distributing "recognition" to ethnic, religious, and other easily identifiable groups. Politics is largely the province of white, middle-class, Anglo-Saxon Protestants. Although the sole Negro elective official is formally a Democrat, he has supported Republican Mayor Norris Poulson in both the 1953 and 1957 elections, despite Poulson's stand against public housing. Neither race nor party are clear determinants of political positions in Los Angeles.

One additional factor should be mentioned. The density of Negroes in Los Angeles has been markedly lower than in either Chicago or New York. Los Angeles, for example, has a comparative absence of apartments and tenements in the central city and instead an immense number of small, single-family homes and duplexes. It has, as a result, a Negro population which is spread over a much greater territory than in Chicago. This relative dispersion has many consequences, but one which is important at this juncture is the greater ease with which district lines can be drawn to exclude Negroes. A widely spread (but generally contiguous) Negro area can more easily be broken up in such a way that Negroes are in a minority in each district. This would be less feasible in a small but densely-populated area.

Detroit is, in many ways, comparable to Los Angeles. City politics is nonpartisan, and genuinely so. Members of the Common Council are elected at-large from the city as a whole. Each voter has nine votes which he may give to as many as nine different candidates, but no more than one vote per candidate. In the primary, eighteen men are selected from a wide-open field frequently of more than one hundred aspirants. The eighteen compete in a run-off election from which nine emerge. There are no ward leaders, and civil service has put an end to almost all patronage at the city and county level. In such a situation it is not surprising that it was not until 1957 that a Negro was first elected to the Common Council.

The Detroit situation differs from that in Los Angeles because of the existence of a large and powerful labor movement in the former city which has tried to operate as a political organization, endorsing slates of candidates and attempting to organize workers in most of the election precincts. Although this organization, in co-operation with other liberal groups and with the regular Democratic party, has been strikingly successful in electing a Governor and two Senators, as well as a host of other state-wide offices (where the elections are openly *partisan*), it has had much less success in the city itself. It was never able to defeat four-time Mayor Albert E. Cobo, a conservative, nor could it dominate the Common Council.[4]

The CIO United Auto Workers, which was first confronted with Negro laborers in Detroit when they were used as strikebreakers in the 1930's,[5] has since succeeded in incorporating them into the union movement with considerable success. Unlike many craft-oriented unions, the UAW has not segregated the Negroes into separate, all-Negro locals. Rather, Negroes are to be found in all the locals in sizeable numbers. Perhaps one-fourth to one-third of the membership of the average local in Detroit is now Negro.[6] In political action, the CIO has concentrated heavily on Negro areas—often with remarkable effect. For example, Negroes are becoming very numerous in the First and

Fifteenth Congressional Districts which now return two white Democratic Congressmen, Thaddeus M. Machrowicz and John D. Dingell. Negro Democrats challenged each incumbent in the 1958 primary, but the white leaders—with CIO endorsement— were able to defeat their Negro opponents by substantial margins. Most Negroes voted the CIO ticket rather than on the basis of race.

Negroes and whites share high offices in the AFL-CIO Wayne County Council (a Pole and a Negro are the two vice-presidents) and Negroes hold office in UAW locals. This has had political advantages and disadvantages for the Negroes. The CIO appeal to Negroes has been reflected in the strong CIO backing which Negro goals usually receive in public affairs. At the state level, a strong FEPC (Fair Employment Practices Commission) statute was passed and implemented. This has been attractive to Negroes while alienating relatively few white workers. The CIO, particularly the UAW, has been a strong supporter of the Detroit NAACP, although the Negro leadership of the NAACP prefers to maintain an image of independence as much as possible. In Chicago, by way of contrast, the labor movement has not been dominated by any single union giant. Individual unions have tended to exclude Negroes altogether (as in certain building trades and railroad unions), relegate them to all-Negro locals (as in many AFL craft unions), or permit Negroes to take over a union almost entirely (as with several packinghouse workers' locals). The politics of Chicago labor are infinitely complex, but the end result is that there is usually no strong union force placed behind various race causes.

There has been a price for the strong Detroit alliance between labor and Negroes. The closer to home a race issue is, the less vigorous the union can afford to be on its behalf. Championing legislation which, if passed, would have few immediate effects on the white workers living in Detroit may be one thing. Championing a law which would, for example, end discriminatory practices in the private housing market is quite another thing. Other groups in the CIO (or who follow CIO leadership politically) must be considered. One of these is the Poles; another is the southern whites. In this very tense area, having an ally as powerful as the Detroit CIO is not enough for the Negro. Lily-white neighborhood "improvement associations," created to keep Negroes out of certain residential areas, often share members with a CIO union.[7]

The other cost has arisen out of the fact of integration in labor. Some Negroes, including some leaders, would prefer to have certain things—such as offices in a union local—given to them as a matter of race recognition rather than as a result of competition on relatively equal terms with white groups for a common set of offices. Negroes cannot control any single local, and although they are present in very large numbers in the union as a whole, many have felt frustrated by what they consider to be a shortage of official positions. If the Negroes were grouped into a few Negro locals, there would at least be some Negro union presidents; as it is, often the Negroes must be content with, for example, the position of recording secretary in each of several locals.

Some Detroit Negro leaders speak of the mixed feelings they have toward their labor ally. On the one hand, a single industrial structure, organized by a single powerful union, has aided the NAACP in reaching Negroes and recruiting them as members. It has provided a source of stability which has given to the local NAACP leadership an unusual freedom from bitter internal struggles. But at the same time, as one Negro leader said, the union "has dulled the effectiveness of Negro leadership to some extent":

Twenty-five years ago when the UAW was a baby we had strong Negro leadership here. It's still remembered. People still talk about the three or four Negro ministers who were so influential at that time in leading the Negro community. . . . I believe it was true. The UAW has reduced the size of this Negro leadership and reduced its importance by providing a more significant, more influential, more comprehensive liberal leadership in the community. It may be a good thing. But it has happened.

On the whole, however, integration into a large and powerful union undoubtedly has worked to the net advantage of most Negroes. The level of conflict between hostile ethnic groups—for example, between Negroes and Poles—might be very much higher if each group controlled its own set of locals and was isolated from the other group. Under the present system, competition for recognition and position between the two groups in the union must proceed within a common organization, much as such competition occurs within a city-wide political machine. Neither side can afford to press too hard for fear of alienating other supporters or even the leadership; neither side can afford to jeopardize the chances for success of the organization as a whole in either union bargaining or political campaigns. The CIO in Detroit acts, in part, as a political machine with two important differences: it has relatively few tangible rewards with which to attract workers and supporters,[8] and it is out of power in the city. Being out of power, and forced to rely on inducements other than material, it has become skilled in raising and agitating various issues which appeal to many of its constituent elements. This, of course, does not deny the evident sincerity of the union leaders who espouse these causes.

An interesting variation of the impact of the system of at-large elections on Negro political fortunes is found in Cincinnati. From 1925 until 1957, councilmen were elected at-large under proportional representation. PR modified the effect of the at-large system to the extent that one or two Negroes were usually elected to the city council by receiving as little as 10 per cent of the total vote. After PR was abolished in 1957 and a system of at-large elections for nine councilmen was instituted, the leading Negro politician was defeated. An important factor in the campaign against PR was the presumed threat posed by the possibility of Negro political power in the city. Theodore M. Berry, the Negro councilman who had been elected Vice-Mayor in 1955 after running second in a field of twenty-one candidates, was the target of much of this attack. In urging Negroes to vote to retain PR, Berry made explicit reference to the Detroit situation as a warning of what would happen to Negro political representation should PR be rejected.[9] The at-large, nonpartisan election system has similarly helped to exclude Negroes from the Boston Common Council. Negroes held office in Boston for over a century beginning in 1776, but by 1910 they had all been displaced. In the 19th century, Negroes were often elected from predominantly white districts by Yankees who, like the Negroes, were Republicans. After the turn of the century, with the entry of new immigrant groups into political life, particularly as members of the Democratic party, this benevolence ceased. Districts were redrawn to split the Negro vote. In 1949, the district system was abolished altogether, and the nine Council members were elected at large. A Negro running for the Council in 1958 finished fifteenth out of eighteen candidates, although he ran first in the most important Negro ward.[10]

The structure of political competition in these northern areas has implications for the responsiveness of white politicians to Negro goals as well as for the organization of Negro politics itself. The relative success in enacting laws embodying Negro race ends in Michigan and New York, for example, has been due to a large number of factors, including the presence of powerful allies for Negro causes. One factor upon which some speculation seems worthwhile at this point concerns the distribution of Negroes in electoral districts. Although no conclusive evidence can be offered, it is interesting to conjecture about the differences in white politicians' attitudes toward race ends which may be related to a large-district political system (such as New York) as compared to a small-district system (such as Chicago).

Manhattan, which was over 21 per cent Negro in 1957, has elected a Negro as borough president. Negro voters in just the four "recognized" Negro districts produced from one third to one half of the majorities won by the top of the Democratic ticket between 1954 and 1958.[11] As the strength of Tammany declines, the pressure mounts on city officials, such as the mayor, to move more and more in the direction of meeting the demands of organized minority groups. Mayor Wagner, for example, was a steady supporter of the proposed "open occupancy" ordinance barring discrimination in private housing even though the *Negro* politicians (with one exception) were silent or unenthusiastic. Here we see the Negro benefiting from what may have been the by-product of political and civic action engaged in by entirely different actors and in part for different purposes. White political leaders, it might be hypothesized, meet demands for race ends in such a situation only in part to attract the Negro vote. Their goal is also to attract and hold liberal *white* voters (for example, Jews) who judge a politician in part on the basis of his contribution to the goals of integration and social justice.[12]

The Negro may be the unintended beneficiary of such a process. But whatever the audience to which the politician appeals, there is little doubt that in New York—in contrast to Chicago—an appeal must be made. Politics in the former city are more nearly two-party (opponents of the Democratic organization can and do win), and hence greater efforts must be expended to be certain of victory.

Furthermore, New York political units (the districts from which councilmen and borough presidents are elected) are relatively large. Sizable numbers of Negroes live in many of these districts and boroughs.*13 Many white politicians must anticipate the reaction of Negroes to city issues affecting the race. What may be more important, *opponents* of race goals find it harder to gain the support of their political representatives against such measures when the districts these leaders represent are so large and diversified. The larger political unit is a factor which works to deter or delay Negro entry into politics, but it may also be a factor which makes it harder for anti-Negro forces to block race legislation which has strong civic backing. Smaller units in Chicago, on the other hand, facilitate Negro entry into politics but also make it easier for anti-Negro elements in local neighborhoods to mobilize support from their politicians to oppose race measures.

---

*13. The six Manhattan Council districts had, in 1957, an average population of slightly less than 300,000. By comparison, the average size of a Chicago ward (in 1950) was about 72,000 persons. At least four of the six Manhattan Councilmen have sizable Negro areas in their districts, and Negroes are to be found in scattered locations in the other two. There are, in addition, important Negro population centers in the Bronx (134,767), Brooklyn (307,796), Queens (116,193), and Staten Island (8,372). The distribution of Negroes in the various New York City boroughs is of great importance. The Board of Estimate on which the Borough Presidents sit has substantially greater power than the City Council. It is composed of the Mayor, the Comptroller, the Council President (all elected city-wide) with four votes each and the Borough Presidents from Manhattan, Brooklyn, Queens, the Bronx, and Richmond (with two votes each). Thus, with twelve votes among them, the city-wide officials can dominate the Board and the important decisions it makes, although the necessary unity can be difficult to achieve. The lack of such unity and its consequences are described in Wallace S. Sayre and Herbert Kaufman, *Governing New York City* (New York: Russell Saje Foundation, 1960), chaps. xvii and xviii.

The Style of Negro Politics

The style of Negro politics in northern cities can be viewed as a function of the felt needs of the organization (its goals and the incentives it must have in order to generate action to attain these goals) and of the character of the constituency to which the electoral appeal must be made.[14] The Negro political organization, like all organizations, has maintenance needs which both arise from within and are imposed from without. One index of the differential effect of internal and external needs on a Negro political organization is the extent to which it finds it in its own interest to use racial appeals in its activities—i.e., appeals to Negroes to realize race ends and elect "race men."

Organizational Needs

The first set of factors involves the needs and position of the organization itself. Negro political action is modified by the answers Negro leaders give to these questions: How can I attract workers to my organization? How can I attract voters to my campaign? Usually, the answer to both these questions is the same for the Negro leader as for his white colleague, but there are interesting variations. Racism, or, more broadly, ideology in Negro politics is often a product of a position outside the established organization, a position of weakness within the established organization, or an absence of material incentives with which to attract and reward Negro supporters. Political conservatism and an avoidance of race issues, on the other hand, often reflects the fact that the Negroes are part of a strong and cohesive political organization.

Some of these differences can be suggested by a comparison of the organizational bases of Negro politics in Chicago and Manhattan. In Chicago, Negro Democrats are part of a powerful political machine; in Manhattan, they work within a weak machine. The position of Dawson as leader of at least five of the six Negro wards in Chicago and the seven Negro Democrats in the Illinois state legislature is thus far unchallenged. In Manhattan, not only the position of any given Negro leader, but of many white leaders as well, is often precarious and fraught with uncertainty and weakness. The Chicago organization bene-

fits from a reservoir of funds and patronage that, although reduced from the early 1940's, has not been seriously weakened
as yet. The Manhattan organization—or coalition of factions
which attempts to operate as an organization—has had many of
its sources of strength seriously curtailed. These differences, and
the consequences for Negro political style, can be seen in a brief
historical comparison.

In Manhattan, Negroes began to enter the Tammany Democratic organization at the district level at a time when the city
organization was alrady under heavy attack. Fiorello LaGuardia
had already led a successful Fusion movement which placed him
in the City Hall, and he was going out of his way to create difficulties for the Sachems of Tammany.[15] The great, restless ferment of the Depression years which expressed itself in Harlem,
in Chicago's Bronzeville, and in other Negro communities in
various protest and separatist movements left a permanent mark
on New York. Tammany for years has had to deal with a series
of insurgents and dissidents. This history of insurgency had an
effect in New York unlike that in Chicago. In the latter city,
the Negroes had already forced an entry *before* the Depression
began; many of them were committed to the political status quo
before a crisis could develop. The regular Cook County Democratic organization was able to sweep the Republicans out of
office and install a strong Democratic mayor—Edward Kelly—
who promptly cast about for a means to cement his alliance with
the strongest Negro leaders. Dawson, until then a maverick Republican, switched parties and became, through his skill and
Kelly's support, the new Democratic leader in the Negro wards.
These years of dramatic change left, in Chicago, a newly strengthened Democratic organization in power—a power it has never
surrendered. In New York, essentially the same upheavals placed
a reform mayor in office whose appeal was personal and direct.
Negroes broke into Tammany just as the posts for which they
were fighting were rapidly decreasing in value. The 1930's in
New York stimulated a pattern of contention and insurgency within the regular organization from which it has never fully recovered,
and one that has caught up Negroes and whites alike.

No strong, single Negro leadership ever developed in Harlem.
Negroes were used, one against the other, by forces in the steady

struggle for place and power; and, in turn, the Negroes made separate and competing alliances to further their own interests. The arrival on the scene of Adam Clayton Powell, Jr., was certainly not the cause of the political debility of Tammany in Harlem, but it was symptomatic of the malaise and in time served to deepen it. When the 22nd Congressional District was, in 1944, created in order to be handed over to a Negro, the principal Negro Democratic district leader in the area was unable to choose the nominee, and in fact was overruled in favor of Powell by Tammany. The weakness of the organization in Harlem continued. In 1958-59, Powell and his followers were able to beat regular organization candidates in the Democratic Congressional primary and in three district leader contests.

Dawson, before being co-opted into the Democratic Party, was an outspoken and vigorous champion of racial causes. Once inside an organization that was strong and which manifestly held the key to the future, race matters were subdued. He was able to provide a plausible, and in many ways correct, rationale to account for the change: The future of the Negro was bound up with political advancement and power. This could best be obtained by working within the Democratic Party and accepting, as a cost, what one could not immediately change. In contrast to this, Herbert Bruce, the first Democratic Negro leader in Harlem, fought the established white leader on the grounds that most of the political jobs were going to whites who no longer lived in the district. Few were left for the Negroes who remained. On entering, however, he discovered a machine which was weak and divided, and it was necessary to fight a steady stream of challengers from within and without. To Bruce, and others like him, race appeals never really became outmoded because the struggle for position never really ended.

In Los Angeles, the forms and nature of city politics are reflected in the politics of the Negro area. The single Negro elected official has a base of support that is personal and of long duration. The attempt by liberal Democrats to revitalize the party in the city and the state through the Democratic Club movement has elicited comparable attempts in the Negro areas. But here the obstacles have been far greater. Negroes have proved to be much more difficult to organize with the intangible incentives and middle-class appeals characteristic of the Club movement. In the 63rd Assembly District, for example, which is about 50 per cent Negro, there are ten Democratic Clubs. Until recently, nine of these were white and only one Negro. The Club movement is not active in the single assembly district (the 62nd) which elects a Negro State Assemblyman. To stimulate political organization among Negroes in the apolitical atmosphere of Los Angeles, a group of Negroes called the Democratic Minority Conference has had to rely more heavily on strictly racial appeals and the demand for race ends such as Negro representation in government. A leader of the Conference explained that it must use a "frankly racial appeal" because Negroes distrust the Democratic Party and feel that the white-led Democratic Clubs can give them little more than the regular organization. The Conference, although allied with the Club movement, has discouraged Caucasians from membership in it. Led by Negroes, it has endeavored to attract Mexicans and Japanese as well.

The Nature of the Constituency

The perceived character of the constituency to which an electoral appeal must be made can condition several aspects of the campaign. Some cities have an electorate thoroughly conditioned and deeply committed to the goal of nonpartisanship. In Los Angeles, this has been carried to the point where until recently the political parties as formal organizations have been almost non-existent. In Detroit, where at least one strong party operates, it is still essential to appeal to the voters in a manner that does not seem to do violence to the ideal of nonpartisanship.

Further, the nature of the constituency conditions the extent to which issues are believed to be relevant. In Chicago, issues in city elections are conspicuous by their rarity. In New York, they are somewhat more common. In Detroit and Los Angeles, candidates often must go to considerable lengths to *generate* issues in order to attract interest to their campaigns for public office. Little else can be offered the voter to induce him to participate in the election than an appeal to his civic or personal interests.

Finally, the nature of the constituency modifies the quality of the candidates offered. Where the organizational strength is weak or declining, it is thought to be more important to offer

candidates who are thoroughly presentable and of considerable
civic luster—i.e., "blue ribbon" candidates. For example, when
Negroes entered Detroit politics, they found none of the common kinds of patronage available to sustain their position. Conditions seemed to be ripe for a political campaign based on the
demand for race issues. But city councilmen and county judges
are elected at large. Only a small portion of the whole constituency is Negro. The selection of the Negroes to run, and the decision as to the style in which their campaign would be waged,
had to take this into account. The support of labor unions and
of the daily press seemed to be essential. The result was the election of a handful of very able, eminently presentable men of
moderate views and unimpeachable character to sit, as Negroes,
on the Council and the bench.[16]

In Los Angeles, the strongest effort made by Negroes to place
a man on the City Council required the mobilization of a broad
cross-section of the Negro community to provide the necessary
support in terms of time, effort, and money. Negro Democratic
clubs which demanded more Negroes in public office were
mobilized. But in appealing to the electorate of the district as
a whole, which has a very large number of whites, a sober, "good
government" platform was devised stressing taxes and city services.
Two separate and different sets of inducements had to be employed: one to attract Negro support for the campaign, and one
to attract white votes for the candidate.

Having said this, it is important to consider precisely how important to Negro leaders such racial appeals may be. Assuming
the existence of conditions which lead the politicians to adopt
their use, it is by no means certain that they will always have the
intended effect. It has been shown in many studies in a variety
of cities that the "Negro vote" is not *simply* a racial vote. Negroes do not vote for other Negroes merely because of race.
The divisions of the Negro community along lines of party, class,
and status are much too profound and pervasive to allow for
the operation of any such uncomplicated response as a "race
vote." Morsell has shown, in his study of Negro politics in New
York, that the Negro tends to register and to turn out to vote in
about the same proportions as whites, and that general party
alignments are often more important than are specific racial con-

siderations.[17] The problem of information is undoubtedly crucial in accounting for much of the absence of a "race vote." Many Negroes cannot identify Negro candidates in an election.

The Efficacy of Organization

These considerations raise squarely the question of the efficacy of political organization among Negroes in northern cities. For instance, what difference does the existence of a strong organization make in the political behavior of Chicago Negroes? What are the consequences of the absence of such organization or the presence of a weak and attenuated organization in other cities? No conclusive answers to these questions can be given, but some suggestions can be made. We shall compare the four cities in several areas of political behavior to see what important discrepancies, if any, exist, and then we shall attempt to relate these discrepancies to the nature of the political organization in the city.

A complete treatment of this subject would require a precinct-by-precinct survey of the relative effectiveness of machine and non-machine politics. Failing that, only a general pattern can be adduced from the over-all data we have. The existence of a strong political machine among Negroes in a northern city has little detectable effect on the size of the vote delivered to Negro candidates, the percentage of the total vote polled by the winning candidate, or the number of straight-ticket votes. Strong organization has greater effect on the ability of the leadership to control the primary vote and to produce a sizeable vote for ballot propositions. Finally, the strength of the organization seems unrelated to, and in some cases hinders, the ability of Negroes to secure important appointive offices in the state and local governments.

The size and percentage of the vote won by leading Negro candidates in four cities is shown in Table 1. Few important differences are apparent. No significant advantage seems to accrue to Dawson for having a strong organization as compared to Hawkins, who has a relatively weak one. If anything, these data suggest that Powell has been able to do slightly better than Dawson in most cases, and that Hawkins has often done much better. All Negro political leaders, by the fact of being Democrats and incumbents, have had little trouble in turning back Republican challengers.

Table 1

Aggregate Vote of Leading Negro Politicians in Four Cities and Percentage of Total Vote Cast

POLITICIAN	1958	1956	1954	1952	1950
Dawson (Chicago)	60,778 (72.21%)	66,704 (64.41%)	71,472 (75.56%)	96,354 (73.45%)	69,660 (62.64%)
Diggs (Detroit)	57,354 (73.01%)	87,383 (69.76%)	64,716 (66.14%)	*	*
Hawkins† (Los Angeles)	19,085 (84.75%)	19,367 (100%)	16,518 (70.78%)	20,914 (79.07%)	14,260 (82.05%)
Powell‡ (New York)	56,383 (90.81%)	59,339 (69.72%)	43,545 (77.55%)	72,562 (69.84%)	35,233 (69.84%)

*Diggs first elected to Congress in 1954.
†Hawkins' vote is for the primary in all cases. Under California law, he has been able to cross-file and has invariably won the nomination of both parties. In 1956, he was unopposed in the primary. Cross-filing was abolished in 1959.
‡In 1958 Powell won both the Democratic and Republican nominations. He was opposed in the general election only by the Liberal candidate, Earl Brown. In 1944 Powell won the nomination of all three parties and was unopposed in the general election. Since 1944, Powell has never received Liberal Party endorsements.

Similarly, there is little evident difference in the ability of the various Negro leaders to deliver a straight party vote in their districts. If the elections are partisan, there will be a relatively small "spread" between the vote received by the top of the ticket (the most popular candidate on the slate) and the bottom of the ticket. The Negro candidate will do neither better nor worse except in unusual cases. The vote will be racially stable; it will not discriminate between Negro and white candidates, nor between whites favorable to Negroes and whites hostile to Negroes. In Table 2 is shown this "spread" in three Negro areas: Chicago's second ward, Detroit's first ward, and New York's eleventh assembly district. The Table suggests that there are few important differences between cities except that Powell has recently (in 1956 and 1958) done better than the rest of his party. Negro voters in all three cities tend to be straight-ticket voters. To a slight extent, the Dawson organization can produce more straight-ticket votes than the Detroit organization. No data for Los Angeles can be presented owing to the absence of voting returns tabulated by Assembly Districts for any office other than that of Assemblyman.

Table 2
Vote for Negro Leader and for Bottom of
Democratic Ticket as a Percentage of
Top of Ticket Vote

	Chicago Ward 2	Detroit Ward 1	New York* 11th Assembly Dist.
1958			
Percentage for Negro Leader	99.12	96.21	126.49
Percentage for Bottom of Ticket	97.83	92.69	97.06
1956			
Percentage for Negro Leader	97.06	93.99	103.76
Percentage for Bottom of Ticket	95.32	90.28	93.42
1954			
Percentage for Negro Leader	97.83	91.43	88.27
Percentage for Bottom of Ticket	96.57	91.34	86.89

*The Powell vote is shown as a percentage of the vote of the leading Democratic candidate. Since the leading Democratic candidate in New York has had in these elections the nomination of the Liberal Party as well, his total vote would be higher than that used here. If one included the Liberal Party vote, Powell's percentage of the top of the ticket would be lower in all cases: 1858, 116.98 per cent; 1956, 91.87 per cent; 1954, 81.56 per cent.

One special case should be noted. The extent of straight-ticket voting varies, not with the strength of the political organization, but with the presence or absence of partisan elections. A straight ticket vote can be found in roughly the same proportion in all four cities where the elections are partisan. Where they are non-partisan, significant discrepancies exist between the votes of different individuals with the same endorsements (by labor unions, newspapers, citizens' committees, etc.). These discrepancies occur most frequently along ethnic and national lines. It can be assumed that one goal of a political organization (either a machine or an endorsing committee) is to produce a winning vote for an entire slate of candidates, resisting the practice known as "ticket-cutting." Ideally, a Negro should do about as well in a Polish area as a Pole, and vice versa. If he does not — if the Polish voters "cut" the Negro candidate on the slate in favor of the Polish candidate—then the organization can be considered less effective than desired. This situation can be illustrated with data drawn from contests in ethnically-heterogeneous, multi-member districts or in at-large contests with large slates of candidates. Chicago and Detroit can usefully be compared in this regard. The conclusion seems to be that there is relatively little ticket-cutting in Chicago (where all elections are in fact partisan) and relatively little in those Detroit elections which are partisan. In nonpartisan Detroit elections, ticket-cutting is widespread.

In Chicago, ten members of the Board of County Commissioners are elected at large, and one Negro has been on the regular Democratic ticket since 1938. Judges of the Municipal and Superior courts are likewise elected at large, and Negro candidates have usually been entered in recent years. In Detroit, members of the Common Council and judges of the Circuit Court are elected at large and Negroes have participated in these nonpartisan races.

Even a cursory inspection of the election returns clearly indicate that ticket-cutting in Chicago's wards is minimal in races for County Commissioner and Superior or Circuit Court Judge, while in Detroit, a very high level of voter discrimination is evident in Common Council and Circuit Court contests. A Negro running for County Commissioner in Chicago, one of ten Democrats on the party slate, will receive 94 per cent of the votes of the leading Democratic candidate (a popular Irishman) in the city as a whole. In Negro wards, he will do slightly better than the Irishman (perhaps 1 or 2 per cent at the most) while in wards where anti-Negro sentiment is notoriously strong he will be somewhat weaker than the Irishman (2 to 15 per cent). A Negro running for Circuit Court Judge in Chicago has shown even less susceptibility to ticket-cutting. In the city as a whole, his vote has been less than 0.5 per cent under the top of the ticket vote, and in anti-Negro wards his vote never sags by so much as 5 per cent. It is important to note that this pattern holds true even in those wards where the machine has historically been weak. In the fifth ward (which is the site of the University of Chicago) and the fiftieth ward (a generally well-to-do north shore residential area), there is hardly any more voter discrimination than in the "river wards" where the machine is powerful. Although neither ward consistently votes Democratic—in fact, the fiftieth is usually Republican—those Democratic votes that are cast tend to be straight-ticket votes.

In Detroit, the situation is completely reversed. Although the Wayne County totals show the Negro Circuit Court candidate lagging less than 9 per cent behind the top of the ticket (an Irish-man), in individual wards and cities the variation is extreme. In the Negro wards, the Negro will receive a vote almost four times as large as that given to the top of the ticket, and he will do even better against a liberal Jewish candidate who is well-known for his activities on behalf of Negro causes. In the Polish city of Hamtramck, on the other hand, the Negro received only about one-fourth of the vote received by the Polish candidate.

In contests for the Detroit Common Council, a Negro was elected for the first time in 1957. He ran eighth in a race for nine seats. In the city as a whole, the Negro received about 56 per cent of the total vote cast, while the most popular candidate (a woman) received almost 90 per cent. The disparity in the over-all totals is far surpassed by the variation in the ward returns. In the Negro wards, the Negro did three or four times as well as in the city as a whole, and twice as well as the top of the ticket. In the white middle-class wards, on the other hand, the Negro received only one-fourth the votes of the top of the ticket. In the Negro wards, the cutting against white candidates was widespread. One man, widely believed to be anti-Negro, was of course heavily cut, re-ceiving only one-fourth the vote he received on the average in the wards. But also cut was a liberal, UAW-sponsored candidate who had worked on behalf of many Negro causes.

Where Negroes have run in *partisan* elections (as candidates for Congressman, State Representative, State Senator, and mem-ber of the Board of Governors of Wayne University), they have done about as well as their white colleagues. The results approxi-mate those obtained by Negroes in Chicago, and differences in organizational strength have relatively little impact. Where Ne-groes have run in nonpartisan contests in Detroit, ticket-cutting is pronounced. The value of partisanship, then, lies not simply in the strength of the machine but more in the traditional party alle-giances of the voter, in the greater ease of straight-ticket voting, and by the presence of well-known state and national figures at the top of the ticket.

This situation raises two questions. The first is whether part of the machine's role in facilitating Negro entry into politics may be due to nothing more than the ability of the organization to bestow on the Negro candidate the official party label. That label alone may be enough to enable the Negro to take advantage of the straight-ticket voting which characterizes most Negro areas regardless of differences in machine strength. The additional services it provides may amount, in the last analysis, to little more than relieving the candidate of the financial and organizational burden of getting the sure vote to the polls. The second question involves the political position of white liberal allies of the Negro. In partisan elections, Negroes do not discriminate against candidates on the party ticket who are personally hostile to Negro interests. In nonpartisan elections, on the other hand, Negroes frequently "cut" white candidates who are widely known as liberal supporters of Negro causes. In the former case, partisan elections work against the Negro's punishing his enemies, while nonpartisan elections reduce the likelihood of the Negro's rewarding his friends. White liberal candidates who had suffered from this situation in Detroit's nonpartisan elections have privately expressed disappointment after the race. "Why stick your neck out for them on race issues if you only get it cut off in the election?"

The electoral advantage of strong machine organization is more evident in primary contests and, to a lesser extent, in the voting for ballot propositions. Here, the evidence is very skimpy, for Powell and Dawson rarely meet serious challengers in their primaries. What limited data there are, however, indicate that the Dawson organization is better able to turn out a large vote in primary contests than the Powell organization. In 1958, Dawson was unchallenged in the Democratic primary. Little interest was shown in the campaign, either in the city as a whole or in his district. His organization, nonetheless, produced a vote of 31,706 for him with no real effort. The same year, Powell faced a vigorous and strongly-backed primary opponent in his New York district. Earl Brown, a well-known Negro leader and one of the two Negroes on the New York City Council, was given Tammany support in the primary in an effort to "dump" Powell. The campaign was intense and dramatic, it received wide local and national publicity, and a maximum effort was made to turn out an overwhelming vote for Powell. Yet in a district similar in size to Dawson's, Powell received only 14,935 votes—less than half Dawson's total—while his opponent received 4,959.

The total vote cast was less than three-fourths of the vote Dawson alone received in Chicago. In Detroit the situation parallels that in New York except that Diggs is more regularly challenged in the primary. In 1958 he defeated one opponent by receiving 82.3 per cent of 23,933 votes; and in 1954 (the first year he ran) he defeated three opponents by receiving 61.4 per cent of 33,530 votes.

The absence of real primary contests is probably as good an indication as any of the power — both actual and imputed — of the machine. Such contests are rare for any office held by a Negro member of the Dawson organization in Chicago. If there is an opponent at all, he is usually a weak one who entered simply to gain publicity for himself or his business. Serious contenders are either persuaded to drop out, sometimes with compensation in the form of money or an offer of another political job, or they are defeated by large majorities. In New York, on the other hand, scarcely a year passes without a real challenge being offered to a district leader or state assemblyman in the primaries. Rival Democratic clubs spring up in Harlem with remarkable frequency and important posts change hands regularly. Here again, machine strength or weakness in primaries in Negro areas is a reflection of such strength or weakness in city-wide primaries. In 1955, Democratic party leader Richard J. Daley challenged incumbent Martin Kennelly for the mayoral nomination in Chicago. The four Negro wards then led by Dawson voted for Daley by over 86 per cent, contributing more than 40 per cent of Daley's city-wide majority. Machine strength in the Negro areas is thus not only an historical product of machine strength in the city, but also one of its most important contemporary supports.

Machine strength may also be a determining feature of the Negro vote for referendum measures. Once more, the evidence is very fragmentary. But Chicago and New York can be compared by the degree to which a sizeable vote from Negroes can be produced on behalf of ballot propositions which would be of benefit to Negroes and which have Democratic Party endorsement. Here the differences, for the few comparable cases at hand, are striking. In Chicago's second ward, in the period 1953 through 1958, a bond proposal to provide additional street lighting received 49.8 per cent of the top of the ticket vote; a proposal to increase County Hospital facilities received 63.8 per cent; and a proposal to pay benefits to Korean War Veterans received 51.3 per cent. During the same period in New York's eleventh assembly district, a proposal to increase the state subsidy to public housing received only 13.8 per cent of the top of the ticket vote, and a proposal to finance additional public housing through a bond issue received only 9.8 per cent. Many qualifications must be made to this picture, not the least of which is that party machines rarely press vigorously for a large vote on the propositions because of the greater importance of concentrating on key elective offices. Nevertheless, the differences between Chicago and New York are so great as to suggest that the Chicago city organization can rely to a much greater extent on a positive Negro attitude toward propositions than can the New York machine.

Presumably one of the important goals of a political organization is to place its members in public office. The appointive offices captured by Negroes in northern cities vary greatly in number. In Los Angeles and Detroit there are probably the fewest, and this would seem to argue for the desirability of organized political strength. But when New York and Chicago are compared, it is quickly seen that machine strength is, if anything, in inverse correlation to the number of Negroes in important posts. Chicago, having about 750,000 to 850,000 Negroes, has only three Negro judges, one Traffic Court Referee, and one assistant to the Probate Court Judge.[18] New York, having about one million Negroes, has seventeen Negro judges: two Supreme Court Justices, one General Sessions Judge, four city Magistrates, three Domestic Relations Court Judges, six Municipal Court Judges, and one City Court Judge. In addition, in New York city (unlike Chicago), many Negroes hold administrative positions at the cabinet and sub-cabinet level. Several factors might account for this discrepancy. One would undoubtedly be the more liberal ethos of New York and the lessened resistance to the entry of Negroes into many areas of public life. Another factor is related to the uncertainty of white political leaders as to the presumed "Negro vote," and the need they feel to develop greater appeals to it in a situation of declining organizational strength. Negro political organization does not necessarily contribute to the placement of Negroes in important public offices; it may actually work against it. The Mayor of New York may believe, for example, that the civic leaders actually speak "for" the Negro community with greater authority and political power than do the politicians, and it thus becomes necessary to gratify them by co-opting some into the administration and by paying heed to the recommendations of others.

The importance of political organization among northern Negroes is, thus, a complex question. The machine seems to make little difference in the size of the Democratic vote or in the number of straight-ticket votes (in partisan elections). It may, in some cases hamper the entry of Negroes into prestigious appointive positions. At the same time, it provides for stronger control of party primaries and perhaps a higher turnout on referendum measures. The deeper significance of organization is probably not evident from election analyses, however. The real impact of strong party organization is in the set of constraints it places on the leaders and members. An organization such as a political machine develops maintenance requirements, and these predispose it to treat issues, candidates, platforms, and election appeals in a manner distinct from that which might be employed by organizations of a different character. The primary importance of the machine lies in the way of life it creates for its members. The fundamental differences between machine and non-machine or weak-machine Negro areas consists not so much in the final election results, but in what must be done to produce those results, what obligations members acquire for having benefited by them, and what rewards exist for those who have contributed to their attainment. The machine conditions political life by the characteristic manner in which it recruits, elects, maintains, and disciplines the politicians. In the next chapters, a powerful Negro political machine, the Dawson organization of Chicago, will be examined to discover the conditions under which it flourishes, the tensions that develop within it, the external constraints it must meet, and the relationships which exist between it and the city-wide organization.

Chapter III

Chicago: Negro Politics

THERE is no single "Negro leadership" in Chicago. Similarly, there is no single structure of influence. Perhaps the Negro community can be regarded, in a general way, as one corner of the "five-acre woodlot" of which Norton Long speaks when he describes civic affairs as an "ecology of games."[1] Within the woodlot are a number of Negro "games" — the political game, the voluntary association game, the newspaper game, the ministerial game, the labor game, and so on. At any given moment it is difficult to tell which game speaks "for" the Negro community — if, indeed, we can conceive of such a possibility at all. The NAACP or the Urban League formulates some campaign as part of its efforts to sustain itself and grow; the press raises an issue in order to build circulation or attract attention; the politicians, who would prefer the issueless calm of partisan harmony, are forced to meet and handle such campaigns or issues; in doing so they frequently invoke the support or provoke the antagonism of ministers and labor leaders. All of these activities proceed simultaneously and rest on different bases of influence.

But this process does not proceed utterly at random. The varied organized forms of Negro civic life are linked together by certain values and goals which form the themes or content of Negro issues — the inescapable consciousness of kind, the inevitable impact of common problems, and the competition for scarce resources from a single community. Not only are there threads which link Negro activities together, a center of gravity is felt within

48

the Negro community. The community is most thoroughly organized by the Negro political organization, and although it is but one of the many games that are played by Negroes, it is also the one whose rules are most widely discussed, whose scores are most generally experienced, and whose managers are most frequently appealed to. It is useful to describe influence in the Negro community by first analyzing the Negro political organization and then the various constraints which operate on it. These constraints are both internal — a changing electorate and restless members — and external — voluntary associations, the Negro press, and mass organizations. It is not our intention to argue that the political organization is all-powerful or inevitably pre-emptive in the Negro community; rather, we begin our discussion with it because it is the weightiest of several structures of influence, and because so much of the efforts of these other structures is directed toward moving it toward certain goals as a means of gaining from the city as a whole those concessions sought by various Negroes.

The Machine

The Chicago Negro political organization is a "machine."* The literature of machine politics is large and illuminating, and insofar as the Negro political organization in Chicago partakes of the character of the classic machine, it will not be described here.[2] But two considerations must be examined. First, the fact that the Negro machine exists and flourishes in Chicago in highly disciplined form in an era in which machines generally have been decaying or vanishing requires comment. The organization of Negro leader William L. Dawson is something of an anachronism; it persists when its counterparts elsewhere have to a great extent either disappeared or undergone a radical transformation. Second, the Dawson machine is not a simple replica — albeit a highly successful one — of any political machine; it is a *Negro* machine, and many of the incentives and constraints to which it responds can only be understood by the fact of its being Negro. The kinds of issues and problems with which it must deal set it apart from,

---

*The term "machine" is used here without pejorative implications. It refers to that kind of political party whose organization is sustained by tangible incentives (largely patronage) rather than intangible incentives (such as appeals to principle, or the lure of being on the inside, etc.).

say, an Irish or an Italian machine; it is a distinctive enterprise because these issues and problems are of a distinctive order of salience and importance in the Negro community.

The Negro machine owes its existence in part to the existence of a city-wide Democratic machine; it is, to use a clumsy phrase, a "sub-machine" within the larger city machine. Although Negroes have held important political office in Chicago since 1915 (when Oscar de Priest was elected alderman), in Cook County since 1871 (although continuously only since 1938), and in the Illinois State Legislature since 1876, the rise of the present Negro machine did not begin until 1939. In that year, Dawson, an independent Republican who had served in the City Council, switched parties and, with the active support of Mayor Edward Kelly, entered the Democratic Party as committeeman of the second ward. Real political power in Chicago is vested in the ward committeemen. Although nominally they are elected by the voters of each ward, in fact, they are selected by the party leadership. All political matters, including the control of patronage, are decided by the ward committeemen, either individually on matters within each ward, or collectively on matters concerning the party as a whole. Negro political strength is coterminous with the number of Negro ward committeemen, and the existence of a single Negro machine is dependent on the extent to which these Negro ward committeemen can be led as a group by one of their number.

The Negro Democratic machine which now exists in Chicago is the product of twenty years of work. Dawson, by virtue of his considerable political skill, the patronage placed at his disposal, and a favorable public opinion, not only secured his own position as committeeman of the second ward, but created a network of obligations and loyalties which brought under his control the organizations of five or six Negro wards. In 1943 one of his followers was installed as committeeman of the third ward, in 1951 another was made committeeman of the twentieth ward, in 1955 another became committeeman of the fourth ward, and in 1956 another was brought to power in the sixth ward. These five wards — the second, third, fourth, sixth, and twentieth — comprise the largest part of the South Side Negro community, and included in 1950 an estimated 420,687 people. Of these, about 241,989 were registered voters. Today, the registration has dropped to 185,368, but it continues to represent a sizeable bloc of votes in the city as a whole. In addition, there are at least ten other wards where large numbers of Negroes live and vote, but which — for a variety of reasons — are not led by the Dawson organization. The voters of the five Dawson wards are as well-organized as any single group in the city through a disciplined corps of precinct captains, most of whom hold jobs in either the city or county administrations. The customary majorities which these wards deliver for candidates on the Democratic ticket are three-to-one, occasionally slipping to only two-to-one when faced with popular opponents or a national surge toward the Republican party. In the 1958 general elections, for example, these five wards produced a total of 84,685 votes for the top of the Democratic ticket (the candidate for state treasurer) as opposed to 29,522 for the Republican opponent. What is important about this vote is that it is a *party* vote, with relatively little ticket-splitting. This means that the Negro vote in these wards is racially stable— it does not, in all but exceptional cases, discriminate between Negro and white candidates. Dawson, the Negro leader and a member of the United States House of Representatives since 1942, receives about the same vote in his wards as do white men running for other offices on the same ticket. Since 1944, he has received between 59 and 75 per cent of the vote, the average being 66.7 per cent.

From each of the wards controlled by a Negro committeeman, of course, a Negro alderman is elected to the City Council. Six of Chicago's fifty councilmen are Negroes, and in four cases, the alderman is the same person as the committeeman. In addition, seven delegates from the Dawson organization sit in the state legislature—one senator and six representatives.

For almost all practical purposes, no real Republican opposition exists.[3] Only two Republican ward committeemen show any signs of vigor at all; the others are merely job holders who usually go through only the motions of electoral opposition. No substantial effort is made to offer an alternative to Negro voters at the ward level. The Republican organizations are weak and lack both funds and patronage. A sense of despair and helplessness is engendered by the consistent successes of the Democratic machine, and many feel strongly tempted to join those whom

they cannot defeat. A prominent Republican politician, formerly
a member of the state legislature, switched parties in 1958 after
his defeat by the Dawson organization. Another politician, a
Democratic Negro alderman, was not slated for re-election by
the machine. For a time, he toyed with the idea of an independent candidacy, and even organized a "citizens' committee"
to work for his election. But defeat seemed so certain and the
rewards of abandoning opposition were so great—including a
promise of considerate treatment by the machine when other
jobs were distributed—that he re-entered the organization and
withdrew his announced opposition. There is no "Republican
Dawson"—i.e., no single Negro political leader responsible for
party organization in the South Side area—and there probably
could not be under the present distribution of power in the Republican party. The Republican party as a whole has no single
leader in the sense that the Democratic party has. Even assuming a man of Dawson's skill could be found, and that the time
is propitious—in terms of a secular change toward Republicanism among Negroes—for an effort on the South Side, the funds
and patronage necessary to sustain a "Republican Dawson" are
not available. A Negro Republican ward committeeman explains
this situation:

> The . . . reason that the Republican party doesn't do this is be-
> cause of the divisions within the Republican party itself. . . . The
> county and state parties are pretty much separate, and on top of that
> [Governor] Stratton has his own organization. . . . There is no central
> patronage source or control, and there is no central leadership. [The
> Republican county chairman] doesn't even know where all the Re-
> publican patronage jobs are. . . . He tried to find out, but that just
> made me laugh. He couldn't find out where all those jobs are. Every-
> body has his own little nest, and they aren't going to give that up
> to some county chairman.

The influx of Negro migrants from the rural South does not
affect the balance of power. Although Negroes often come to the
North to escape the privations and hostilities of the South where
the Democratic party is in power, none of the evidence indicates that these migrants bring an antipathy toward the Democratic party which makes itself felt in local elections. On the contrary, there is every indication that they replenish the Democratic

precincts which have been vacated by those Negroes with greater means who have moved to the outskirts of the community. A Republican politician admits that any appeal to these people on the basis of their Southern experience has been ineffective. Searching for an explanation, he observed:

> I think in part they tend to join the strong force in the community, the winning side. Why join the loser? What can they do for you? Plus, the economic situation. The Democratic party has sold the Negro on being for the little people. . . . Also, a lot of these people have relatives here. They vote the way their relatives advise them to, or if not relatives, at least old neighbors from the South.

Such a statement probably underplays the importance of the Democratic organization, but at the same time it suggests the pessimism with which even energetic Republicans view their prospects.

The Dawson machine, like all machines, is an organization whose purpose is the election of men to office and which is sustained mainly through the distribution of tangible incentives to its members. To a greater extent than any other Negro organization which acts in the public or civic arena, it is "issue-free." It holds the loyalties of the voters in large part by virtue of their general commitment to the Democratic party, but also in part by providing services (or the illusion of services) to the voter and by the personal relationships of loyalty and mutual favors which exist between the voters and precinct captains. Although in its formative years, the Dawson organization—and Dawson personally—used appeals to race pride and race unity as a technique for building strength and gaining adherents, the organization has for some time been in a position of security and established success which have made such appeals largely unnecessary. The mass meeting or street corner rally of voters has been replaced as the central feature of the campaign, for the most part, by the regular meeting of the organization workers. The appeals made at those meetings are intended to instill enthusiasm but not to win votes—the listeners are already committed. The workers themselves are most commonly instructed to appeal, in speaking to the voter, to his sense of party loyalty, to the personal qualities of the candidate, and to national issues of a nonracial sort. Only rarely are frankly racial appeals made at party meetings, and the precinct captains themselves are divided as to the importance of race in soliciting votes at the grass roots. Dramatic race incidents, such as the Trumbull Park or Cicero riots, a brutal Southern lynching, or the obstructionism of Governor Faubus, are of course commonly discussed; but the civic issues which the Negro protest and improvement associations define as important—open occupancy, fair employment practices, medical integration—are not common topics in the politicians' contacts with the voters.

The machine can flourish in the Negro wards largely because of the status and needs of the Negro. The incentives it can offer are still attractive to many Negroes, whereas they have largely lost their appeal to other ethnic groups which have risen farther. Low-paying jobs, political favors, and material assistance are still as important to many Negroes as they once were to foreign-born whites. The Negroes, unlike the Irish, have not priced themselves out of the market. The importance which Negro precinct captains often attach to the money available for election-day expenses reflects this. Buying votes is a relatively uncommon procedure, but hiring workers with large families for precinct work is not. A highly placed figure in City Hall described his first-hand impression of the attitude of party leaders towards the Negro precincts:

It is important to emphasize the role money plays in the Negro wards. The only factor which interests many captains and committeemen is how much money will be put into those areas on election day. Negro precinct captains often refuse to accept brochures and other literature we print up for the campaign, although it is very easy to move this literature elsewhere in the city. A Negro captain's typical reaction is to wonder whether accepting the literature will mean a cut in the amount of money they're going to get. . . . If the organization has half a million to spend, the big boys are likely to put half of it in the Negro wards. A typical procedure is to wait until noon or one o'clock on election day, until precinct reports begin to come in. If the vote seems weak in certain precincts, additional money is sent out in a bag. . . . It is used to hire more workers, although, of course, some of it winds up in the pocket of the captain himself.

The abuses of authority fall more heavily on the Negro, and hence he is more in need of a buffer which can, in a politician's phrase, "stand between the people and the pressure." Contacts between Negroes and police officers or relief workers are more apt to be harsh or abusive (or felt to be harsh and abusive), and a mediator is more commonly in demand than among people who have less contact, or less discriminatory contact, with such forces.

Access to other levels of civic influence is very often denied the Negro. Negroes have little effective voice in the influential white civic associations, and Negroes, if they are present at all are not a weighty factor in the ranks of the city's important businessmen as they attempt to determine the course of public affairs. Politics, for the Negro, has long been one of the few regularized avenues of influence. Their Southern experience, where lack of political power seemed to be the reason why the laws were administered to their disadvantage, brought many Negroes to awareness of the value of the vote. At the same time, politics has been for the Negro—as for other ethnic groups in the past—an opportunity for upward mobility. When the Dawson machine was in its initial stages of construction, few Negroes of the business or professional classes entered politics for advancement, but today, the machine is filled with lawyers and young professional men who see the advantages of contacts in influential quarters and the publicity and prestige which office can bring.[4] One young lawyer in a ward organization observed:

> You get to know people and you get known yourself. You can open a few doors and walk in . . . and talk to people on more friendly terms. Important people, I mean. You get a few cases referred to you out of this. . . . It all helps.

Most Negro lawyers depend on a flow of "little people's" cases, with few opportunities for large corporate practice or entry into important law firms. Of the lawyers included in the group of Negro leaders surveyed for this study, more were active in politics than were active in race organizations or nonpolitical civic affairs, although many participated in both categories. Politics has tangible rewards for the Negro lawyer that the Urban League, for example, cannot offer. According to one Negro lawyer:

> Politics is the best thing for a person who has to build a practice among acquaintances; who can't move into a big law firm. Politics gives you those acquaintances. . . . There are rewards in terms of

getting a political job, too, as an assistant state's attorney or in the corporation counsel's office. The rewards are great for a lawyer.

Indeed, a regular pattern of advancement can be seen among Negro lawyer-politicians. After successful work as a precinct captain and after having, as a young man, perhaps attained office in the ward Young Democrats organization, an aspiring lawyer is given a political job in one of the legal sections of the city or county administration. Continued good faith and hard work on behalf of the party, and the lawyer may be slated for representative in the state legislature.

Negro Democratic precinct captains, by and large, are more able than are those in other wards where the native and foreign-born whites have found more attractive and less arduous routes for personal achievement. The manpower the Negro machine can recruit is on the whole better than the manpower non-Negro machines can recruit, and this contributes in no small measure to its durability.

The ward organizations of the Negro machine continue to make themselves helpful to the voters in their precincts in the traditional manner. There is no need to detail the well-known services a political machine renders except to observe that these services persist in the Negro wards. In one ward before Christmas, 168 families received some free clothing, about 5,000 children were entertained at theater parties, and turkeys were distributed to large numbers of needy householders. In another ward, $400 was raised for a family burned out of its home. Political intervention with the police, bondsmen, lawyers, relief workers, and other city officials on behalf of voters is still common, although the ability of the machine to render important services in these areas has steadily declined over the years. The importance of this fact is discussed elsewhere in this study; here, it is necessary only to note that the ward organizations continue to supply information about such services and have generally been successful in maintaining the belief among voters that political intervention is of value.

In addition to the traditional bases of machine influence, there are also certain prevalent attitudes in the Negro community, which can be detected among Negro civic leaders, that are favorable to the political organization and preserve it from serious attack. Civic leaders who might represent a potential or actual challenge to the machine are for the most part not a challenge at all. This is in part a result of the machine's influence—the network of obligations with which the machine has entangled would-be rivals— and in part the result of favorable attitudes. Let us discuss some of these attitudes first.

First, there is the general allegiance of the northern Negro to the Democratic Party. Most Negro leaders not members of the political organization proclaim the virtues of political independence, but in fact, the majority appear to be fairly consistent Democratic voters:

> I wouldn't hesitate to vote for a Republican if I thought he were the better man. I've voted a split ticket before, and I can do it again ... some Democrats are SOB's that I wouldn't vote for if my life depended on it. . . . But I believe, on balance, that despite the Southern element, the salvation of the Negro lies with the Democratic party.

Second, there is the general conservatism of Negro leaders. The Democratic party in Chicago represents the status quo; it is the entrenched power and the target of reformers. Although the Republican party is closely allied with business in the city, an ideological choice on local issues (a choice between conservative and liberal positions) does not correspond necessarily with whatever ideological alignment may exist between the adherents of the two parties nationally. In Chicago, the rebels, the reformers, and the independent liberals tend to be forced into opposition to the controlling forces—the Democratic organization. Negro leaders tend to be conservative, and to share (with the exception of the importance they attach to race) the values of white conservatives. Few feel that there is anything at stake important enough to warrant an attack on the status quo and the political party which controls and supports the existing arrangements. Few operate enterprises of sufficient size to raise for them real estate and taxation problems of a magnitude which would elicit efforts to achieve "economy" in government and produce attacks on the city administration.

Third, there is a distinct and evident aversion to politics among Negroes of the middle and upper classes. Except for those who are attracted to it for its rewards, or those few who are temperamentally inclined to practical politics as a way of life, Negro leaders tend to withdraw from electoral politics for the same reason they withdraw from controversy in general. Working with, or against, a political machine means working in an area widely believed to be "dirty" or corrupt and coming in contact with the large numbers of lower-class people who make up the backbone of the machine in the precincts. Politics is not respectable, and respectability is highly valued. In addition, overt partisan activity can alienate friends or hurt business. A Negro businessman and civic leader observed that most of his colleagues shied away from politics:

> Politics is too controversial. The only way you can even get them to let you use their name is to set up an independent citizens' committee of some kind. . . . The Negro businessman, he won't even vote in primary elections much less join the regular party organization.

An aggressive and militant civic leader agreed completely with that statement, and offered an explanation of why few Negro leaders will participate in organization politics, much less oppose the machine:

> Politics is completely unrespectable to the middle-class Negro. . . . Our feeling of respectability is very precarious. . . . It is too easy to lose it, and politics can threaten it, we seem to think. Politics is bad, so we withdraw from it. . . . The middle-class Negro is satisfied just to hear people talk about the "great challenge" and the need for "action." But there is never any action. It never occurs to them to do anything themselves. . . . The aversion is there, built in, and it is probably deeper than this, but I don't know. It has something to do with a loss of respectability. We have to maintain that respectability come hell or high water.

Although several Negro ministers support or oppose the machine regularly, there is a sizeable group of ministers who consider themselves advanced, educated, or upper-class, to whom politics is anathema. In part this reflects the general withdrawal from politics of this entire group, but in part it reflects the widespread belief that the store-front Negro preacher has been bought and sold politically with utter venality. The college-trained, well-paid Negro minister with a large congregation of "respectable" people is anxious to avoid any identification with his lower-class brethren. Said one:

> Politics is filthy. . . . My argument is that the minister loses something by getting into that. My job is to inspire Christian laymen to get into it and help clean it up. . . . I don't want to get into names, but if half what I hear about Dawson is true, then it's filthy. . . . You are judged by the company you keep. The preacher is still a leader, *the* leader, and he has to avoid the very appearance of evil. . . . No politicians will speak in my church.

In return, the Negro politician regards such people with considerable contempt:

> In Lake Meadows [a private interracial apartment development], you can't tell those people anything. They're upper class, or think they are. They mark their ballots with the word "yes," or a check, or write their names on it. . . . They don't know that you're only supposed to put in an "X" mark, and you can't tell them. . . . Those people refuse to vote in primaries. You can't get them out at all.

A fourth attitude which contributes to the power of the machine is the wide-spread *imputation* of power to it by other Negro leaders. Whatever power it has is in part due to the fact that people believe it has power and act on the basis of that belief. Constant references appear in almost all interviews to "Dawson's power" or "Dawson's machine." No doubt Dawson has influence, but often influence is conceded to him in what appear to be excessively generous portions. "This whole city is hidebound politically," said one Negro businessman. "It's under tight political control. Other than the politicians, there's no contact possible with the people who make the big decisions." Negro leaders, particularly those who are anxious to change things but feel frustrated in their attempts, believe that most other leaders are in debt to or live in fear of the machine. "Who is going to do it?" asked one. "Everybody in this town is under some obligation to the city machine. . . . You name me a person who could do it, and I'll tell you what their obligation is." One particularly shrewd civic leader felt that this was the correct way in which to act. You get more done if you recognize the existence of power:

> Now in ———, where I have a farm, I might very well be a Republican there. . . . You have to support the person who can get things

done for you, and if the Republicans have the power, then you have to be a Republican. . . . But I can't see being anything but a Democrat in Chicago. I've never been anything but one here even though I don't like [a certain politician] at all, and can't work with him.

There is a fifth and final attitude which contributes to the maintenance of the machine that in some ways is peculiarly Negro. Whatever their attitudes toward the Negro boss, many Negro civic leaders admire him—with varying degrees of reluctance—for being a Negro who has achieved something, who has attained power and status, and particularly for being a Negro who has accomplished this in a white-dominated world. Only the most militant would insist that the Negro boss was, as a boss, utterly bad; to most, he is a source of subtle pride. For example:

William Dawson is a politician, but you can't despise him. I don't support everything he does or what people claim he does, but as a symbol of political leadership I think he's terrific. We have to have a man like that.

Another Negro leader described the covert manner in which such sympathy is sometimes expressed:

Dawson represents something for the Negro people: achievement, status, the power of the ballot. . . . When you have a racially-mixed group meeting here, for instance, and some bright whites start to sound off about Dawson and attack him, the Negroes present will sort of look down, and mumble, and maybe even add in a small voice . . . other criticisms of Dawson. . . . That's the way they act, but that's not how they feel. . . . It's not just politicians who don't want to lose Negro representation in government.

Another very well-known Negro civic leader who had fought Dawson vigorously on an issue in which he had a personal stake remarked, in the midst of the controversy, that he had "tremendous respect for Dawson." Asked why, the civic leader said:

He is a man who gets things done. If you get his word to do something, then it's as good as done. You can count on him once he makes a promise. . . . And he is intelligent. That counts a lot with me. There aren't many men these days whose word you can count on. . . . He's not afraid to work, either. I saw him working in his office on Easter Sunday once. I figure any man who will work on Easter works hard enough to deserve my vote, I don't care how many times they say he has been away from his desk in Congress.

But these bases of the machine's influence—its virtual monopoly of electoral strength on the South Side and the attitudes which are favorable to it—are not the only grounds of its strength. There is in addition a network of personal relationships and obligations which radiates out from its leadership to that of other civic enterprises and to the heads of other important Negro organizations. The machine can forestall public attack on it because it is in a position to reinforce the natural moderation or conservatism of most Negro leaders with favors and benefits which place them in its debt. The Negro press is an important Negro organization which could choose to subject the Negro politicians to much more criticism than they now receive at its hands. The publisher of the principal Negro paper is a man who is naturally moderate in his views, with no trace of the militant style. For a number of years he has had a fairly close personal relationship with Dawson. The publisher has been a member of several prestigious state and national public agencies, including the Virgin Islands Commission. Dawson, as Congressman and a vice-chairman of the Democratic National Committee, has been in a position to have blocked some of these appointments had he chosen. He permitted, and perhaps encouraged, them instead. He has been helpful to the publisher in business matters on a number of occasions. The Negro press is also the beneficiary of heavy Democratic political advertising during election seasons. Although such revenue is probably important to the newspaper, no one believes that the advertising will change any votes. The newspaper, it seems clear, would lose more than the machine if the advertising were withdrawn.[5]

Occasionally there is formalized co-operation between the Negro press and the Democratic organization. When Chicago police seemed to be conspicuously harassing Negroes on the South Side during a few months in 1957-58, the Negro aldermen and other politicians met in a group with the officers of the Negro newspaper to decide on what should be done. For a period, these meetings occurred fairly regularly, and there continue to be informal, off-the-record contacts between editors and politicians on matters of mutual interest. This co-operation does not preclude criticism of Negro politicians by the Negro press. On occasions of race issues of particular importance—such as anti-Negro violence or brutality, or overt and widely publicized cases of discrimination—the politicians will be criticized if they fail (and they usually do fail) to take a strong *public* stand. Such criticism, however, is sporadic and specific in content. There is not found in the press the steady antagonism toward Negro politicians which is characteristically exhibited by Negro protest leaders.

Negro businessmen in general, not just publishers, need to proceed cautiously in any civic actions which would be interpreted as a threat to the machine. Whatever criticisms they have of politics, Negro politicians constitute an important and sometimes vital source of influence which the businessman (or labor leader or minister or publisher) may some day need. It is rare that a businessman does not have some interests which on occasion could be furthered by political assistance—interests ranging from securing a building permit to resisting an urban redevelopment project that might displace his property or attract strong white business competition. Property owners are liable to the critical attentions of building and fire inspectors. Negro businessmen and property owners approached the politicians for aid in defeating a plan to place a large, white-owned shopping center in the Lake Meadows redevelopment project. On another occasion, a similar group sought the assistance of the aldermen in helping them produce a neighborhood conservation program which would both raise property values and resist further redevelopment involving large-scale land clearance. There are, on the other hand, some Negro businessmen and large property owners who have vigorously campaigned against the Negro Democratic machine with regularity. But some of these hedge themselves so as not to alienate the machine completely. When the associate of one Republican businessman was asked whether the Republicans had felt any reprisals because of political campaigning, he replied:

Oh, no. There are no repercussions of that sort. You know, we are heavy contributors to everything out here. . . . We have a fund, which [X] channels through me so there won't be any need for his dealing with or accounting for it, which we use to give to the Democrats. They come wanting $500 or so for something, we give it to them.

There is no way of knowing how typical this is, but there can

be little doubt that the business civic leadership of the community has good reason for avoiding unnecessary conflict with
the machine. A group which often has good reason for *seeking*
conflict with the machine, on the other hand, is the local branch
of the NAACP. The NAACP, when officered by Negro protest
leaders, is an organization in search of an issue, and the issueless character of Negro politics renders the politicians a prime
target. The differences in ends between the NAACP and the
Negro machine come to the fore most clearly in those cases
where a dramatic instance of anti-Negro action occurs. The advocacy by the NAACP of a race position on such issues is a
constraint on the machine's latitude of action, and as a constraint it will be discussed later in this chapter. At this point,
we are interested in what controls the machine can exercise over
the NAACP to reduce its impact.

Since the NAACP has a mass membership which elects the
officers, it is susceptible to the influence of those groups which
can manipulate its elections. Many groups in the Negro community attempt to do this—labor unions, churches, and others.
None has the resources for this purpose which the machine
can command. Only when it feels itself to be strongly provoked
does the machine act to alter the leadership of the NAACP,
but then it acts with great effectiveness. An aggressive labor
leader was the NAACP president for two years, and during this
time had criticized some Negro politicians for what he felt were
failures to act on race issues. In addition, the leader had been
active in South Side politics, both as a candidate some years
before and as an organizer of political opposition to the machine. When a moderate businessman was proposed as a candidate to replace the labor leader, the machine moved to assist
him. One experienced Negro politician described the process:

[X] is an old friend; I've known him for twenty years. . . . He came
to me and some of the boys and said he'd like our help. We helped
him as a friend, and we didn't like [the labor leader] at all. He was
using the NAACP for his own purposes, just as he used [his union].
. . . We don't want to control the NAACP. . . . We just ran in a few
votes for an old friend who we thought would do a good job.

By taking out memberships in the NAACP for its precinct
captains, workers, and job holders, the machine was able to

place around four hundred votes at the disposal of the candidate it favored. He was elected. Once the new president was in office, the machine did not attempt to interfere in or direct the course of the NAACP's affairs. The new president was not an agent of the machine; he was only an acceptable alternative to a thoroughly unacceptable leader. When, at the end of his first one-year term of office he faced re-election, he began by attempting to mobilize his own supporters without calling upon the machine for organized assistance. Labor leaders, ministers, and businessmen who were favorable to his candidacy were asked to supply votes from their organizations. Shortly before the election, however, it became apparent that he might not be able to enlist enough votes to defeat the challenge of the militant groups opposing him. He turned once again to the machine. A Negro politician describes this situation:

> He called us about a week before the election. He must have woke up and saw that the people he had counted on weren't going to deliver as they had promised. . . . His personal help didn't seem to be too formidable, at least as compared to the other side. . . . His supporters [some ministers and labor leaders] were supposed to deliver 150 or 200 votes each. But it was closer to 50 or 75 each. . . . So we sent in some people from our wards. . . . If it hadn't been for the organization, I think he would have lost the ball in the weeds.

The machine sought no particular policy ends as the price for its support; it merely wanted the "right kind of person" as president. This man was supported again because "he seemed to do all right last year, so we figured he would be all right again this year." In addition, his opponent was known to be hostile to the machine, and this hostility was explained by some politicians as radicalism. "The big thing is to keep the pinkos out. . . . Those other people are pretty red."

This network of obligations which the machine can weave in the Negro community embraces not only the press, businessmen, and the NAACP, but includes ministers, labor leaders, and others. Many observers believe that the machine is also related at certain points to organized crime, receiving campaign funds in exchange for protection from police. This is a subject about which little is known and which in any case is not relevant to our center of attention—influence relations among civic and political leaders in the area of public policy. Few, if any, strong political machines are entirely free of corrupt elements; at the same time, it is unlikely that the Chicago organization is as venal as its most hostile critics claim.*6

Tensions in the Machine

Both external and internal constraints operate on the actions of the Negro machine. The internal constraints are largely a function of shifts in the Negro electorate and the restless and unrequited ambitions of members of the organization. The increased prosperity of the Negro community and its continued differentiation in terms of class, education, and place of residence have placed new demands on the machine. A substantial Negro middle class with a relatively high level of education and a greater awareness of issues is conspicuously emerging in

---

*6. The relationship between the Dawson organization and crime is a favorite topic of speculation everywhere in the city. There is no doubt that at one time gambling, particularly the policy racket, flourished on the South Side, with evident police and political protection. Since that time, policy has declined in scope for a variety of reasons. Nevertheless, there are to the author's personal knowledge at least fifteen separate policy "wheels" on the South Side, and probably two or three times that number in actual fact. Narcotics and prostitution are widespread.

Dawson is well-known for his tolerant attitude toward small-scale gambling. "Betting is a human frailty, but it isn't an evil in itself . . . Negroes don't create money. They usually go outside their area to work for it and bring it back to their community. And a corrupt system, growing out of gambling, drains them dry. . . . If anybody is to profit out of gambling in the Negro community, it should be the Negro. . . . I want the money my people earn to stay in the Negro community." (Quoted in John Madigan, "The Durable Mr. Dawson of Cook County, Illinois," *Reporter,* August 9, 1956, pp. 39-40.) Several investigations, one by a Federal grand jury and the Department of Justice, have been made into Negro political and police links to crime in Chicago. No findings have ever been announced, and no important prosecutions have resulted. Most law agencies confess their inability to develop substantial evidence of improper connections. The sole Negro police captain was indicted on a perjury charge arising out of an investigation, but the case was dismissed for lack of evidence.

In any case, the days of the Negro "policy kings" have gone. These men were rich and flamboyant citizens who often contributed substantially to church and race organizations, such as the NAACP, using money gained through gambling. See St. Clair Drake and Horace R. Cayton, *Black Metropolis: A Study of Negro Life in a Northern City* (New York: Harcourt, Brace and Co., 1945), pp. 470-94.

Chicago as elsewhere, and fragmentary evidence indicates that it is raising political problems which the machine has not as yet solved. The high-price, middle- and upper-income apartments of the Lake Meadows project were constructed in the center of the oldest all-Negro ward in the city, and brought in many well-to-do Negroes who would otherwise have been living on the periphery of the Negro area. In the 1958 judicial election, an election which for all practical purposes was uncontested by the Republicans, the precincts which comprise the Lake Meadows area went Democratic but only by comparatively small margins. Of the seventy-six precincts carried by the machine, the Lake Meadows precinct had the lowest percentage of Democratic votes. In the 1958 Congressional election, when Dawson was running for his ninth term, he lost only three second ward precincts—two in Lake Meadows and one in which the Illinois Institute of Technology is located. This is particularly striking when it is realized that he lost only five precincts out of his entire district (which includes over 350 precincts).

As the Negro area has expanded to the south and west along its periphery, it has begun to enter areas of single-family, owner-occupied dwelling units (homes and duplexes) that offer a marked contrast to the tightly-packed multiple dwelling units (apartments and rooming houses) which have characterized most of the South Side Negro area in the past. Part of this area, known as Park Manor, is a community which offers some of the same kinds of challenges posed by the Lake Meadows project in the heart of the Negro quarter. Middle-class home owners have settled here, and the Negro machine has not, by and large, been able to organize them as successfully or with such facility as it organized the slum dwellers in the core of the Black Belt. Future expansion of the Negro area will continue in this direction, provided that a general level of prosperity continues. More sophisticated appeals will have to be made to many of these people for their votes, and the ability of the machine to depend on a steady majority regardless of its posture concerning race issues may easily decline.

A study has been made which contains a breakdown of the Negro vote by class of neighborhood. In an area of single-family, owner-occupied homes in a stable neighborhood, the Negro vote shows both a resistance to machine control and a sensitivity to national issues as compared to "machine" Negro wards in the center of the more congested areas. Between 1951 and 1955, the Negro vote for Mayor in the machine wards changed radically, owing to organization activity. When the machine decided to "sit out" the 1951 election as a sign of hostility to Mayor Martin Kennelly, the Negro precincts delivered only 49 per cent of their votes to Kennelly. Four years later, when the machine went all-out for Richard Daley, these same wards delivered 87 per cent of their votes to Daley. At the same time, the so-called "middle-class" Negro precincts outside the machine's area remained stable—voting 57 per cent for both Kennelly and Daley. For national candidates, however, the middle-class precincts showed a much wider range of fluctuation. In 1952 they delivered a 70 per cent vote for Adlai Stevenson, but in 1956 this fell to only 51 per cent. In general, the Democratic percentage of total votes has declined most in the middle-class precincts and least in the machine precincts in the period 1947 to 1957, although the *total* vote in both areas has dropped. The Democratic majorities in the machine precincts have declined 11 per cent, while the Democratic majorities in the middle-class precincts have declined 23 per cent.[7] Movement of Negroes to middle-class neighborhoods is rising steadily, and the implications this may have for machine influence cannot be predicted with certainty, although a loss seems inevitable.

This demographic shift has another implication. Those who move to better residential areas are those who once lived in the crowded centers of the Negro community. The most congested wards on the South Side, where the densities at one time were upwards of 70,000 persons per square mile,[8] have lost population over the last ten years. In part this has been due to the partial relaxation of some barriers—particularly restrictive covenants, made unenforceable in 1948—to the freer movement of Negroes in the city; in part it has been due to postwar prosperity which has given Negroes greater opportunities to seek better housing; and in part it has been due to the large-scale land clearance projects in the second ward which have displaced many thousands of Negroes, replacing them with far fewer in such projects as Lake Meadows, public housing, the Illinois Institute of Technology campus, and the Michael Reese Hospital development. This population loss has been reflected in a drop in numbers of registered voters. In 1950, the second ward had an estimated 108,761 inhabitants, of whom 58,445 were registered voters (about 32,000 to 33,000 voted). In 1959, the total registration was only about 35,000, despite strenuous efforts on the part of the organization leadership to encourage registration. The center of Negro population appears to be shifting southward in Chicago; correspondingly, the absolute size of the vote the Dawson machine can contribute to the party as a whole has declined.[9]

An additional and perhaps even more important source of stress within the machine arises from the ambitions of its members. The enthusiasms which built the machine are beginning to fade; the sense of accomplishment which accompanied the early successes in gaining political recognition for the Negro is being replaced with a sense of frustration and doubt. In the general competition of ethnic groups for a place on the Democratic ticket, the Negroes (along with the Poles) have not gained in accordance with their numbers in the city. No Negro has ever been slated by the party for one of the politically important posts—those posts in the city and county administration which control patronage. The number of Negroes elected to well-paying and prestigious judgeships has been far fewer than the Negro proportion of the total electorate would suggest. Despite tremendous population gains since 1940, the Negro group continues to elect only one state senator. Although all ethnic groups complain of an unfair distribution of the rewards of political activity, Negroes see in it a sign of racial discrimination. The decline in the importance of organization politicians—the weakening of the ability of the aldermen and the precinct captains to control the allocation of favors—has made it appear to many Negro political leaders that the virtues of party regularity have been exaggerated and that new appeals must be sought. To a Negro, an alternative appeal can only mean one thing—the use of race issues. The Negro majorities for the party, it is widely felt, have been taken for granted, and as a consequence the rewards bestowed on Negroes are not as great as those which might be offered to more marginal constituencies. If there were a real challenge to be overcome by the machine, then it might claim a greater price for its services. To some Negro politicians, these complaints are intensified by a belief that the "Old Man"—Congressman Dawson—is getting too old and that he has lost his vigor. One remarked:

> There's a lot of things I can't get, or have to pay more for than you do . . . just because of my skin color. And jobs are one of those things. A white ward committeeman can go down there [to City Hall] and from top to bottom put his boys in. . . . Hell, they have enough jobs out there to take care of the Republican captains . . . if they want. We can't get anything. . . . We have two municipal court judges, but we should have more. There was recently an opening on the bench, and the Old Man didn't ask for a Negro to be put on it. I don't know why; maybe he's slipping.

Another Negro politician could understand how Dawson felt:

> I know how he feels. I'm a half century old, and you start to lead a new life then. I don't want to hatch a fight anymore, although I won't dodge one, either. I would much rather be cautious. I prefer. . . the least conflict possible. I can see how an old man is mostly interested in preserving power, not risking it by trying for more.

Many members of the organization believe that Dawson has kept his old friends from the early days of the machine in office too long and has not made enough room at the top into which younger men might advance. One Negro elected official is disliked by a number of his Negro colleagues. "If Dawson didn't have his arms around him . . . he wouldn't last a minute," said one. "But for some reason the Old Man likes him. . . . They've been around together for a long time."

These tensions, which can be found in any political organization, are important for our purposes because they often lead the restless members in the direction of the manipulation of issues as an expression of their discontent and as a means of insuring against the future. Younger Negro politicians are beginning to look beyond Dawson, and some are experimenting with an appeal based on race issues or at least on modern public relations as a means of establishing themselves as leaders in their own right. Great care must be exercised in attempting this, for the limits of permissible action are clearly defined. One Negro alderman, who is also a ward committeeman, has attempted to create an image of independence and issue leadership in the Negro community. He became co-sponsor of an open occupancy ordinance with a white alderman from an adjoining ward and received a great deal of publicity as a result. The other Negro aldermen, under Dawson's leadership, have shown great reluctance in supporting the measure, least in its present form. Friction developed between Dawson and the alderman, Holman, over this issue, among others. At the same time, Holman desired to retain the advantages of organization membership; this required walking a fine line between defiance and compliance— a tactic which may or may not prove successful. Rumor repeatedly held that Holman would be dropped from his posts, but nothing occurred. It is widely believed that he aspires to the Congressional seat now held by an aging white man whose district includes Holman's ward. The district also encompasses the predominantly white University of Chicago ward, and an image of independence and civic leadership, including a strong stand on civil liberties, would be an almost indispensable asset for a politician hoping to carry that ward in a Congressional election. Other Negro politicians, who are less venturesome than Holman and whose ambitions are not caught in such difficult cross-pressures, nevertheless are beginning to feel that in the newer Negro communities, a greater appeal to issues must be made.

These tensions are largely incipient rather than actual, and should not be overestimated. The Chicago Negro machine continues to rely on the traditional methods of politics. "This isn't California," said one politician. "Elections are still won by precinct captains. The Negro wards aren't newspaper wards by a long shot." Lake Meadows is an island of four thousand people in a sea of half a million. The peripheral Negro communities still vote Democratic, although with reduced majorities. Few Negro politicians are yet in a position where the risks involved in an appeal based on issues would be offset by the probable benefits. Old allegiances are still strong. But the leader, the Old Man, *is* an old man—seventy-three years old—and tensions and rivalries now latent will, on his death, erupt into a period of political warfare which will convulse the Negro machine before a new pattern of leadership is established.

External Constraints

Those groups which can assert and maintain race issues can set limits on the machine. The machine rarely raises issues, but issues—once raised—are forces which it can ignore only at a cost. In many cases, the cost is deemed acceptable; in other cases, it is not. The machine might not advocate such issues, but it can only with difficulty avoid responding to them. It might not submit a hospital integration ordinance to the city council, but it cannot work against such an ordinance once submitted.

Many Negro politicians, particularly the older ones, admit the machine's reluctance to become embroiled in issues where sacrifices might have to be made and argue that this is proper. Politics is politics, not civic leadership. "I'm a *politician*," said one Negro leader. "I know what can be done and what can't." Another Negro politician felt that the most effective Negro leaders were not politicians at all:

The most effective leaders, or leadership, comes from people who are not politicians. . . . Politicians are limited, they have to watch out for their jobs; there is only so much they can do. You have to go outside the politicians to find good leadership. . . . But the Negro politician has done the thing which is necessary before anything else: *organization*. . . . He has organized the Negro and taught him how to use the ballot. Of course, he's taught them that for the benefit of the politician concerned, but then you have to expect that.

This man believed it was unreasonable to expect politicians to do more than this. The rewards of issue leadership were few and the perils many. The Negro politician must not risk party disloyalty and antagonizing unduly the white machine leader. The possible rewards—limited popular appreciation, grudgingly given and soon forgotten—cannot compensate for an intraparty fight, possible sanctions from the boss, and the instability caused by having unsettled the electorate. Junior politicians may seek issues to accelerate their rise, but older leaders do not. To the Negro politician, peace is a great virtue:

My people are not very well educated yet, and they are a hot-headed group . . . . I could rouse them if I wanted to. There was a time when I could and did make impassioned speeches on the streets. I knew how to reach them . . . . But we have to admit it, these people, a lot of them just up from the South, they aren't mature citizens yet. They are good people but they are excitable. What these people need is help in the little things. . . . There are very few interests that concern them.

This attitude has been formulated, by Dawson and others, into an explanation of their conception of the function of politics. Politics, to the politicians, is the art of organizing a community for the purpose of electing men to office. It is not a vehicle for the public expression of grievances:

> These people don't understand what politics is all about. I want to teach people how to organize and elect public officials so that we will have someone in power who can speak for us in the party councils and in government offices where it counts . . . . Talking about all these problems won't get you elected and won't help your cause any when you get in office . . . . These other groups raise a lot of fuss, but when the chips are down they come to me . . . . I won't pick a fight with anyone . . . . But if they understood what politics was all about, they would help us build this organization rather than criticizing it so much.

As young organizations value change, so mature organizations value order, and the leading Negro politicians have so completely moved from youthful change to present order that the aversion to issues, publicity, and protest action has become ingrained. The constraints of the political situation alone are inadequate to explain the unwillingness of the politician to make even minimal concessions to public relations. Dawson's dislike for publicity is legendary. It goes far beyond that which is called for simply by prudence. He feels that he has been mistreated by an essentially hostile press, that even friendly reporters are not allowed to print stories favorable to him, and that publicity invariably ends by embarrassing him or those political leaders with whom he works. Silence is golden: "I don't like publicity. . . . They can't hurt you for what you don't say."

The relationship between the Negro machine and race issues can be described along two dimensions: salience and divisiveness. Salience refers to the perceived relevance of an issue to the needs of the political organization. Divisiveness refers to the impact such an issue will have on the organization. The machine has some ends which are compatible with race ends, and it will champion them when that is apparent. The race issues which are adopted by the machine spring, by and large, from those immediate relations with its constituents who express or feel a direct concern over tangible problems. The machine can be moved to interest itself in concrete, proximate ends, but only with difficulty moved to absorb itself in the search for more remote, intangible, or ideological ends. The merchants of the second ward were able to impress upon the machine the disadvantages to Negro business which would result from a large Lake Meadows shopping center controlled by white corporations. Property owners were able to obtain machine support for efforts to maximize the prices they would receive for their condemned properties. Men who are out of work can gain machine help, and the machine can describe its efforts in terms of an attempt to reduce employment discrimination. But some *thing* must be sought. Where the voluntary association would see land clearance as representing a perpetuation of residential segregation in its effects, the politician sees it as:

mainly a case of organizing the property owners in the area in order that they could get more for their property. We managed to stall Lake Meadows for two years, and we got something for it . . . . The people who stuck with us in that got as much as twice what others who dropped out got for identical properties.

The politician is not oblivious of the political advantages of such a program:

I fought [a land clearance project] . . . . There were hundreds, thousands of Negroes in [that building]. It was a police precinct all by itself. I kept them from tearing it down for eight years . . . . We insisted that they had to have a place to move all those people to before they could tear it down. Of course, I wasn't exactly a knight on a white horse about it. Those people were all Democrats, and I was a Democrat, and I was playing politics.

It is hard, on the other hand, for the politicians to detect any benefits to them from an issue which has an intangible, remote, or diffuse end. An open occupancy ordinance is not yet "good politics" in Chicago; too few constituents are concerned about it, too few will benefit from it in any immediate sense, and too many people will be upset by it. Politics, of course, does not impose an unalterable mold on the activities of its participants. Politicians operate, as do others, on the basis of imperfect information and calculations of risk. The old-line Negro political leadership displays strikingly the characteristics mentioned above; younger men may or may not, depending on where they think the future lies. The sponsors of the Mid-South Chicago Council, in an effort to develop a conservation program for the Negro community, sought the aid of the Negro aldermen. Their reactions were varied. One supported it strongly, although with doubts as to its success, as a means of avoiding further land clearance and the disruption of established constituencies. A second also supported it strongly, but more as good public relations that would enhance his efforts to rise in the area as a whole, beyond merely his own ward. A third saw no political value in it to himself — to him, civic activities of this kind would only create commitments that might later prove burdensome. A fourth was suspicious and hostile, owing in part to the bad experiences he had had in his own ward generated by the conservation efforts of another group. One alderman did not like to unsettle his constituents for an uncertain result; another alderman had a survey made and discovered that there was such a high level of transiency among the residents of his ward that losses arising from conservation would be relatively meaningless. The degree of co-operation the Council's sponsors could obtain, therefore, varied widely among members of the same machine. To induce them to contribute, the Council endeavored to put them before the public in meetings. Although there was no common pattern of response from the politicians as politicians, their responses could be accounted for on the basis of what each felt to be the needs of their political ambitions — each saw the "facts" of his own ward's position as they affected his own special set of aspirations. The "hard-headed realism" often imputed to professional politicians is not always a realism that disposes them to see the same facts in the same way.

The second dimension of the political response to issues is the extent to which an issue will divide the party. There are two principal areas of political combat in Illinois: the Chicago City Council and the Springfield state legislature. In the City Council, the Mayor and his Democratic party are supreme — the party's decisions are the city's policies. (Of the fifty aldermen on the Council in 1959, forty-seven were Democrats.) In Springfield, the

Democrats may or may not control the lower house, depending on the fortunes of electoral politics, but they never control the Senate. Here the Democratic party does not enforce its will. This difference means that the kinds of issues which can be fought out in the City Council are not of the same character as those that are fought out in Springfield. In Springfield, the party can allow its members the luxury of catering to the demands of their constituents with such special-interest legislation as a strong FEPC law or a school redistricting law without fear that it may be embarrassed by its passage. Such legislation is regularly defeated by the Senate where the Republicans are in the majority. After nearly fifteen years of seeing an FEPC bill defeated in Springfield, one Negro politician exclaimed that "FEPC is a farce." Another observed:

> Let's be frank about that .... They [the white Democrats] vote for it first because they want to keep the Negro vote and that's a good way to do it. Second, they knew it wouldn't pass .... so they don't have to worry about getting it. They are against it anyway, really. Let's not kid ourselves.

On most race matters, the Negro politician in Springfield is a free agent. No party clearance is needed to propose any kind of legislative solution to the ills of the Negro people. It is rare for a Negro state representative to receive orders from the Negro boss. In the two most recent sessions, such orders only came twice — in both cases on vital intraparty matters such as redistricting and patronage. The officers of Negro voluntary associations are aware of this and know they can take their favorite bills to the Negro politicians, confident they will be received and sponsored. One militant leader said:

> They don't like us, but I can't think of a bill we've given them that they haven't supported .... I think that deep down inside they think I'm right .... On most matters they are free agents.

In Chicago it is a different matter. Here the Democratic party is on the spot: it must bear the responsibility. Few white aldermen and ward committeemen can be described as liberal on race issues, and few can afford to be. The proceedings of the Chicago City Council are generally undisturbed by the advocacy of race ends. When such ends have been advocated and as a result the Democratic majority has been forced to divide, this advocacy has come from independents or Republicans. Proposals to build public housing on vacant land sites in white wards and ordinances to ban racial discrimination in housing built with public assistance (e.g., land clearance and urban renewal projects) were urged by non-machine aldermen. The latter, the so-called Carey Ordinance, was defeated by a vote of thirty-one to thirteen after a heated controversy in which Mayor Kennelly intervened in opposition. The Negro machine politicians do not raise such issues, but neither, of course, do they oppose them. One described his philosophy in this regard:

> He [another Negro leader] was always raising the race issue and antagonizing people. . . . Me, I never raise the race issue. . . . I certainly didn't in the Council. I would let the other fellow speak and put the burden on him of proving that all Americans aren't entitled to the same rights . . . . But I wouldn't raise it. I would just defend our rights if somebody else tried to raise it.

Chapter IV

Chicago: Negro-White
Political Relations

THE leader of the Chicago Democratic machine is the effective
head of the city government, regardless of the title he may
hold. Since 1955, the head of the Democratic organization (that is,
the chairman of the Cook County Democratic Central Committee)
and the head of the city administration (the Mayor) have been
the same person. The Democrats have held uninterrupted control of
Chicago since 1931, when Anton Cermak was elected Mayor. In
1933 Edward Kelly was chosen Mayor by the City Council upon
the death of Cermak. Kelly promptly began to take advantage
of the national trend toward the Democratic party, and, with the
aid of large amounts of patronage, began to build a strong organization in Chicago. One of the important ethnic blocs in the city
was the Negro group.

Of great importance for the political history of Chicago was the
fact that the Negro population was, from the first, concentrated in
contiguous, all-Negro tracts which grew by peripheral expansion.
This residential concentration took place in a city whose political
subdivisions were small and tended to follow ethnic lines. Before
1921 there were thirty-five wards in a city of 1,367,515 adult
citizens; after 1921, the number of wards was increased to fifty.
Each ward before 1921 elected two aldermen; each ward after
1921 elected one. The city was fractionalized politically from the
very first, and this meant that as early as 1915, the Negroes con-
stituted a majority of one ward, and that year the first Negro was
elected to the City Council. By 1918 the Negroes were able to

elect a second alderman from that ward. When the ward lines
were redrawn in 1921, two wards — the second and the third —
were each able to elect one Negro alderman. A Negro entered
Congress from Chicago in 1928.

The importance of bringing the Negroes into the political organization of the city was first recognized by the Republicans.
Under Mayor William "Big Bill" Thompson, Negroes were provided with patronage jobs, appeals were made for Negro electoral
support, and promising Negro politicians were brought into the
Republican party. The Negro wards responded generously. In
1927, for example, the Negro second ward gave over 91 per cent
of its vote to Thompson, the Republican candidate for Mayor.
The early and decisive entry of Negroes into Chicago politics made
them an important factor to be considered by any aspirant to power
in the city, and their firm Republicanism made their conversion to
the party of Kelly difficult. When Kelly came to the Mayor's office,
there were more than 150,000 Negroes living in just the second,
third, and fourth wards on the South Side. In 1934 and 1935,
Mayor Kelly was in search of a man who could successfully organize these Negroes for the Democratic party. At the same time,
William L. Dawson, a maverick Republican in the City Council,
was in search of political support. Kelly realized that the white
committeeman of the second ward was finished; the choice had
to be made as to successor. Kelly became convinced that Dawson
was the best prospect. In the February, 1939 aldermanic elections,
Dawson ran third in a field of four in a close race and then
announced that he was switching parties. Henceforth, he said,
he would be a Democrat. Kelly agreed to give him an opportunity
to take over the second ward organization. For this purpose, the
power to clear city patronage appointments was put at his disposal.
Then Dawson began the task of winning over his rivals within the
Democratic machine. Dawson assured them their positions in the
party would not be swept away by an influx of his ex-Republican
followers and, indeed, they were not. Dawson soon acquired control over the balance of the patronage appointments in his ward,
and the transfer of power to the new ward committeeman was
accomplished.[*1]

_____

[*1]. The transfer of Negro voters' allegiance from the Republican to the
Democratic party was not, as some have argued, a simple function of the

As time passed, more and more wards became "Negro" politically as well as demographically. Logically, the city machine could organize these wards in one of two ways. They could select a series of Negro ward committeemen, each of whom would be independent with regard to the affairs of his ward, owing his allegiance directly to the County Central Committee. Or, the party could permit the rise of a single Negro leader who would exercise general authority over all the Negro wards and who would be responsible for the political organization of the Negroes in the entire area. Stated metaphorically, the Negroes could be allowed to produce a number of feudal barons in the kingdom of the Democratic boss, or a process of subinfeudation could be followed, with one Negro standing between the boss and the individual Negro wards. What is important here is that the existence of a city machine made the second alternative possible. The city leader, who was the single source of authority and patronage for the city Democratic organization, could support a sub-leader. If there had been no city machine, if power at the top had been diffused, it is most unlikely that a single Negro leader would have emerged. The

---

impact of the New Deal and Roosevelt's great personal attraction. Gosnell presents figures which demonstrate that shifts to the Democratic party occurred faster in those Negro areas of Chicago with higher median rentals and fewer unemployed than in the depressed areas where relief cases were the largest in number. The most depressed area in the Negro community has generally been the second ward, where Dawson began his rise to power. Although a Negro Democrat has carried the first Congressional District (which includes the second ward) every year since 1934, it was not until 1944 that Dawson could carry the second ward for himself, and it was not until 1948 that he was able to win a larger percentage of the total vote in his own ward than he won the District as a whole. Since that time, however, the second ward has been the stronghold of the Negro machine, and it has never failed to give Dawson a larger percentage of its vote than the District as a whole. The most depressed Negro areas in Chicago changed party allegiance more slowly and reluctantly, but when they did change, they changed much more decisively and completely. Most Negro politicians explain this by noting that the second ward had been the greatest Republican stronghold, personal loyalties to well-established Negro Republican precinct captains and officials were strong, and the area had always been a "dumping ground" for new in-migrants from the South who for many years continued to bring Republicanism with them from their native country. On the early history of Negroes in Chicago politics, particularly in the Republican party, see Harold F. Gosnell, *Negro Politicians* (Chicago: University of Chicago Press, 1935), esp. pp. 34, 63-92.

absence of a "Republican Dawson" is in part attributable to the absence of a single Republican organization in the state.

In reality, it is extremely doubtful that any rational process of choosing between these alternatives occurred. Rather, Dawson's power grew as a result of a whole series of specific and limited decisions in which his authority was challenged by others, and from which he consistently emerged victorious as a result of his superior skill in the political arts. In each case the Democratic leadership was confronted with a choice: shall we side with Dawson, who has given us certain support and produced results at elections and whose advice we have generally found to be reliable, or should we side with his challenger, who may be a man of untried prowess, or who has not been as successful, or who seems to be lacking in skill? In retrospect it is easy, and perhaps true, to say that building a single Negro machine was the most rational course to have followed, in terms of an economic calculation that judges the efficiency of patronage and money spent in terms of votes and elected officials produced. But had a weaker or less effective man than Dawson set out to be the Negro leader, it is possible that in a series of challenges others would have triumphed and no single Negro machine would have emerged. In any case, the existence of the city machine is probably a necessary explanation for the existence of the Dawson machine, but it is not a sufficient explanation. As a politician close to both Dawson and the city leaders observed:

Kelly did not build Dawson by pre-arranged plan into *the* South Side boss; he made him head of the second ward, and after that Dawson just grew. In each showdown, Dawson was seen to be the better man and was supported. In fact, Kelly didn't want Dawson to run for Congress; he felt that in Washington Dawson would not be able to build his local organization. But Dawson always had had his heart set on Congress.

Since 1939, Dawson's power on the South Side has grown steadily, with hardly a single important setback. Negroes objectionable to him were removed from their posts as ward committeemen in other Negro wards and replaced with men in whom he had greater confidence. Dawson was seen by his followers as a stern father, quick to punish insubordination or incompetence, but quick to forgive. He made few lasting enemies, although he frequently dealt very harshly with rivals. An illuminating example is that of another Negro committeeman, a lifelong Democratic politician, whom Dawson summarily removed from both his ward and elective offices and stripped of his powers. At the same time, Dawson permitted him to retain the important patronage position he held. He eliminated a rival without creating an enemy, and soon the other man was taken back into favor and slated for another elective office which he was able to win.

After a slow beginning against the obstacle of decades of heavy Republican majorities in the Negro wards, Dawson and his organization began to return Democratic majorities that have more or less steadily increased in size. In 1942, Dawson won the Congressional race by fewer than one thousand votes. By 1952, he was winning by over sixty thousand votes. The majorities the organization could produce for the city, county, and state Democratic tickets continued to grow and the influence Dawson wielded in party councils expanded in proportion. In 1955, he was one of the leaders who induced the County Central Committee to drop Mayor Martin Kennelly and slate instead Richard J. Daley. By this time, Dawson was not simply another ward committeeman, he was one of the "inner circle" who ran the affairs of the County Central Committee through its executive committee. In the mayoralty election, when Daley had to meet heavy opposition from the popular Republican, Robert Merriam, Daley's majority of about 125,000 votes was produced for him by the Negro wards. It appeared that Dawson and his organization were at the zenith of their power.

In fact, this power was already beginning to decline. At the same time as his influence in Negro politics seemed supreme and unchallengeable, his influence in the conduct of the affairs of the city was being eroded by a shift in the pattern of politics in the city as a whole. In 1947 the Democratic party had elected a "reform" Mayor, Martin Kennelly, after Kelly had been persuaded to step aside as a concession to the growing swell of public (or at least newspaper) discontent with his extravagant management of public affairs and the evidence of corruption that was beginning to accumulate. Martin Kennelly surrendered control of the party machine and sought to govern solely through the official powers at the disposal of the Mayor. Kennelly presided over the morality

82

of the city administration while real power was divided among the "big boys" of the City Council and the County Central Committee. Kennelly's impotence had its effect on the party, however. The number of patronage positions was reduced as Kennelly gave away to the Civil Service Commission the elements of political power. The ability of the ward politicians to sustain their favor-dispensing systems was curtailed; correspondingly, the ability of the Mayor to govern was drastically reduced, and policy control was dispersed among competing leaders. Furthermore, and of great importance to the Negro wards, Kennelly revealed, in the face of acute cases of race violence in Cicero and Trumbull Park, an inability or unwillingness to act decisively to restore order and protect the Negroes. Negroes began to compare Kennelly unfavorably to Kelly, who had on occasion been forthright in his response to anti-Negro actions and had been known as a supporter of public housing for Negroes. By 1951 the situation had deteriorated to the point that the political machine in the Negro wards "sat on its hands" in the Mayoralty election, and Kennelly's vote fell off sharply in those areas. By 1955, Dawson and others in the party had succeeded in obtaining nearly unanimous agreement in the County Central Committee that Kennelly would have to go. Richard J. Daley, former majority leader in the state senate and then Cook County Clerk, was selected for party backing in the Mayoral primary in February, 1955. Daley was a "party man," a regular member of the inner circle of the Committee and a ward committeeman in his own right.

Daley was elected after a hard fight, with all-out party support. But the era of Edward Kelly did not return. The number of patronage positions was increased but did not approximate that available under Kelly. Daley came to the Cook County Democratic Central Committee with the slogan that "good government is good politics." He saw that shifts in the electorate — the decline in first-generation ethnic groups, the rise in standards of living and levels of education, the movement of voters to the suburbs — made the old style of politics obsolete. New appeals would have to be made to attract these voters, appeals that traditional precinct work could not achieve. These new appeals were of two kinds: "blue ribbon" candidates for important offices, and the development of a strong and attractive set of civic projects. Where Kelly had appeared to be strong but corrupt, and Kennelly had been clean but weak, Daley would be strong *and* clean.

The new appeals were not attractive to the older politicians in the Negro wards. Appointments of "blue ribbon," newspaper-endorsed civic leaders to public positions meant fewer such posts would be available for the persons sponsored by the Negro machine, an organization the metropolitan newspapers thoroughly disliked. The impact of the new civic projects, such as urban renewal, would fall most heavily on the Negro community, where people would have to be displaced and property condemned. The civic campaign to reduce crime through stronger police efforts meant that the Negro districts, which were among the highest in reported crimes and which were widely believed to be infested with criminal types, would feel most keenly police harassment. The Mayor's efforts to distribute city services directly to the people through impartial administration meant that the value of the alderman as a man to whom voters could turn for favors and the redress of grievances was correspondingly reduced.[2]

The Negro machine was strong and vigorous, but the Democratic organization in other parts of the city was becoming weaker and more flabby. Patronage jobs which typically offered low pay were no longer as attractive to whites as they once had been. To improve the salaries for these positions would require politically unacceptable tax increases, and to expand the number of such positions would weaken the public image of good government which the Mayor was anxious to create. While the Negro machine was approaching the peak of its effectiveness, the requirements of city politics as a whole seemed to be compelling the party to direct more and more of its appeal to voters who were not organized by an effective machine.

The men upon whom Daley drew for advice, facts, and plans — the professional city planners, the businessmen-civic leaders, the downtown voluntary associations — were the kind of men who had opposed Dawson and the Negro machine and whom Dawson himself distrusts and suspects. The passions and ideological fervor of Dawson's early years as a rising young politician, which then he vented on racial injustices and the inequities of the Democratic party, had cooled somewhat, but not entirely. In part, they only shifted their targets to the men of wealth who were felt to be the manipulators of civic affairs and whose views were embodied in such institutions as the Republican Party, the University of Chicago, the Illinois Institute of Technology, and big business. Dawson has said:

I don't think the Negroes really hate me, no. . . . Now these white civic leaders, well, that's a different story. I won't even break bread with them. They invite me to big dinners and the like. I won't go. Why should I? I know what they want from me. I don't need a meal from them, and I'm not flattered by their company. A lot of people are, though.

To the Negro political leaders, these "civic leaders" were men who more and more seemed to make up the planning groups which surrounded the Mayor and from whom the Mayor took his cues. One leader said:

The Mayor inherited a bad situation from Kennelly . . . . He had set up these . . . advisory committees to pick people for these agencies. They would send him three names for each job. They never put any people on these committees who have done any political service or who deserve anything from politics. They all look down on politics . . . . So who do you think they pick for these jobs? People who have never done anything to deserve them.

Particularly annoying to the Negro politicians has been the partial loss of their ability to influence the appointment of Negroes to important or prestigious jobs on public boards and agencies. Negroes selected for membership on such bodies as the Board of Education, the Land Clearance Commission, the Community Conservation Board, the Chicago Plan Commission, and other groups are the "token leaders" described in a later chapter, and control over their appointment has in part passed out of the hands of the Negro machine. When the Negro member of the Board of Education retired, a great scramble ensued in the Negro community to provide a successor, and the machine submitted its recommendations. They were not taken. Similarly, a Negro attorney was appointed to the Corporation Counsel's office without the approval of the Dawson organization. The machine has been able to get its recommendations adopted for prestige appointments in only a few cases. An appointee describes one such case:

I have known all the Negro aldermen and committeemen for many years . . . . The six Negro aldermen recommended me to Mayor

Daley. I was called by one of them and asked if I would serve. He said that if I would agree, then all of them were pledged to support my nomination . . . . I think they wanted to make it sort of a test case, to see if they could get Daley to take a man through their united efforts.

An issue in which the Negro organization felt its interests were being subverted by the actions of the Mayor was judicial reform. The Illinois courts, and particularly the courts of Chicago and Cook County, had long been a jumble of competing jurisdictions and cumbersome procedures that usually delayed justice and sometimes denied it. The courts, and their attendant administrative systems of court attaches, bailiffs, clerks, and so on, have also been important sources of political jobs. Mayor Daley endorsed a plan to reform the courts, along lines proposed by a citizens' committee, through a popular referendum on a constitutional amendment. To the Negroes, as well as to many other ward organizations, the plan was dangerous, a step in the direction of liquidating the Democratic party in Chicago in favor of the Republicans. One Negro politician said:

You know this judicial article? Now that article to me isn't worth a damn. . . . It would kill the Municipal Court, and the jobs we have in that court are the backbone of our organization.

Another powerful Negro leader saw this as another move in the process that would ultimately "reform" the Democratic organization out of existence:

It's foolish. There's only one Municipal Court in the state, and that's in Chicago. Why should we give it up? We have all those jobs . . . and the bailiff . . . and the clerk. All we would be doing would be to give more judges to the Republicans. They are the only ones who would benefit by all this . . . . Somebody has taken Mayor Daley up on the mountain again and sold him something. The people who will gain have gotten to him . . . . The Republicans will gain everything we lose . . . . I won't oppose Daley on it, I won't split the party. But it's so foolish.

Despite their objections, the Negro Democrats in the state legislature were induced to vote for the amendment. It was one of those occasions when Dawson gave direct orders. He was called and given certain assurances that his organization would not be affected adversely by the proposal in order to induce him to bring the Negro representatives into line behind the bill. In retrospect, however, the Negro political leaders feel they were disadvantaged by the bill. When it came before the voters in a general election in 1958, certain Negro wards did not back it despite the Mayor's official endorsement and his commitment of the party to it. Precinct captains either did not mention the judicial reform article, or, if asked about it, told the voter he should be against it. Despite the fact that the organization "sat on its hands," the article carried the Negro wards and came near to winning the necessary two-thirds majority to carry the state.[3] In every conversation concerning it, Negro politicians who opposed it referred repeatedly to the shadowy "they" around the Mayor who "had his ear" or who had "sold him a bill of goods." The new sources of influence on the city administration were sensed, but not understood.

Another issue which set the city machine, to some extent, in opposition to the Negro machine was urban renewal. When the University of Chicago sought to invoke certain provisions of the national housing act to improve its neighborhood, it soon became evident that it would require the destruction of a large number of housing units, many of which housed Negroes. These Negroes, who regarded the area as a desirable residential location, would be forced to leave because the prices of new sale and rental housing would be prohibitive to the great majority of them — a fact of which the University was not unaware. The first steps in the direction of urban renewal were resisted by some Negro political leaders who raised objections to it in the City Council and in public statements. Charges were made that many homes slated for demolition were in better condition than those scheduled to remain standing, that the reason for this discrepancy was that the University was engaged in Negro clearance rather than land clearance, that Negroes were being unjustly treated by being artificially excluded from an up-graded neighborhood, and that adequate relocation housing was not being provided for Negro and other lower- and middle-income families. Negro political opposition was almost completely confined, publicly, to the activities of a single alderman, who had apparently made housing issues his specialty.[4] The issue became one of those in which the ends of the Negro race organizations — the Urban League and the NAACP — coincided to some degree with the ends of the politicians. Almost all Negro leaders, of whatever type or style, revealed a distrust of the University and its motives. The Negro press vigorously and consistently opposed it in its editorial pages and in its news columns, and the matter became — at least publicly — a race issue. The Negro alderman was prepared to join the issue on those grounds.

Dawson himself opposed the plan, although he never made a public statement about it. There is little doubt that he, as well as other Negro politicians, genuinely felt that a powerful and hostile force was acting contrary to the interests of the Negroes. In the University area (the fifth ward) there were large numbers of Negroes, particularly in the western and southern portions. They had begun to enter in 1948-49, and by 1958 accounted for half the population. Some observers felt that Dawson had a political interest in the urban renewal issue. The fifth ward had a white alderman and ward committeeman, and it was the key ward in the second Congressional district, the fifth state senatorial district, and the twenty-third state representative district. Opponents to Dawson argued that he took his stand in order to maintain growth of the Negro population in the ward in the hopes that it would eventually "go Negro" politically and that white possession of these elective offices would be undermined. There is no evidence for this charge, however, and no way of telling how important this consideration was to Dawson. In all likelihood, Dawson would have taken a dim view of the University's plans regardless of the political stakes which might have been involved.

But Mayor Daley wanted the urban renewal plan to go through. This being so, the Negro politicians could not hope to block it. Again, it seemed a case of the Mayor acting against the interests of his own party. The men elected to public office from the fifth ward and its allied districts were rarely "organization" Democrats; more often than not, they were liberal independents who either opposed the machine from within or bolted and joined the Republicans. Once again the Negro politicians believed that Daley was under the influence of downtown interests and businessmen:

It's not the Mayor's plan, although . . . he has a certain amount of influence which he has used to help it . . . . He's not the real force behind it, though. The thing to do is get the real force, Julian Levi and those men . . . . But if he [the Mayor] keeps letting his influence be used for these purposes, then he is just creating ammunition that can be used against him later.

The Mayor has centralized political authority in his hands to a remarkable degree, and many Negroes who are not politicians and who seek certain civic goals are fully aware of this. It is becoming common knowledge in the city that the Mayor is the man who can cause things to happen. This fact, combined with the dislike of politicians that is found among the more militant — and hence more issue-conscious — Negro civic leaders, has led them to seek the Mayor's aid directly, circumventing the Negro political organization. The head of the NAACP speaks directly to the Mayor in hopes of persuading him to eliminate job discrimination in the fire department and police department. The head of the Urban League finds that the Mayor is "very accessible" and that problems in race relations can be discussed with him. One association officer explained:

We try to get to the politicians through the Mayor. He is the boss in this town, and what the boss wants, others want. . . . The politicians have a job to hold, and their problem is to figure out how to do their job without losing their job.

But despite his power and accessibility, the Mayor does not see race problems in the same light as do the officers of the Negro voluntary associations. Moving him to act can be just as difficult as moving the Negro politicians. Time and again Negroes have approached him, either directly or through intermediaries, seeking action to curtail the Negro-harassing activities of the police department's task force, eliminate the sources of racial violence in integrated housing projects, end Negro difficulties in obtaining fire insurance, promote the hiring of more Negroes in the police department, and so on. The Mayor relies on his own judgment or takes his cues from his advisors, who include officials of the Chicago Commission on Human Relations. This agency is part of his office. In turn, these advisors respond on the basis of cues they take from him: they tend to share his image of a peaceable city, steadily improving in race relations, with no cause for precipitous action — a city often unjustly criticized in unfair ways by the Negro protest leaders. Further, they display great sensitivity to what they feel is the explosive quality of the Negro question in white areas.

The Mayor earnestly desires to create and maintain a favorable reputation for the city, and he tends to resent charges that it mistreats Negroes. Descriptions of Chicago as "the most segregated city in the world," made by some militant Negro leaders in public statements, disturb the Mayor and lead officers of his Commission on Human Relations to reply, denying or qualifying the charge. One such officer described what he felt the proper policy should be:

> Facts and figures shouldn't be given out to influence people in a negative way. This information can be given out so that it is constructive . . . but it shouldn't kindle popular feelings and all. . . . It's simply a case of good human relations requiring good public relations, and vice versa. . . . Accenting the positive is the best way to bring about better understanding. There are times when you have to talk about the negative side . . . but our philosophy is that you can catch more bees with honey.

The Mayor is more receptive to Negro moderates than to Negro militants. When he can be induced to act on race problems, however, the action is effective. For example, some Negro and white organizations were attempting to integrate Chicago's private hospitals by eliminating discrimination in patient admission and medical staff appointing practices. They secured passage of an ordinance that made it illegal to deny hospital care to those in need solely on the basis of race, color, creed, or national origin.[5] A year later, the City Council was persuaded to adopt a resolution calling upon the Mayor to confer with physicians and hospital administrators as might prove necessary to end discrimination in the appointment of Negro doctors to hospital staffs. Both measures were passed with little opposition after desultory hearings; the real matter at stake was not, it turned out, whether the Council would pass such measures, but whether the Mayor would act decisively to gain compliance from private hospitals and the medical profession. More than eight months passed and the Mayor took no action. Meanwhile, Negro and liberal white doctors within the Chicago Medical Society were calling for action by the Society's leadership to deal with the problem, and the

Commission on Human Relations was urging the Society to take the initiative in the matter. During this period, the Mayor had sought the advice of highly placed medical advisors and had been told to avoid the issue if possible; "it's dynamite — don't touch it."

Suddenly, however, the Mayor decided to move. He called a meeting of the important people involved, and—well-briefed in advance by the Commission—dealt with the protests and denials of the medical society representatives. A problem existed, said the Mayor; he wanted it solved. He refused to consider explanations. By demanding to know what the doctors proposed to do about it, he brought them to promise that they would attempt to deal with a list of qualified Negro doctors seeking appointments in private white hospitals.

This is one of the few cases in which significant progress has been made in Chicago toward some race end. Although the absence of many such instances (which in itself is significant) makes generalization difficult, this, with other similar cases, can be the basis for the observation that the conventional model of Negro protest action in the North is not always applicable. That model sees Negroes as more or less spontaneously organizing to protest some felt injustice, and carrying that protest — through publicity and organized demands — to authorities formally vested with the power to redress the grievances. In fact, the process is more complicated and the flow of action often is in the reverse direction. An alternative model would argue that in many cases the initiation of civic action begins with an existing organization and that the organization is often (though not always) white-led rather than Negro-led. The organization sustains the issue to the extent that its professional staff finds it in its interest to do so. The agitation of the issue requires (1) mobilizing and stimulating some semblance of Negro protest action, (2) assembling the political power necessary to resolve the issue by influencing or co-opting other leaders and public officials, and (3) maintaining the flow of communication between all parties in order that the differences between them do not become so deep and rigid that no solution is possible at all. When a single organization attempts to perform all three functions, tensions and inconsistencies inevitably arise.

Ideally, two or more organizations would perform these tasks individually.

In the field of race relations, a tidy division of labor is rarely possible. In Chicago, the Commission on Human Relations has played all three roles — protest-stimulator, power-assembler, and communicator. Negro doctors, on whose behalf the medical integration campaign was waged, were not generally involved. Some interested and militant Negro physicians did participate through a group called the Committee to End Discrimination in Chicago Medical Institutions (CED). Many of the members of the CED were white liberals, with a high proportion of Jews. The Commission, however, found that one of its greatest problems was maintaining pressure from below. It had difficulty in recruiting Negro doctors who were willing to press for admission to private white hospital staffs, and it had difficulty in keeping "the heat on." Speaking of his role as protest-stimulator, a Commission representative said:

> Our weakest point in the whole thing has been the lack of pressure from the Negro doctors themselves. . . . What we want, of course, is for these people to put the heat on *us* so we can then go to the Mayor and others and tell them we "have to act" and something "must be done." Also, we want the Negro doctors to keep the pressure on the Medical Society.

In its role as power-assembler, the Commission's staff acted both as the agent of the Mayor and as a source of pressure on the Mayor. It could claim to be speaking "for" the Mayor at the same time that it was pressing the Mayor to take a strong stand on the issue and throw his influence decisively on the side of the Commission's goals. As one staff member put it:

> It is nice to be able to sit down and write a letter to somebody on the Mayor's stationery, and then send it over to his office and have him personally sign it and mail it out. It impresses a lot of people to get letters from the Mayor. . . . I think Mr. [X] was impressed by this. He called me up and said, "I just got a letter from the Mayor thanking me for pushing this . . . business." Of course, I wrote that letter, but he doesn't have to know that.

At the same time, the Commission staff had to convince the Mayor to act against the doctors in the face of recommendations from other advisors that he ignore the issue. In part, the Mayor may have personal feelings regarding injustices that ought to be corrected. But he must also assess the political costs. For an experienced and able politician, this may be almost a subconscious process. The responsiveness of the Mayor most often appears to depend on the character of the ends sought. Some race issues, such as the demand for Negro doctors on white hospital staffs, involve relatively few people. Large symbolic victories can be won with few practical concessions. Twenty or thirty Negro appointments might be scattered over fifty hospitals. Little organized opposition exists outside the hospitals. Results would be visible to Negroes but not outrageous to large numbers of whites. Little public controversy was generated over the issue. Worthwhile gains — good relations among some Negroes, a feather in the cap of the Mayor's Commission, a vindication of some principle — could be won at relatively small political costs.

On the other hand, such issues as integrated public housing, open occupancy in private housing, and school integration involve ends which are hotly controversial and elicit responses from conflicting, often irreconcilable, interests. Great public concessions would be necessary for what a politician sees as largely intangible or symbolic gains. The political costs might be heavy. The Mayor is not so powerful that he can act in a way that disregards the strongly-held convictions of, and the political pressures on, his associates. It is far better to act when everyone gains a little, and no one sacrifices a great deal. The ends being sought by the more militant race organizations are not yet of that character; the situation is too explosive in the eyes of the politician to permit of reasonable political consideration of changes which would be, in Chicago, radical. In the meantime, Chicago politics does not require the Mayor to wage dramatic fights for the rights of Negroes, even when Negroes are almost one-fifth of the population. The Mayor's position can be enhanced somewhat by performing modest services for Negroes, but it will not be destroyed if he fails to perform spectacular ones. Further, there is no Negro organization, and no group of Negro leaders, who are in a position to, or want to, force these larger issues by mounting a massive, vocal, and sustained demand for race goals.

Finally, the Commission acted as communicator. It not only prodded Negroes, white doctors, and the Mayor, but it tried to act as a clearinghouse for the relay of information among factions which would have difficulty in talking to one another directly. It is a delicate role, and strains develop easily. The agency begins to wear out its welcome with those it prods; it runs the risk of premature publicity jeopardizing its position; and each faction begins to suspect that the Commission "really" has the other fellow's interests at heart.

This model of the multiple functions that must be served in such civic issues, and the tendency for them to be served by the paid staff of existing organizations, is not always applicable. It is, however, a frequent case. The functions discussed are not logically compatible. In many kinds of civic issues, different organizations and individuals perform them. In race relations, however, there is a paucity of professionally-staffed organizations in Chicago and it is more common for a single organization to have the entire burden. In the next chapters, we shall discuss issues in which other groups have become involved. Thus far, however, we have (1) seen that issues in race relations tend to bypass the Negro politicians and (2) raised some doubts concerning the accuracy of a conception of Negro civic action as involving a simple push-pull relationship between organized protesters and entrenched public authorities.

PART TWO

THE ORGANIZATION OF
NEGRO CIVIC LIFE

Chapter V

The Context of Negro Civic Life in the North

THE civic life of a Negro metropolitan community, as its political life, is strongly influenced by the character of the city as a whole. But the relationship between the city and its Negro sub-community, although important, is not as directly influential in civic affairs as it is in politics. Negro civic activity will be powerfully shaped by the nature and vigor of the white liberal civic leadership in the community, the access which liberal causes have to the politicians, and the character of the local labor movement. At the same time, factors are at work among Negroes which are largely independent of the city as a whole. Civic activity is more diffuse and variegated than politics, and it is less certain that Negro civic leaders will follow the cues of white civic leaders in any given case.

Among the determinants of civic life among Negroes are the extent of Negro business activity and the time and resources these businessmen can or will place at the disposal of civic enterprises, the quality of the Negro press, the unity (or fragmentation) of the principal Negro voluntary associations, the size and rate of growth of the Negro population, and the pattern of segregation. In this chapter, some of the factors which distinguish one northern Negro community from another will be sketched; then, in succeeding chapters, a close look will be taken at the civic life of Negroes in Chicago.

Negroes throughout the North have entered, particularly since 1954 (the year of the Supreme Court school desegregation decision), into a new period of militant civic activity. There is greater ferment among northern Negroes today than at any period since the Depression. In most cities, Negroes are better organized for race ends than ever before, and these organizations are devoting more and more attention to the problems of the Negro in the northern city than they have in the past. *Local* issues in the North are coming to have an importance that rivals the continuing national issues of race relations.

But this civic activity is uneven. In some cities, Negroes are vigorous and outspoken; in others they are divided and confused; in still others, they are virtually silent. In some cities, Negroes have joined with white allies to seek, and attain, race ends; in other cities, they have resisted or been suspicious of white allies. In some cities, the most prominent Negro leaders remain simply *Negro* leaders, "representing" the race and acting in those situations which call for a Negro to be present as a Negro. In other cities, some Negroes are aspiring to more generalized leadership functions — that is, they seek to act as individuals who endeavor to serve a community purpose without reference to their racial identity. Finally and most importantly, in some cities Negroes are attaining some of their goals; in others, they appear to be as far from them as ever.

The reasons for these variations are extraordinarily complex. No simple explanation can be given that will account for all, or even most, of them. But the most important point that emerges from a cursory survey of various northern cities is that the vitality of Negro civic life is not necessarily related to the ability to attain race goals, to the magnitude of the problems which confront Negroes, or to the obstacles to progress raised by the white community. These obstacles are significant, of course, but an understanding of Negro civic life cannot begin with the assumption that Negro leadership will be the simple reflex of external conditions.

The city-by-city variations which exist in the extent, frequency, and vigor with which Negroes raise, agitate, and resolve race issues are readily apparent to the investigator but difficult to document. In New York, for example, Negroes are more evidently aggressive than in Chicago. In New York, the Negro press and civic leaders level a steady stream of criticism against the city regarding school segregation, inadequate school facilities, alleged police brutality, slum conditions in Harlem, and various discriminatory acts. Legal suits against the city seeking the correction of alleged racial injustices are more common in New York than Chicago. The number and strength of the voluntary associations dealing with race issues are higher in New York. Negroes holding important public offices in New York are more likely to take strong — and often public — stands on race issues.

To explain the differences in Negro civic action between, for example, New York and Chicago would probably involve, in the last analysis, an explanation of the differences between the two cities as a whole. This is plainly an impossible task. But short of this, useful comparisons of a lesser order do emerge from a survey of various northern Negro communities at the level of civic leadership.

One of these is the simple matter of size. Smaller Negro communities — as in Boston, Minneapolis, and Denver — lack the resources that come with larger numbers for supporting a vigorous civic life. But even more important, the white community is less likely to regard Negroes as a serious threat except in isolated cases. The northern states with the most liberal legislation from the standpoint of Negroes are often states whose largest cities have only a small proportion of Negroes. These laws were clearly not won by militant Negro leadership, although in some cases Negroes contributed to such causes. More commonly, liberal laws (such as FEPC, open occupancy laws, and other anti-discriminatory measures) are "good politics" in these states because (a) they satisfy the demands of other liberal groups (such as church, labor, or Jewish organizations) and (b) they represent a small threat to whites who believe that there are only a few Negroes who will take advantage of their increased opportunities.[1] And, of course, when these laws are passed, they often work to reduce the motivation among would-be Negro leaders for further civic action. Boston Negro leaders, for example, appear to be more concerned with taking advantage of their presumed opportunities in the community as a whole than in advancing themselves through acting strictly as "race men." Size is thus important in two ways: (a) it reduces the resources of the Negro community for civic action, making it less likely that ambitious

Negroes will be content to attempt to build a career *within* the Negro community; and (b) it increases the likelihood that the community as a whole will offer proportionally less resistance to race legislation sponsored by white liberal groups.[2]

When the Negro population is large, as it is in Chicago, Detroit, and New York, it becomes much more difficult to create a situation in which liberal measures become good politics. In this study, it will be suggested that success in attaining these ends is closely related to the extent to which there are powerful white liberal groups in the community. When seeking the broadest, most controversial ends involving the status of Negroes, the quality of Negro leadership is rarely the most significant factor in determining success or failure. When the changes sought involve high perceived costs to large segments of the community (as in laws barring discrimination in private housing), there is a need for a strong white liberal civic leadership and an appropriate climate of opinion before there is much chance of progress toward realizing these changes. Negro civic leadership here can be no more effective than the liberal civic leadership of the city as a whole. Given at least minimal representation of Negroes in such causes, success or failure will often depend on other, non-Negro factors.

The existence of a white liberal civic leadership means that it is possible to obtain action on behalf of Negro interests without having to organize Negroes. Many liberal white civic leaders, particularly professional staff executives, complain of the difficulty they experience in mobilizing Negro support for causes involving Negro goals. In many cases, their complaints are well-founded but misdirected. It may be true that Negro resources are harder to find than, say, Jewish resources. But more often than not, success does not depend upon the level of Negro activity, unless the divisions or apathy among Negroes are so manifest that opponents of the goal being sought can exploit this situation by mobilizing Negroes against the proposal or capitalizing on the lack of Negro sentiment for the plan.

On the other hand, as the scope of the goal narrows, the importance of Negro civic action as a factor determining the outcome increases. When the ends involve fewer felt costs for the community as a whole, when the goals are more concerned with bettering the condition of the Negro community or correcting specific abuses or injustices, then the vigor of Negro leadership becomes of greater importance. This is true when issues involving the quality of public services provided to Negroes (such as schools, public housing, police protection, etc.), arise. Finally, the effectiveness of Negro leadership becomes all-important when the ends sought involve the control of Negro behavior. Little can be done about problems of crime and delinquency without strong and continuing leadership from within the Negro community.[3] In short, the character of the ends being sought is a prime consideration in assessing the role of Negro civic leadership. This is particularly important when it is realized that the thrust of Negro civic life today is precisely towards the broadest, most controversial goals even though (in some cases, *because*) narrower goals remain unattained. When one approaches these broader problems, agreement on ends and means becomes more difficult; resources are harder to mobilize; enthusiasm is harder to sustain; and Negroes are most in need of effective allies.

Ecology and Civic Life

One important factor which has implications both for the effectiveness of civic leadership on behalf of Negroes and for the quality of Negro civic action itself is the racial ecology of the city. We refer to the extent to which the city has an extensive and rigid pattern of racial segregation. Segregation, for this purpose, is conceived broadly as the existence of barriers based on racial identity to the contact between people in all areas of life — residence, business, society, and civic affairs. The existence of high and strong racial barriers is not only a sign of the failure of liberal civic leadership, but is in part a cause of that failure. Politicians, who tend to defend the status quo, are more concerned with the size of the obstacles to change than the possible rewards of such change. Rigid segregation creates the expectation among whites that it will endure. Segregation may be eroding in the long run, but unless a real breach has been made in the wall (for example, by a strong anti-segregation law), the wall is held to be "natural" and permanent. If segregation has been supported by violence, and that violence has gone unchecked (as it often has in Chicago and, to a lesser extent, in Detroit), there develops a tradition of violence which many whites come to believe has at least the tacit consent of public authorities. Defense, even violent defense, of a changing neighborhood on the periphery of the Negro area is rarely successful for long, but even though the neighborhood may be surrendered to the Negroes, the system permits whites to believe in the right to resist. The greater the segregation of Negroes, the greater that right.

The Negro population of Chicago, which in 1955 numbered about 630,000, is concentrated in a few large contiguous areas which are expanding along the edges as it continues to grow. The largest and most important of these is the South Side community, often called "Bronzeville" or the "Black Belt," which extends south from Chicago's Loop for perhaps ten miles. As the Negro population of Chicago increases at an annual rate of about thirty thousand, this Black Belt — together with the other Negro concentrations on the west and north sides of the city — expands at the periphery at a rate of about 250 housing units per week.[4] This expansion has been, and continues to be, taking place in areas settled for the most part by working-class white families, often Catholics of Irish, Italian, or Polish extraction, who have resisted Negro encroachment by a variety of tactics including violence. The great outburst of violence which has become known as the Chicago race riot of 1919 took place along the geographical line which separated the white and Negro families on the South Side. Since World War II, three large-scale riots have occurred where Negroes were moving into white areas. Between 1956 and 1958, 256 incidents of racial violence were reported, including five deaths and thirty-eight cases of arson. Most incidents occurred in neighborhoods undergoing racial transition.[5] The competition of Negro and white for living space engenders the strongest and most irreconcilable passions, and these antagonisms are one of the most powerful single factors conditioning the pattern of civic life in Chicago.

The civic issues in which most is usually at stake are those involving the disposition of real estate, and the Negro is often at the center of such problems. Land clearance, public and private housing projects, and institutional construction all frequently, if not invariably, raise questions concerning their impact on the racial composition of the neighborhood for which they are proposed. City planning in general is inherently bound up with the question of which races will use which parcels of land, and the "objective" professional standards which are supposed to govern the development of land-use planning will often run afoul of the racial problems which defy objective solution or, it often seems, any solution at all. Whatever procedure is adopted for dealing with civic issues that involve the Negro, the Negro usually participates only in a token role, and the on-going voluntary associations which do so much to generate and agitate civic issues are often careful to exclude Negroes from positions of prominence for fear of reducing the organization's effectiveness.

Los Angeles, by way of contrast, has virtually no tradition of violence in race matters. Residential segregation, for example, has been maintained almost entirely by legal measures (such as restrictive covenants) and by real estate practices. When these covenants were held, by the Supreme Court, to be legally unenforceable, whites fell back on the only weapon that remained: control by agreement in the real estate market. And, equally as important, the high rate of geographical mobility in Southern California has probably meant that whites feel they can always cut their losses and move out of changing neighborhoods into new suburbs without great burdens or risks. The growth and prosperity of the area, or at least, a *belief* in that growth and prosperity, may have been important factors in the relative absence of bitter and violent resistance to the expansion of the Negro community along its periphery. Northern cities generally can be distinguished in terms of the intensity of the competition for living space. That competition is probably in part related to population densities. In Los Angeles, at one extreme, there are only about 4,400 persons per square mile in the center of the city. At the other extreme, densities in Chicago are at least four times as high and in New York City about six times.[6]

Boston is another important city with a comparatively low level of overt Negro-white friction and a general absence of interracial violence. Prosperity clearly is not the explanation for this state of affairs. A complete explanation would have to take into account several factors. Some of them are the conditions that seem relevant to the Boston situation. There, the expansion of the Negro area (South Roxbury) has occurred in large part into older Jewish neighborhoods where vigorous anti-Negro sentiment has been relatively absent. Further, the total number of Negroes in Boston (an estimated 60,000 in 1959) and the proportion of Negroes to whites (about 7 per cent) is so low that white neighborhoods may feel less threatened than in, say, Chicago or Detroit. One could speculate that Negro-white conflict is intensified by the perceived magnitude of the "threat." Where the size of the Negro population is low and its "visibility" in the city as a whole is proportionally small, the entry of Negro families into white neighborhoods may not be regarded as seriously as when the white areas feel inundated by a spreading Negro area of overwhelming proportions. Finally, Negro-white job competition as a source of interracial conflict might be less in cities where there are few heavy industries with a large unskilled labor force. Boston Negroes are found in service occupations (such as domestic service) to a greater extent than in Chicago, and here economic rivalries between ethnic groups may be significantly less than in, say, steel mills or automobile plants.

A pattern of relatively strong segregation has important implications for the Negro, the would-be Negro leader, and his relations with possible white allies. First, living in a highly-segregated, densely-populated Negro community impedes the natural processes of spatial differentiation. The ecological forces which tend to differentiate a community by class and status, which separate geographically one stratum from another, are crimped and thwarted by high segregation and dense population patterns. The consequences this fact has for Negro civic action can be suggested in some hypotheses which seem to conform to the data but for which real evidence cannot, as yet, be offered:

(a) Potential Negro leaders are constantly confronted with the overwhelming magnitude of the problems of the Negro area. The daily contact with slum life by the Negro middle and upper classes who are compelled to live within that slum usually works to lower the level of expectations and the intensity of motivation for civic action. Strong civic leadership may very well require an underestimation of the magnitude and a simplification of the character of the problem to be resolved — at least on the part of the initiators of civic action. (The leader who is the initiator of civic action must believe that solutions are *possible* in some measure.) Living in isolation from the city as a whole, pressed daily by the weight of disadvantaged people dwelling in squalor, and desiring to differentiate himself from these people who have — by their manner of life — given to him a reputation he does not want, the middle or upper class Negro can see few rewards in civic leadership. The obstacles to success seem insuperable, and action on the behalf of others would only increase his identification with them in the eyes of others.

(b) The patterns of life in a dense, highly-segregated community which is heterogeneous in terms of class and status tend to reduce the extent to which community life stimulates and reinforces civic action and leadership. Civic activity requires rewards of some kind, and most often those rewards are the approval of others who place a value on such activity. This kind of stimulus and reinforcement may be found, for example, in a suburban community which is relatively homogeneous in the class and status of its various neighborhoods. If community action is regarded as at all desirable, those who engage in it are rewarded to some extent. They are often prompted to lead by the example of others whose good opinion they cherish. Relatively stable patterns of expectation about civic contributions exist as well as a fairly steady system of reinforcement for such behavior. Within a ghetto, where the struggle for survival is felt to be more intense and where the greatest rewards seem to come from material success, those who are desirous of civic action often receive little encouragement from their fellows. Life in the ghetto is one so manifestly lacking in *things* — material comforts — that to many inhabitants it is absurd to seek the intangible and seemingly non-existent rewards of civic leadership.

(c) A dense, socially heterogeneous ghetto increases the probability of conflicts of interest between various classes and strata in the community. When lower-income and upper-income groups live side-by-side, advantages won for one group must often be at the expense of another group. It becomes difficult to act disinterestedly toward community goals when the costs of those goals are so evident and so personal. For example, if a ghetto is heterogeneous in terms of class, it means that a public housing project for lower-income Negroes will disadvantage upper-income Negroes. The former desire, presumably, decent shelter at low cost. The latter desire to improve their neighborhoods, exclude lower-income and undesirable elements, and protect their property values. Public housing involves few costs for this latter group if enough distance separates it from the site of the project and the lower-income groups who will live in it. In a dense, highly-segregated area, such distance rarely is available. Upper-class Negroes are led to oppose, as they have done in Chicago, public housing projects slated for sites near their homes. In Los Angeles, on the other hand, where the density is far lower and where great distances often separate lower-income Negro "ports of entry" (such as Watts) from desirable neighborhoods (such as those in the Crenshaw area), Negro middle- and upper-class groups need not feel threatened by public housing placed in lower-income areas. Similarly, urban renewal or other land clearance plans designed to clear or thin out slum areas need not disturb more desirable areas *if* they are some distance apart. (Some effects are certain to be felt even if the areas are separated, of course. One of these involves neighborhoods which might be threatened by the relocation of Negroes displaced from clearance sites into more desirable Negro areas.)

A second general consequence — in addition to the lack of spatial differentiation — of relatively high levels of segregation is the extent to which it reduces the number and alters the character of contacts between Negroes and whites in the city. We do not necessarily imply that problem-solving is a function of communication. In fact, in many cases greater communication heightens conflict, reduces "understanding" and exacerbates the problem.[7] What we do mean is that civic leadership requires a certain minimal level of sophistication, comprising a set of skills, habits, and knowledge necessary to carry out civic tasks. This sophistication is often the product of repeated contact with or an involvement in on-going civic enterprises in the city. In general, the enterprise precedes the leader. The existence of functioning, formal civic organizations is an important factor in creating civic leaders. To the extent that Negroes fail to engage in such work, they reduce their chances of acquiring the attributes of what the city as a whole regards as a civic leader — attributes such as a certain camaraderie, flexibility, and business-like attitude. Initial contacts between white and Negro civic leaders are usually tense and unsatisfactory in Chicago. The Negro is either "unrepresentative" or he is a "race man" who is "hard to handle." Negro civic leaders in New York, on the other hand, have had a longer history of moving in such worlds. Negroes have been brought into relatively high political office from outside the political machine, and hence have gained experience in public life free from some of the constraints that operate on members of such a machine. The large number of white liberal voluntary associations in New York has meant that a proportionally higher number of Negroes have been co-opted into community-involved groups. Although the ends these associations serve might be decidedly more liberal than the ends of, for instance, a chamber of commerce, the skills acquired by successful civic action in the former realm are not completely inappropriate to the latter.

A third consequence of segregation is that life over a long period of time in a rigid ghetto situation tends to produce a stake in that ghetto. Institutions, organizations, and business practices develop which benefit from the fact of segregation. Negro responses to their exclusion from community life generate commitments to all-Negro institutions. For example, more Negroes appear to be in positions which involve some stake in the ghetto in Chicago than in Los Angeles. These commitments are not entirely due to ecology. Historical accident can powerfully condition present attitudes. For example, the creation of a large all-Negro hospital in Chicago has had consequences for commitments different from other cities (such as New York) where — for a variety of reasons — no all-Negro hospital was ever provided. In business, important differences probably occur in the extent to which Negroes themselves manage slum properties, convert buildings into "kitchenettes," and speculate in transitional neighborhoods. Although data are hard to develop on this point, Negro leaders themselves in the four cities believe that these differences exist and are important. Negroes in Chicago, even moderate Negroes, speak with feeling about the involvement of Negro businessmen in real estate practices which prosper through "tipping" neighborhoods and encouraging scare selling. And it is true that the real estate market in some cities is more conducive to such practices. Where Negroes are slowly expanding into tense or hostile white neighborhoods that are characterized by multiple-family dwellings the opportunities for profit are greater than where

Negroes are encountering relatively less resistance to their movement and where they are entering areas of single-family, owner-occupied homes that cannot conveniently be converted into high-density tenements. Such appears to be the case, for example, in Los Angeles where even militant Negro leaders are less prone to accuse other Negroes of exploitation than they are in Chicago.

Less rigid — or less obviously rigid — segregation patterns not only have benefits for Negroes, but they have some costs as well. The existence of a less densely populated Negro community spread out over a considerable space, coupled with a general level of prosperity and an optimistic view of the future tends to reduce the number and intensity of Negro demands for change. Los Angeles Negro leaders, for example, speak of their city and its problems with a tone and rhetoric that is in marked contrast to that employed by comparable Chicago leaders. Problems in Los Angeles are not felt so keenly nor is the status quo viewed with as much despair, even though the denial of opportunities to Negroes may in fact be every bit as high. The city government takes little interest in race relations causes and only in the last year or two has the state provided any liberalizing legislation. But here the prosperity, or rather the subjective commitment to prosperity, filters out many of the remarks of bitterness and anger that characterizes the conversation of important Negroes elsewhere. The motivation for civic action is probably reduced appreciably by this fact.

An important aspect of race relations in Los Angeles is not only that the Negro population is less dense and that the level of prosperity and mobility is higher, but also that the Negro population is of very recent origin. The ten-fold increase occasioned by World War II took place in a city in which there were (in 1940) only about fifteen Negro lawyers, some twenty physicians and dentists, and correspondingly small numbers of other professionals. The potential Negro leadership group was minute. Today these numbers have risen to about 150 lawyers, perhaps 300 physicians and dentists, and a host of teachers, social workers, and other professional people. In the words of an important Negro civic leader in the city, the sudden and enormous rise in the Negro population "overwhelmed" the leadership group among both Negroes and whites. No established pattern existed for handling Negro problems, either among influential whites or would-be Negro civic leaders. No organizations existed, no points of access had been developed, no political relationships established, few Negroes had been co-opted into the public agencies as token leaders, and no strong trade union movement existed with a base in the Negro community. In response to this situation, many Negroes have endeavored to build leadership in alliance with other large minority groups, notably the Mexican-Americans. Whites have encouraged this to some extent by giving the sole minority-group City Councilman (Edward Roybal, a Mexican-American) a district with almost as many Negroes as Mexicans. At the same time, the co-option of token leaders has proceeded on the understanding among whites that *any* minority group representation is a form of recognition for *all* minority groups. Thus, Japanese, Chinese, and Mexican judges are considered to be "non-Caucasian" and a concession to non-Caucasian sentiment generally, including Negro sentiment. In such a situation, the development of strong Negro leadership becomes doubly difficult.

Not all cases of a low level of Negro motivation or concern for race relations problems can be explained by such factors as seem to be relevant to Los Angeles. In Boston, for example, many Negro leaders speak of the extent to which social equality is an accepted part of the city's tradition. Negroes held political office in Boston as early as 1776, and they had been enfranchised since 1764. Negroes held state office as early as 1866. Further, the abolitionist background of the city, the early passage of anti-discrimination measures of various kinds, and the less dense pattern of residential segregation have all encouraged Boston Negroes to believe that they have moved farther along the road to integration than their brothers in such cities as Chicago. Nonetheless, the material condition of the bulk of the Negro population of Boston is deplorable. Many Negroes ascribe this situation to economic, rather than to caste, distinctions and, as a result, manage to excuse the city in part from responsibility arising out of anti-Negro sentiment. In Boston, the small size of the Negro population, the relatively greater degree of Negro dispersion (as compared to Chicago or New York), and the belief in a tradition of social equality may all contribute to a

lower level of concern for local race goals and enhance the
desire of middle-class Negroes to seek a place in the community
as a whole on equal terms with whites. Boston Negro leaders are
frequently anxious to *sever* connections with the Negro community — residentially and professionally — and explain this desire in part on the grounds that the relative absence of discrimination makes this both possible and desirable.[8]

This situation might be quickly altered by a sudden and dramatic increase in the size of the Negro population in Boston. As
white resistance mounts to an increasingly visible and sizeable
Negro population spread, so also Negro leaders may come to
see their opportunities as lying more within than outside the
Negro community.

Chapter VI

Negro Civic Forces in Chicago

T HE Negro in Chicago places few effective demands on his political organization that reflect community goals. The politician rarely feels pressure of this kind. The Negro civic leader who threatens white politicians with a popular reaction among Negroes against him if he fails to act on some race demand is largely bluffing and knows it. "They are pretty much empty and idle threats," said an NAACP leader, "but we make them anyway. . . . We are aware of how little white people really know about us [and] the politician is never quite sure how serious our threats are." Protest action requires preferably the reality but at least the image of solidarity among the protesting group; for the most part, Negro protest leaders have been trading in images only.

Given this state of affairs, Negro civic organizations have been endeavoring to develop other forms and patterns of leadership and influence. Most importantly, they have been attempting to adjust to the bipolar world of the white civic leader and the white politician. The growing importance of voluntary associations and the centralization of political power have set a standard for Negro civic action. Negroes are trying to create and sustain a modern voluntary association leadership based on paid staffs and fund-raising boards. The Urban League has been most active in this respect, but works under the inevitable constraint that the resources for such an organization must come in large part from the white community. There is, in short, an effort

111

to professionalize race relations much as civic action generally
has been professionalized in the city as a whole. A professional
staff can raise issues, provide facts, stir action, and draft (or even
create) civic leaders. These leaders must be functional, rather
than personal, leaders; men who can be attracted by a particular
issue rather than by aspirations to. broad inspirational leadership
of the whole community. The professional staff seeks white allies
among other staffs and endeavors, through these staffs, to make
civic action on the problems of race relations attractive to influential leaders. This is a slow and difficult and expensive task,
but there seems to be no reasonable alternative. Further, Negro
voluntary associations hope to bypass the Negro political machine
and deal directly with the boss of the city, the Mayor.

Most of the voluntary associations active in race relations are
operated by whites, and thus represent a form of white influence
on the Negro community — the American Civil Liberties Union,
the Commission on Human Relations, the Anti-Defamation
League, and others. The Negro voluntary associations — the
NAACP and the Urban League — contribute to this process of
influence, in part through their own efforts, and in part as channels of communication between the white agencies of liberal reform
and the Negro community as a whole. Whatever the source of
the ideas, however, the voluntary associations exercise a profound
influence on the thinking of the "attentive" segment of the Negro
community. Two important race issues — a Fair Employment
Practices Commission (FEPC) and open occupancy — have become slogans in the Negro community in great part as a result of
their continuous assertion by voluntary association staffs. When a
Negro civic leader is asked to suggest a solution to some race
problem, he will usually either grope for a reply out of the in-
tuition of the moment, or will repeat what he has been told as a
board member of some voluntary association — told by the paid
executive of that staff. The Urban League, as the Negro voluntary association with the largest and most vigorous staff, is coming
to have the greatest influence in this regard, although many conservative Negro leaders react unfavorably to its ideas and tactics.

The politicians are a prime target of voluntary association
activity. Many persons in such associations visualize their tasks
as in great part putting "heat on the aldermen" or "building a

fire" under the politicians. The political organization and the voluntary associations have dissimilar ends and tactics, and this produces a considerable amount of mutual suspicion and distrust on both sides. The voluntary associations attempt to impose constraints on the machine which the machine attempts to resist without placing itself in the position of public opposition. The reactions of Negro politicians — particularly the older politicians less inclined to cultivate good public relations — to the efforts of voluntary association staffs and officers who are endeavoring to move the political organization toward certain race ends in the city are sometimes openly hostile:

> [The executive of the Urban League] and those people who talk out of their mouths instead of out of their heads just don't know anything. They talk .... Some people who have been in this city for a few months think they know everything.

The statements of the associations are resented. Militant protest is disturbing and raises matters to which the machine must sometimes respond in order to avoid further criticism. In its relations with the party and the government as a whole, such statements make the machine's job that much harder. Although the associations are often ridiculed as groups which "just talk," it is apparent that the talk itself is an unwelcome disturbance. For instance:

> You can take what [a voluntary association executive] says just for what it's worth. He hasn't, those people haven't been in the city very long. He came here two years ago, from someplace out West. They don't own property. He rents .... They don't pay taxes; they don't even own their own building yet .... What do they do? Nothing. Just talk and making statements. They don't know what they're talking about.

The politician who made that statement was confronted with an issue — a proposed branch of Cook County Hospital for the South Side — which he hoped to dispose of on non-racial grounds but which the protests of officers of the Urban League had converted into a sharp racial issue. "Just talk" was a problem for him.

In general, the politician feels he is in a better position to assess the possibilities for change than are association leaders who are free of the responsibility for action.

If the NAACP and that crowd wants to run around shouting about this, let them, but I'm not. *I'm a politician.* I know what can be done and what can't. Right now things are too hot. Everybody's on fire, and running around waving their arms. We need a cooling-off period first.

Exploiting issues is, to the politician, a form of political meddling. Politics should be left to the politicians. The politician, like the race moderate generally, has a clear image of the proper roles of race organizations, and does not want to see those rather limited roles transgressed by people who are more committed to certain race ends and issues. The NAACP should be simply a legal defense organization, and the Urban League should be merely an employment and social service agency on behalf of Negro in-migrants. Although one Negro politician was a member of the Urban League board for several years, no real liaison between the two groups resulted. Indeed, the politician rarely attended the board meetings, and eventually he was dropped from membership. On the other hand, the only Negro Democratic politician who was active on the Urban League board during this period was finally dropped from the machine, which refused to slate him for re-election. Although some members of both groups would like better co-operation, the most important leaders on both sides see little common ground. One is committed to the party that administers the status quo, the other is dedicated to altering the status quo. Occasionally, their ends can become compatible. Both sets of leaders express doubts and reservations about slum clearance and urban renewal plans that displace Negroes, but there is little real co-ordination of this opposition — each is suspicious of the motives of the other in asserting its opposition and each is conscious of the great differences in political style which separate them.

The politicians and the voluntary associations divide on both ends and means. The NAACP — then under militant leadership — caustically attacked Congressman Dawson in 1956 for opposing the Powell Amendment in Congress (which would have denied Federal aid to education to those schools which practiced racial segregation), for supporting the weak civil rights plank in the Democratic party platform in a speech to the national convention, and for failing to make a more voluble public protest over the Emmett Till lynching case. An NAACP leader said in Chicago that "Mr. Dawson has finally revealed himself, not as a statesman, not as a leader of the people, but as a tool of the Democratic National Committee in its machinations."[1] After much discussion within the NAACP as to the proper methods to employ, that organization finally sent to the newspapers an "open letter" to Dawson which excoriated him for his alleged inaction and "softness" on race issues. Publicly, Dawson replied that he had "nothing to say. . . . I will not enter into controversy with Willoughby Abner."[2] Privately, he was furious. He felt he had acted properly in all the cases cited in the open letter. He felt he had been right to oppose the Powell Amendment, because its passage would have defeated all hopes for aid to education. He believed he had pulled important wires in the Till case which were more effective than public protest. He stated:

> Sending an open letter to Congressman Dawson! Who do they think they are? They don't know what politics is all about. What business is it of theirs whether I make speeches or not? The NAACP should stay out of that . . . . What good could it possibly do to make speeches about that [the Till case]? . . . I called [Attorney General] Brownell from this office while the widow was here . . . and said that I wanted protection for her. . . . She got it. . . . I gave her money out of my own pocket to travel down there. . . . This is better unpublicized.

It is widely believed among almost all Negro leaders that Dawson's prestige was hurt by the episode. In the Congressional election of November of that year, in which he ran against a weak opponent who did not campaign, his vote slipped by about 7 per cent from the 1954 election (and about 31 per cent from the 1952 presidential-year election); while his opponent scored more than a 50 per cent increase over the vote of the 1954 Republican candidate (although only a 6 per cent gain over 1952). Nevertheless, Dawson still was the victor by almost a two-to-one margin, and in the next election (1958), the vote of his opponent — who this time conducted a noisy campaign — lost all that had been gained in 1956. Indeed, it is not by any means certain that Dawson's 1956 vote loss had much to do with race issues at all, since the Republican slate that year was headed by President Eisenhower who probably gave to the Republican Congressional candidate the advantage of more straight-ticket votes than usual. What is certain is that specific and personal charges of having let down the race, brought against him by NAACP leaders at the local and national level, were insufficient to weaken Dawson's hold over his constituency to any substantial degree. Dawson's local political power is sufficiently great to allow him the luxury of considerable political latitude on race issues at the national level.

In what sense, then, do the NAACP and similar race organizations pose a constraint on the politicians? On the local level, dealing with local issues, it can be of much greater importance. It can press measures which the machine cannot avoid, even though it has no enthusiasm for them and even though it has endeavored to sweep them under the carpet— complex, often intangible goals such as open occupancy or hospital integration. On simpler, more tangible ends — such as race violence, police harrassment, and overt cases of discrimination — the voluntary associations can move the machine simply by making these things public knowledge. They are issues which the machine's constituents can feel directly, and they are issues upon which both moderates and militants can agree.

It is not only in the area of issues that there is friction, however. The machine sees the voluntary associations as rivals who seek to speak "for" the Negro community. The Negro political leader feels that Negro patronage, particularly important Federal positions, should be allocated like all other patronage — on the recommendation of the organization politician concerned. At the national level, however, the NAACP sees itself as a spokesman "for" Negroes, and is gratified when its favorites are placed in positions of prominence.

In the city, a latent rivalry smolders between the machine and the Urban League as to which will represent the Negro community. The politician feels that on matters such as political appointments, the machine is the only proper agency for recommendations — although its ability to influence political appointments has declined somewhat. The Urban League (and many other voluntary associations) challenges this, and when important appointments are to be made, it offers candidates of its own.

A final zone of friction arises from the different means employed by associations and the machine in approaching even common objectives, and the misunderstandings that can arise as a result. Voluntary association tactics involve publicity, branding issues with the race label, and various forms of lobbying and persuasion. The association thrives on issues; issues are its life blood. The machine proceeds by intra-party haggling and trading; public attacks and outspoken antagonisms only "rock the boat." Issues are obstacles to be overcome, not opportunities to be sought; open controversy is anathema. To the machine politician, it is not clear why the voluntary association must act in the way it does, or, having acted this way, why it does not then labor to reward politically the politicians who have supported its cause. One has reported:

> None of these groups like the NAACP or the Urban League . . .
> help us. You ought to ask them, directly, why they don't. These
> groups don't follow up politically. All they do is make public state-
> ments, take a position, and that's that.

Another politician stated that associations, both white and Negro, unreasonably demand efforts from the politicians without fair compensation:

> What these organizations should do that they don't is to activate
> more in the primaries when the Republicans are up for nomination.
> They should show more activity on behalf of the people who voted
> for FEPC. Some legislators have complained to me that they voted
> for FEPC, and then these people didn't help them in his campaign,
> while other groups used his vote for FEPC against him.

The Negro Press

In many Negro communities, and in Chicago in the past, the Negro press has been an important source of civic protest, and has often set the tone of public discussion of race issues and defined the constraints under which others worked. The Chicago Negro press — principally the *Chicago Defender* — is no longer an organization devoted to single-minded protest. Over fifty years old, and in the hands of a man who inherited it from its founder, it has become more moderate. The personal relationships which exist between its publisher and the Negro political leaders have already been sketched. What is important at this juncture is the relationship between civic protest and the organizational needs of the press.

Certain trends are discernible in the history of the *Defender* over the past ten or fifteen years. Foremost among these has been its decline in circulation. From an estimated high for all editions of almost a quarter million copies per week,[3] it had fallen to about 63,111 in mid-1958.[4] About 50,000 of the total are sold in Chicago. Various expedients, including the establishment of regional editions of the *Defender* in various parts of the country, have generally failed to recoup the circulation losses. At the same time, the volume and scope of the advertising has increased. In the weekly *Chicago Defender* the majority of the large advertisers — firms which purchase one-quarter page or more of display advertising — are white. Only about one-fourth of this kind of advertising is purchased by Negro firms. The result has been a reversal of the economic balance which sustained the paper in its early years. Previously, the paper was supported for the most part by circulation.[5]

At the same time, the character of its ownership has shifted. The founder, Robert S. Abbott, was an independent Republican who focussed attention on race issues and visualized the paper as a crusading — and lucrative — enterprise. His nephew, John Sengstacke, who inherited the bulk of it, is a Democrat for whom the paper has been both less lucrative and less crusading. The problems of survival and reorganization have been more pressing than racial protest. Early in his career as publisher, a hard and protracted internecine battle broke out within the paper, with control of the firm at stake. One dimension of that conflict was a political cleavage within the editorial board. All of these trends have had a cumulative impact on the nature of the paper. An officer of the *Defender* feels that the paper must attempt to obtain a broad base of readers through the appeals other papers have found successful:

We used to have big campaigns in our national edition.... Big screaming red headlines, week after week, talking about [racial] injustice.... We still have stories about injustices, but we don't display them like we did.... Our heads aren't like that,... they are the same as the ones you find in the metropolitan press.

When asked what made this shift from protest to sensationalism possible, he replied:

> Psychologically, I think the Negroes have changed.... We used to get a lot of complaints about the type of headlines we ran.... People said they got tired of that stuff, so we are trying to give them what they want.

Another editor of the paper was more vivid in his analysis of the basis of the change:

> We have to change our paper to keep up.... Now we have every sensational murder on the front page.... We printed a picture of that woman who had been decapitated in some murder over there. We got criticized for it, but we sold 60,000 copies, three times our usual figure [for the daily edition]. We couldn't print enough. What can you do? That's what they seem to want.... But then, there are not many issues of a local character that strike deeply into the core of our readers.... You can't write about segregation and discrimination every day. You get a surfeit of this. People get tired of it. You have to stay away from the constant note of protest, protest, protest.... But it's hard to do, because the Negro press was born out of protest.

Race issue news continues to be carried, particularly in the weekly edition, but protest is loud only where the issue appears to be both clear and dramatic — a Negro allegedly framed on a vice charge, a Negro boy denied a position as page boy in Congress, or acts of race violence. No extended or systematic coverage, by trained reporters, is given such areas of importance as housing or employment. Most editors concede freely that the mainstay of the paper is the coverage of society news, night-life gossip, and neighborhood events of social significance. Reducing that coverage in favor of more race-issue news appears to be a dubious investment of available resources.

Although the *Defender* pursues a fairly consistent policy of supporting the Democratic party, Democrats — including the Negro politicians — are not immune to criticism. The paper was critical of Dawson at the time when he was under fire from the NAACP for his public silence on race issues, and the Negro aldermen occasionally are taken to task for their lack of aggressiveness. Just before the 1959 aldermanic elections, for example, the paper ran a series of editorials in its daily editions accusing the aldermen of "moral hypocrisy," describing them as "dancing like helpless puppets at the end of invisible strings." Moreover:

> Our aldermen are politically eating high on the hog, with the
> ravenous, unquenched appetite of a fat-bellied Caliph of Baghdad.
> They create the indelible image of a happy-go-lucky aggregation of
> irresponsible politicians more addicted to concentrating around a
> poker-table than to serious meditating on unresolved community
> problems.[6]

The editorial page, however, is distinct from the rest of the
paper, and any reader who looked for items in the news columns
that would give meaning and content to these charges would
search in vain. There is a division of labor at work which con-
fines moral indignation to the editorial pages, and these have
little direct political influence. Few Negro civic leaders give serious consideration to what is said there. The politicians ignore
it because their constituents ignore it. All the Negro precinct
captains, of both parties, interviewed in another study agreed
that the Negro press in general had "little if any influence on . . .
voting behavior" and cited the case in which an opponent of
Dawson, backed by the *Defender,* was defeated by the customary
three-to-one margin.[7]

The Negro press defends but does not control the Negro
community. It will respond vigorously to outside attacks or presumed outrages, but it rarely attempts to criticize any specific
group of Negroes. The exception to this is the steady editorial
and cartoon campaign against the mores and manners of lower-
class Negroes, principally rural in-migrants, whose dress and behavior is offensive to the middle-class Negro. Negro misconduct,
other than crimes that appear on the police blotters, is rarely a
subject for news treatment. When Negro organizations encounter
difficulties, these are seldom treated in detail. The periodic con-
vulsions that seize the local NAACP, for example, in which bitter contention for office rages, are given the sketchiest treatment.
The collapse of the Chicago Urban League and its subsequent reorganization were barely alluded to, and the copy which was
printed was often written or thoroughly edited by officers of the
Urban League itself. This posture is justified by editors of the
paper by the need these associations have for protection in order
that they might retain the confidence of the community:

> We didn't want to hurt these organizations . . . . We feel they have

an important job to do, and we don't want to break the confidence of the community in them . . . . The organizations are too valuable to weaken by publicity like that . . . . We just gave it straight news coverage.

This protection is facilitated by the fact that usually the *Defender* will have one or more of its officers on the boards of both the NAACP and the Urban League. Rarely does an issue arise involving any tangible stake that would prevent social and business colleagues from helping one another through difficult periods by refraining from public criticism or exposure. Besides, such material is not circulation-building.

The absence of real political impact by the Negro press and its abdication of the control function in the community should not be taken as conclusive evidence that it is without any influence and does not produce any constraints. Clear racial issues are cultivated. The slogans of race issues — for example, open occupancy — are given wide currency and they tend to set the tone and provide the rhetoric of public discussion of issues. Civic leaders, whose positions are not as secure as those of the machine politicians, cannot ignore the effects on their reputations which their public utterances may have when printed in the press. Only infrequently are two sides of a civic issue publicly taken by civic leaders — for the most part, it is far easier to subscribe publicly to the race position and reserve one's doubts for private discussion.[8]

The quality of the Negro press varies widely among northern cities. It varies in the extent to which a newspaper is issue-oriented, in the extent to which it is defensive or critical of the Negro community, and finally in the extent to which it is well-edited. The Negro press in Chicago tends to devote less attention and less thorough coverage to race or civic issues and goals than do the leading Negro papers in New York or Detroit. Criticism of Negro leaders is less frequent in the Chicago press than in one or two Los Angeles or New York papers. A paper in one town will print its front page directly from the police blotter; a paper in another city will devote more attention to civic issues. All Negro papers to some extent reflect their origins in Negro protest, but beyond this point there is great variation — even in political party allegiance.

The most vigorous and militant Negro civic leadership is usually found in cities with the most issue-conscious and critical Negro press; the least militant leadership is found in cities with a relatively muted or sensationalist press. Militancy, of course, is not a homogeneous style: militants can be either nationalist or integrationist, intelligent or unintelligent, selfless or self-seeking. Nor can it be argued that a militant Negro press "produces" militant Negro leaders; both probably spring from anterior causes. But a militant and critical press can make it more difficult for Negro leaders to take *public* stands reflecting a gradualist or moderate approach and can provide an additional element of reinforcement for those who choose to be aggressive.

Relatively few Negro newspapers have thus far attempted seriously to pursue "control" ends. Few have focussed attention on problems for which Negroes are in part responsible (crime and deliquency, for example) or urged that Negro leaders attempt to deal with them. Such an attitude would involve criticizing the Negro community in some measure. In Detroit, the Negro newspaper ventured into this area, editorializing on its front page the fact that Negroes were responsible for a "shockingly high percentage" of crime in the city. It called for Negro leadership to "lift its head from the sociological sand and unite in one strong, widespread, and positive effort to do something to wipe out lawlessness."[9] Such a group was formed, and the paper discovered relatively little race criticism greeted its announcement. Even so, there remain limits to the extent of possible Negro press criticism. Privately, some Negro publishers and editors will admit that they do not feel at liberty to be frankly critical of certain Negro leaders whom they consider a disgrace, to discuss openly the use of quotas as a possible way of stabilizing interracial neighborhoods, or to fail to defend Negroes who are involved with white police.

The Mass Organizations

The Negro community possesses two principal mass organizations, other than the political machine. They are the labor unions and the churches. Their impact on civic and political leadership is very hard to assess, since the influence they wield is often the product of the attitudes they create among the rank-and-file of Negroes. Their hold over their followers is a subject which would require research of a different character than that employed here, but other studies, such as the work by Drake and Cayton, suggest that their influence is considerable. All that can be observed here, however, is the activity of these leaders in relation to other sources of influence in the Negro community and the relationships which seem to exist among them.

The hope of Negro writers in the 1930's that the entry of Negroes into organized labor in positions of leadership would mean the beginning of a new liberal force working on behalf of race ends has proved to be overly optimistic. The role of *labor* leader is more specific and demanding than the role of *Negro* leader, and the constraints of office in the labor movement are usually more powerful than the illusive attractions of militant civic leadership. Nowhere is this better illustrated than in the almost Florentine subtleties of Chicago labor politics.[10]

Negro labor leaders tend in most cases to reflect the political and civic positions of the parent organization. Although the presence of a large number of Negroes in a union local is an important constraint on the actions of the leaders, it must not be assumed that a Negro membership or Negro officers inevitably propel the union into militant participation in civic and political affairs concerned with race ends. Both the AFL and the CIO are divided between liberal and conservative locals and inter-nationals. Chicago has white-led liberal unions (such as the United Auto Workers) and white-led conservative unions (such as the United Steelworkers); there are Negro-led liberal unions (such as several locals of the United Packinghouse Workers) and Negro-led conservative unions (such as several "Jim Crow" locals of AFL craft unions).

The general argument being made here is that the attitudes and actions of a Negro labor leader with respect to race issues are more a function of his position within the union than of his position in the Negro community. The constraints imposed by the organization are usually stronger than the demands of the race. In this respect, the Negro labor leader is in much the same position as the Negro politician or businessman for whom the organizational situation is more relevant to action than the vaguer role of being a "Negro civic leader."

The participation of any Negro labor leader in civic action cannot be understood apart from the internal politics of his union. One such leader, in the past identified with liberal race causes, finds it more difficult to be so identified today. He is engaged in competition for county and state union office, and this requires alliances with many of the conservative elements in labor. He has been under pressure from governmental agencies seeking to uncover possible radical affiliations. Finally, his participation in causes which attacked the local political organization led to apparent harassment from building inspectors. These factors account in part for his taking a more conservative stance in the community and for his associating his union with the moderate, business-oriented leadership of the NAACP. Another Negro leader, on the other hand, is endeavoring to advance in a union in which very few Negroes have risen to top-level positions. Despite a large Negro membership, few of the higher executive or staff positions are held by Negroes. The Negro labor leader in such a situation is faced with a choice: either abandon his ambitions or seek support for them. This Negro has developed strong political support within his union and has taken the leadership in creating pressure from various locals with large Negro memberships on behalf of greater Negro representation in the union hierarchy. The Negro leader's independent base of support within his organization has both made possible and encouraged his activity on behalf of Negro-involved goals and has permitted him to give expressions to personal convictions which are not always received with enthusiasm by his superiors and colleagues.

Labor in Chicago in recent years has been engaged in a pattern of shifting alliances. For several years, the United Packinghouse Workers (UPWA) was widely considered to be Communist-infiltrated at the same time when Negroes were entering its locals in ever-increasing numbers. The UPWA at this time was not active in the Cook County CIO. After World War II, as a result of the Taft-Hartley Act and the anti-Communist drive of other CIO unions, notably the auto workers, the UPWA was (formally at least) purged of Communist officers and brought into the CIO in full standing. Within the CIO a struggle for power was in process between the steel workers on the one hand and the auto workers on the other. The UPWA became allied with the auto workers in this contest. This alliance has meant that the Chicago CIO has been divided, beneath the surface, between the more conservative steel unions and the more radical group of automobile and packinghouse workers. Negro labor leaders reflect this cleavage. In campaigns to control the NAACP and in relations with the political machine, conservative groups (Negro businessmen and organization politicians) have been able to draw upon the support of the so-called conservative unions (the steel workers plus most AFL unions), while the more liberal groups (Negro protest leaders and white liberals and independents) have been able, for the most part, to draw on the more liberal unions (the UAW).

Direct political action in the Negro wards by labor has largely been the product of the UAW Political Action Committee, of which an energetic Negro, Willoughby Abner, is director. A precinct organization, created by Abner from union personnel beginning in 1948, directly challenged the Democratic party in the 1950 primary election to decide upon the party candidate for state senator. A white man was the organization's candidate, and he received support from the Negro machine. Abner became the opposing candidate, backed by the UAW and a white liberal group centered around the University of Chicago. The Negro union locals split in their attitude toward Abner. The United Transport Service Employees — the red caps — headed by the prominent Negro leader, Willard Townsend, rejected Abner's candidacy. Other conservative unions, including clothing, building, electrical, and shipbuilding locals, followed suit. For another group, however, Abner was not radical enough — some packinghouse workers' locals were cool to him, possibly because of his anti-Communist efforts.[11] Abner was defeated by over two-to-one. Members of the United Auto Workers have continued to engage in precinct work in the Negro community, sometimes supporting the regular Democratic candidate and at other times supporting white and Negro challengers. Abner's own candidacy, his subsequent opposition to machine candidates for alderman and congressman in the Negro wards, and his outspoken attacks (as NAACP president) on Congressman Dawson were some of the principal reasons for the opposition of the political organization to him in the NAACP elections. One Negro politician observed on that occasion:

I had a score to settle with Abner. . . . He got out and fought me in this ward, even going to the extent of hiring a sound truck and driving around asking people to vote for [my opponent]. . . . And he had no reason to oppose me. I had a clean record, there was nothing against me . . . . It was all because I was a member of a political organization . . . . So I was glad to lend a hand to get Abner out.

Abner himself, of course, places a different interpretation on these events. To him, opposing the Negro politician had nothing to do with the qualities of the politician himself. Rather, it was an organized expression of opposition to the political machine as a whole which, in Abner's view, was stifling the "natural expression of the needs and aspirations of Negroes."

Challenges to the political organization of this nature are only offered by a relatively small segment of the labor movement. By and large, the city-wide labor leadership endorses and works with the candidates of the Democratic party. Congressman Dawson invariably receives official endorsement from labor, and is regarded — on labor issues — as having a commendable voting record in Congress. Opposition to Dawson comes from points below the highest leadership level. This is occasionally a source of friction between such Negro labor leaders as Abner and his superiors. The friction results, in great part, from the differing organizational interests of the two sets of leaders. One set, the labor leaders in charge of the locals, must meet the bread-and-butter needs of their unions and maintain good working relations with those who control the city administration. There are few causes which would provoke an open break between labor and political leaders, although privately they may disagree on many matters. Another set of leaders, who function at the *staff* level and who are concerned with creating a political action committee, must find and distribute intangible rewards for their followers. Labor political workers are for the most part volunteers, and the enthusiasm with which they participate in any given election is in part dependent on the character of the candidates whom they endorse and the issues in the contest. These labor leaders, to sustain an organization which has political rather than strictly union ends, almost inevitably find themselves occasionally in conflict with those higher leaders who seek a different, *apolitical* set of ends. Although the beliefs of the various leaders are not unimportant, the overriding consideration governing their attitudes toward political and civic life springs from the varying influence relations and organizational maintenance needs that exist within the highly diversified labor movement.

On some civic issues, the more liberal unions are able to persuade the city labor leadership to speak in accordance with their desires. Criticisms of the city's urban renewal plans, for example, were expressed by the Cook County CIO Council. On other issues, however, unity is more difficult to obtain. When there were white-instigated acts of violence against some Negroes in a Chicago neighborhood, a Negro labor leader was unable to get certain affiliated unions in the area to take effective action on behalf of strong police measures:

> The [union out there] is headed by [X]. He operates purely on the basis of political expediency, just like . . . the alderman down there. . . . I called him up first thing on this ——— but he wouldn't stand up and be counted. He has to play politics with his union, so he stays quiet.

The Negro ministry is also divided in its attitude toward the political machine. Several prominent Negro ministers who have large congregations never fail to support the Dawson organization and are personally close to him. These ministers are characteristically Baptist or Pentecostal, with large followings among lower-income Negroes. Another group of ministers, often better-educated and with wealthier congregations, are suspicious of Dawson in particular and of politics in general. Some are drawn into campaigns on behalf of the Republican opposition, but they become quickly disillusioned. Most avoid electoral politics. The class bias is felt strongly among Negro ministers, and generally corresponds to attitudes toward the Negro machine. One upper-class minister argued that he could not be the kind of civic leader he wanted to be because of distrust:

> I couldn't do it. I am unacceptable to the average Negro minister. I am an alien, I am accused of pastoring a [high-brow] church. . . . These other Negro ministers, they never went to college, or if they did, they didn't finish and go to a seminary . . . . They are uneducated, and they have segregated themselves . . . . The Baptists just jump up and start preaching.

The educated, upper-class ministers of the socially-preferred denominations — the Congregationalists, the Presbyterians, the Episcopalians — together with the "better" Baptist and Methodist ministers form the group from which civic leaders are drawn. These "better" Baptist ministers — men who have built large and prosperous congregations and who have a college education — discuss what they feel have been the important changes they have wrought in their religious leadership in past years:

When I first came here, I'd shout 'em. I'd get 'em hollering. They were old and wanted to forget. But I couldn't do that now. If I did that, they'd say, "My, the reverend must be sick today." You wouldn't know this place —— years ago. It was so different. There's no shouting or hollering here anymore.

Another Baptist, who had risen from "store-front" preacher himself, now was contemptuous of demonstrative religious leaders:

Only the illiterate preachers, it seems, get on the radio. I can't even let them preach in my church. *My* people will come up to me and say, "Reverend, we don't want that trash in our pulpit." Personally, I think they should be closed down by law. If you say I said that, I'll deny it. You say something like that on the South Side, and everybody will be after you.

Everyone agrees, however, that the lower-class Negro minister has a great hold over his following. "A social agency which wants to work in that area," said one minister, "has to come to terms with [X] or with men like [Y] or [Z]. You can't ignore them. They are deeply entrenched in their areas." Equally, everyone says that the Negro minister, the most powerful force in the community, does not act in civic leadership roles. The upper-class minister is drawn into a plethora of Negro organizations, although rarely into protest organizations such as the NAACP. He is also active in many interdenominational and white-sponsored activities, such as the Church Federation of Greater Chicago. The average Baptist minister is not engaged by such activities. The church defines the boundaries of his behavior. Some of the more powerful of these ministers have built their churches into huge social service agencies, distributing food, clothing, and fuel in virtually wholesale lots to the needy. But, with some notable exceptions, they are not attracted by the rewards of civic leadership. They are rarely in interdenominational groups or interracial groups.

A prominent NAACP officer, not personally a militant, described his efforts — and failure — to attract Negro ministers to responsible positions in that organization:

Everywhere, the church exercises very great influence in the Negro community. But this leadership is not being well used at present. The church men have not wakened to their responsibilities . . . . What did somebody say? They said the church lifted its skirts and tiptoed through the problems. They weren't nice . . . . We send literature every month to the churches, but we rarely ask them to do anything, except read pronouncements or offer up a prayer. . . . We *never* ask them for money; we'd be embarrassed by the quarters we'd get in response . . . . Last month we managed to get seventy-five ministers out to a meeting, all denominations. This is the first time in my tenure anything like that has ever happened . . . . The NAACP can bring them together, but only by appointing a lay chairman of the church committee. That worked.

In 1945 there were between four and five hundred Negro churches in Chicago, but perhaps three-fourths were "store-front" churches operated by part-time ministers with very small congregations. Weekly church attendance was estimated at about 20 per cent of the South Side population.[12] Only a few Negro churches, perhaps two or three dozen, are sizeable institutions today. The church is an important part of life in the Negro community, but it is not, as Drake and Cayton point out, the center of that life any longer. Most of these churches are marginal enterprises, with few resources and little organization. But even among the larger churches, many of which claim to have over ten thousand members, support for race causes like the NAACP is spotty. In 1958 48 Chicago Negro churches secured 4,500 members for the NAACP who paid a total of about $12,000 in fees. This was the largest such contribution in the history of the churches.[13]

On occasion, the denominational and personal rivalries which exist among many Negro ministers can be overcome in the seeking of civic goals. Ministerial participation in an NAACP rally in support of the Montgomery bus boycott was obtained by inviting almost all of the important ministers and giving over a large portion of the program to a prayer service led by each of them in turn. Similarly, when the NAACP sought to hire a new executive secretary, a young minister was considered (and eventually hired). Although personally well-qualified, he had to meet other tests as well. He had to be liberal (to earn labor support) but not *too* liberal (in order not to alienate conservative groups). He could not be a "competitive" minister — i.e., one who might be seen as a threat by certain other ministers. This was solved by picking a man who was young and who had no church of his own. Both militant and moderate NAACP leaders agree on the difficulties inherent in working with church groups, although recently church support of membership drives has improved markedly.

The politicians themselves are, at least privately, skeptical of the ministers. Many regard them as outright rivals who "mislead" the Negro people. Others feel they are corrupt, a feeling tempered by admiration for those who perform the kind of social welfare function that the politician has used to build his organization:

> I'm suspicious of the churches in the Negro wards around here. I've always believed that the preachers were getting a cut out of their church contracts.... But you take Reverend [Y]. He probably rakes off, but at least he distributes free food, clothes and all to the people, and helps them get jobs. He may take, but he puts back as well. And besides, he is a Democrat.

Apart from those few Negro ministers who take part in civic activities (usually of a non-controversial sort), and that slightly larger number who help the NAACP extract memberships from their congregations once a year, the Negro ministers are by and large not a significant source of civic impetus or political constraint. When the organizational goals of the minister are affected by a civic enterprise, of course, he can be expected to respond. The minister of a large and powerful Negro church which was threatened with demolition by a land clearance project did not hesitate to remonstrate personally with the highest officials. The church was removed from the clearance plan. Other aspects of the plan, which touched Negroes but not Negro members of his church, did not concern him. Finally, Negro ministers provide an important source of prestige leaders, men who perform the functions described under that label in Chapter X.

The gulf that separates the Negro politicians on one hand, from the more militant NAACP, Urban League, and labor leaders is in part created by both groups. Neither group fully understands the role of the other, and this is partly inevitable. The maintenance needs of political organizations, labor political action committees, and voluntary associations are so radically different in Chicago that it would be remarkable if the respective leaders could see clearly and dispassionately each other's functions and problems.[14] These differences are expressed in fundamental disagreements over the value of conflict, the role of politics, and the selection of ends. To a militant labor leader, conflict is an inherent part of social change. Concessions are forced by bringing pressure to bear on appropriate governmental agencies. Compromise is possible only in the sense that one can accept partial concessions as a step in the right direction, but it is impossible in the sense of exploring and approving mutually advantageous solutions. It rarely occurs to the more militant leaders to discover ways of appealing to the self-interest of the politician in order to induce him, rather than compel him, to move. Politics, for these groups, ought to be implicated in all phases of Negro public life.

To the politician, politics is one important segment of public life, but not the only one. Politics involves attaining office and governing, and it ought to be possible — in this view — to exclude many issues from its purview. When civic associations raise issues that involve party matters, then he believes that these groups are "interfering" in politics. Politics can be a road for race advancement, but it can only deal with certain kinds of ends in a certain way. The politician cannot understand why militant leaders do not understand this or why they insist that the politician ought to seek *all* the ends of the race with equal fervor. To the militant leader, the Dawson political organization stands as a great and probably corrupt barrier to the natural expression of the needs and aspirations of the Negro community; to Dawson and other Negro politicians, the organization has rendered a great service to the Negro community by organizing it under a single leadership in order to make its weight felt in the councils of the party and in the offices of government. The militant leaders feel the politicians are derelict for not espousing the race ends they feel are important; the politicians, on the other hand, hold these leaders in disdain for "interfering" in politics (i.e., raising issues and making charges) but not "participating" in politics (i.e., joining with the organization in strengthening its position in the party and the city). This fundamental line of cleavage in the Chicago Negro community is deep and probably un-

avoidable. It would exist, in some degree, regardless of what individuals occupied the leading posts in each group. It gives rise to
many conflicts over ends and means which will be discussed in
later chapters.

Chapter VII

Negro-White Civic Relations

I N very few instances can one discover a case in which a Negro or a Negro-led organization altered the course of civic affairs in Chicago by intention. Nevertheless, it is evident that many civic affairs would take a different form if Chicago had no large Negro population; in some sense, Negroes do make a difference. This difference, however, arises most usually from the mere *presence* of Negroes rather than from their concerted activities. The existence of a great and growing Negro population in Chicago is taken into account, responses are anticipated, and the ecology of the Negro is carefully and exactly studied in order to determine the Negro impact on proposed civic developments. The broadest and most controversial civic projects typically involve the use of real estate, and it is precisely in this area that the Negroes, by their very presence, are an important—sometimes an all-important—determinant of the resolution of the issue. In problems of public housing, neighborhood redevelopment, institutional construction, area conservation, and the development of public facilities, often the most crucial questions asked reduce themselves to one: "Will the Negroes be in this?"

Negroes are, in a very real sense, the objects rather than the subjects of civic action. Things are often done for, or about, or to, or because of Negroes, but they are less frequently done *by* Negroes. This state of affairs has several important implications for Negro civic leadership. It tends to lend credence, in the eyes of many moderate Negroes, to the argument of the militants that only outspoken protest action can have any effect whatsoever on decisions that will shape the Negro's destiny. It creates a sense of defeatism among many Negro leaders who despair of accomplishing anything at all in the city. Events are out of their hands; they seem to be powerless to alter conditions that affect them. Those few Negroes who have been economically successful and who come in contact with influential whites, aware that race is a controversial and unpleasant subject in such circles, avoid it and confine themselves to the specific transaction that concerns them and their affairs. It seems to them that the race is collectively maligned and mistreated; the individual must get for himself what he can.

But this picture of inefficacy is not completely accurate. Certain forms of leverage can be exerted by the Negro to alter at least the conditions in which civic action occurs. Some whites seek a reputation for brotherhood and humanitarianism which can be endangered by acts which arouse Negro opposition and condemnation. Some whites have political aspirations beyond their own white precincts, and conspicuously anti-Negro acts must be avoided. The Governor, for example, may aspire to national office, and such hopes may lead him to espouse, at least publicly, race ends such as FEPC with somewhat more enthusiasm than formerly in order to cultivate a broader constituency which includes important Negro groups. Other whites seek civic ends justified in terms of the general phrase, "good government." "Good government," for the middle-class civic reformer, is government that appears to benefit all at the expense of none but the boodling politician. If a project, such as a plan to build a branch of the County Hospital in or near the Negro community, is suddenly attacked by a reputed spokesman for the Negro community, then the enterprise becomes tarnished and doubts are raised in the minds of those whites who formerly thought it to be a "good thing." Further, criticism from the Negroes may provide a weapon in the hands of those who oppose the project for other reasons, but who cannot admit those reasons without appearing to act from purely selfish motives. Race is rarely discussed publicly by white civic leaders. If an issue can be settled without public reference to race, then it is less controversial, less nasty, than issues which become branded with the race label. Less controversial issues can attract more white civic leaders to them; the greater the controversy, the more respectable civic leaders are likely to fall away or shun it. And some Negroes, as will be discussed later, are often eager to apply the race label wherever they can. Other civic projects, which clearly involve the interests of the Negro community, cannot be launched without at least the semblance of Negro support. Efforts to promote conservation in a Negro neighborhood, even though they are primarily supported by white businessmen in the area, must give at least the appearance of Negro leadership. If the project becomes branded as anti-Negro, it becomes harder to recruit the kind of Negro spokesmen that is preferred; indeed, it may not be possible to get any Negro spokesmen at all. The problem of recruiting token leaders is made harder if organized Negroes publicly oppose the plan.

All this makes the Negro significant, even if he does not wield "power." Few civic issues are initiated by Negroes, but many are responded to by them; Negro civic leadership is more often defensive than assertive. Negroes, to use Riesman's phrase, are often—though not always—a "veto group." When they are not a veto group, the reasons can most frequently be found in the constraints that affect Negro civic leaders themselves—constraints which this study will describe. In this chapter Negro civic relationships with white businessmen—civic leaders and white liberal allies—will be analyzed.

The Negro and the White Businessman

Communication between Negroes and white businessmen-civic leaders tends to be minimal and to concern matters other than race. Almost all Negro civic leaders agree that they have little or no opportunity to discuss problems of importance to the race with white businessmen and those few Negroes who do have influential white contacts generally agree that racial issues are not raised and that they prefer not to raise them for fear of the complications it would cause. A prominent Negro businessman, whose business requires him to meet white businessmen, often at the highest corporate levels, describes the attitude with which he approaches such contacts:

> I have been considered a businessman, not a race leader. In fact, I emphasize to our salesmen that they are to avoid discussing the

race problem. People get excited about it, and we might lose business through that.... I don't raise race issues with these people [that I meet]. I attempt to evade discussion on things like Paul Robeson, even though I disagree with Robeson thoroughly.... The whole problem with this matter of communication between Negroes and whites is that the leaders meet at teas. The whole meeting is surface and veneer only.... No one really knows what the other fellow is thinking.... All you do is exchange pleasantries with each other. Mr. [M] has been down to lunch here, and I have had lunch with Mr. [K] and Mr. [L]. But I don't know what they think about social problems. We never come to grips with the basic problems.... I could talk to them if it came about in a natural way. I couldn't make an appointment for business and then switch the conversation to talk about race, though.... I'm not ashamed of my position but I will avoid talking about it if I can.

Another Negro, a member of several white-led civic associations whose fields of interest included problems which touched race matters, mentioned that these groups were interested in mortgage financing for home construction. But the Negro, moderate in style and a token leader by type, realized that his position as a member was in part dependent on conforming to that style and type:

I never dealt with these people on an economic basis. I didn't feel it would be right. I knew them on a social basis, and we talked about what we were supposed to talk about.... I never went to them about these matters.

Another Negro, more militant in style, had struggled for some time to gain entry to a white association which had formerly excluded Negroes. When in, however, he quickly discovered—in truth, he had hoped to discover and was not disappointed—that entry into such white circles was to be on their terms and not on his, and he became restless. The process of "luring" Negroes is one which is widely described among more militant Negroes as "brainwashing":

That kind of pressure is hard to resist. They will call you by your first name, and invite you into their homes, and invite your wife to parties.... They give you social acceptance and slap you on the back and tell you what a fine fellow you are.... They just calm you down, and make your forget any race issues. We're all buddies, that sort of thing. It's a softening-up process.... The white people want you to be a regular guy and put your head in the sand and work hard.

Whatever reservations they may have, this kind of acceptance is nonetheless a genuine lure, and some voluntary associations are able to attract Negro support by inviting them to well-publicized benefits or theater parties attended by prominent whites.

The business and professional contacts of Negroes and whites have been limited, but they are slowly widening. Negroes participate as members of such organizations as the Association of Commerce and Industry, the Chicago Bar Association, the Chicago Medical Society, and labor unions; they are excluded from the Chicago Real Estate Board and comparable organizations concerned with the appraising, selling, and financing of real estate. At the same time, Negro real estate brokers are heavily dependent upon these white groups for real estate listings and mortgage money. In the area in which Negroes feel the greatest problems lie, there is the least Negro-white organized communication, and most Negroes resent this. In the Negro community itself, however, interracial organizations do exist and are concerned with business problems affecting Negro-occupied real estate. Such forums, however, are strictly for business purposes, and most Negroes as well as whites respect this focus. One younger Negro broker, however, wanted to raise civic issues in the organization:

I'm on . . . its board. It's 95 per cent white, and there's where you find the big kitchenette and other property owners on the South Side . . . . I can't talk to anybody there . . . . I was on the board for a while, and proposed that we try to push for an improvement program out here to get things cleaned up. Hell, man, that was voted right out the window in short order.

When whites come to grips with problems affecting their real estate holdings in Negro areas, private Negro advisers are brought in to help; the problems are not taken to voluntary associations. Younger Negroes who seek to inject race into the affairs of business or professional organizations are cautioned by older Negroes that this is not done; the value of Negro-white contacts in these associations lies in the fact that should the whites need advice on race problems, they will turn to those Negroes whom they know and feel they can trust. Temperate behavior by Negroes in business groups can create that trust. One experienced Negro adviser described a younger colleague in these terms:

[X] is still young. He fights all the time, that's true, and he is all

bound up in his own community.... But he will come along. I am
trying to draw him into the Association of Commerce and Industry
more. Now we are getting him to go to committee meetings. We
are always pushing people to get them into this. Then, when people
in the Loop need advice or just want somebody to talk to from out
here, they can turn to someone they know in the Association.

When the structure of the professional or business association
is federal, however, local units can be "captured" by Negroes and
then used to press for race ends in the larger organizations. The
Medical Society is so organized, and its South Side branch is composed almost entirely of Negroes who have, under unusually
vigorous leadership, pressed in the medical society as a whole
for hospital integration and other reforms. When the association
is unitary in form, with only one meeting-ground in which whites
predominate, Negroes are far less outspoken.

In the Negro-led voluntary associations, such as the NAACP
and the Urban League, white civic leader participation may
lend the organization varying qualities — prestige, or status, or
influence, or support. The NAACP began in Chicago as a white-
led organization. Its first president was the father of a recent
chairman of the board of the First National Bank, and Harold
L. Ickes was also an early branch president. Over the years,
and particularly since World War II, Negro domination has grown
to the point where whites form a small minority, excluded from
all but one or two offices in the association. Nationally, the
NAACP has acquired a practical monopoly of Negro protest
action — something it did not have in the past, when protest
was shared with, or usurped by, more radical Negro groups such
as the March on Washington Movement, the National Negro
Congress, and others. As it has become identified with Negro
protest and explosive issues such as school integration, the
NAACP has become suspect in the eyes of influential white businessmen and civic leaders. "Too radical" is a common description
of it among these men, and the whites that are found in it today
are largely liberal union leaders, intellectuals, and housewives.

The Urban League, on the other hand, has had better relations
with whites. It was founded and to a great extent is financed by
white businesses which have a stake in the Negro community
owing either to a dependence on a Negro labor force or a Negro

market or both. In Chicago these businesses include meat pack-
ing, steel, telephone, merchandising, and others. The white business representatives to the League, many of whom are directors,
have generally been public relations vice-presidents for their respective firms, and not by any means the most influential men
in either their own corporations or in the city's civic affairs. In
part, their jobs require them to maintain good relations with
important groups in the city, and — given their businesses — the
Negroes are an important group. Most Negroes who are board
members are in the League for less tangible reasons, and occasionally one will make some unfavorable comparisons:

I can't see it . . . . [Z] and these others, they get paid for coming
to these meetings. And Sears and the others want the Negroes to put
up money if the Urban League expects to get white business money.
Why should we? They've got the money; we'd have to go out and
beat our brains out for it. I'm not about to start ringing doorbells
for the Urban League . . . . If they just want to create an impression,
they can pay me for it. I'll impress, at my usual fees. The others get
paid, why shouldn't we? If not, the hell with it.

Such outbursts reveal latent tensions that exist in any such
interracial association. The Urban League staff sees its task as
one of "selling ideas" to the white members, and through them to
influential whites in the city as a whole. The same ideas have
to be sold to the Negro community and the continued support
of both groups, white and Negro, has to be maintained through
service programs in the field of employment counselling, youth
guidance, and other bread-and-butter projects of a welfare nature.

White business supports the Urban League because it has a
tangible stake in the Negro community — the need for Negro
labor, a desire to upgrade the quality and skills of that labor, the
relations between Negro and white workers, and the need to protect plant investment in Negro areas. But this should not lead one
to conclude that white businesses can or do dictate a conservative
policy to the Urban League staff. In fact, the staff is often able to
persuade white board members to endorse fairly advanced race
positions. The determinants of the positions which board members can be led to accept are more than simply the liberalism
of the end itself, but involve further the style or manner in
which it is pressed and the relevance of the issue to the economic

and community position of the business. White civic leaders, and particularly civic leaders who are concerned with public relations, often measure success in terms of the interests of their businesses and the level of favorable publicity which civic enterprise can attract. There are many race ends which, simply because they are so remote of achievement, will disturb neither business interests nor public relations *so long as* they are not sought by protest or agitational tactics.

Shortly after the reorganization of the Chicago Urban League, the question arose as to whether it should endorse the FEPC bill then before the state legislature. Several of the white businesss were known to be opposed. Within the Urban League itself, however, the issue was presented to the white board members in terms of the needs of the Urban League as an association. To maintain that association in the eyes of the Negro community, endorsement of FEPC was essential; without endorsement, the Urban League would be accused by Negroes of being under the domination of the Loop, and its effectiveness would be severely hampered. A Negro director described the situation:

[X] was really on the spot. He didn't know what to say. So he went back to [his company] and said that the Urban League has to come out for FEPC or it will go under, and that the law won't pass anyway.... He [then] came back and stood up and said, "Well, we're on the horns of a dilemma here, and if we have to take one horn, we might as well grab hold good." He proposed [the bill] and we adopted it.

At the same time, other white business representatives voted against endorsement. The assessments made by white members of the maintenance needs of the association versus the effects endorsement would have on their own interests depended on the kind of business and type of businessman involved.[1] Most of the white businesses involved had large numbers of Negro workers: FEPC would not greatly affect them even in the unlikely chance that it should be passed. Since political obstacles prevent the Urban League, or any other race relations group, from forcing unwelcome legislation upon them, what remains is the delicate and complex field of public relations.

Between 1947 and 1955, the actions of the Negro executive of the Urban League brought on a chronic state of crisis in the relations between the League and its business sponsors. Many Negroes charged that the management of the League was characterized by administrative disorder, but at the same time the public actions of the League staff were militant and often radical in many areas of race relations. Through public statements critical of white neighborhoods which would not accept Negro residents, the League Negro executive became identified by some — probably wrongly — as a person actively engaged in "blockbusting" — i.e., encouraging and financing the entry of Negroes into all-white neighborhoods. The League staff became involved in a whole range of race issues, many of which were outside the defined scope of the Urban League.

The result was a steady loss of support for the League. Moderate Negroes, including the Catholic representatives and right-wing labor leaders, dropped off the board of directors. The Community Fund, which provided the bulk of the League's financial support, began receiving complaints from donors about the use of Fund money for the League. Businesses lost confidence in the League's employment services which had been placing Negroes in industrial jobs. The Welfare Council, a federation of Chicago welfare and social service agencies, began to inquire into the management of the League. A prominent Chicago corporate executive, who was the chairman of a section of the Community Fund during one year, felt that his fund-raising efforts were meeting resistance because of the League's membership in the Fund.

White business and civic organizations began to withdraw support from the League. The subscriptions committee of the Association of Commerce and Industry threatened on several occasions to withdraw its endorsement, an almost essential prerequisite for fund-raising activities among Chicago businesses. Some board members asked the National Urban League to step in with a full-scale investigation. A committee of inquiry was selected from the Welfare Council and the Association of Commerce and Industry to consider the whole matter.

Certain League directors, Negro and white, were able to persuade the board to close down the League and to fire the executive and almost all of the staff. For six months the League was in limbo, existing in name only. A committee of Chicago businessmen was brought together to consider ways and means of rehabilitating the League on sounder principles. Feeling in some quarters was so strongly against the League that many felt that its name would have to be changed in order to regain the confidence of business and political circles. The Mayor was consulted. The public relations vice-president of a company, whose chief executive had been the Community Fund chairman who encountered fund-raising difficulties because of the League's presence, took the lead in recruiting a new board with representatives from key industries. In effect, the League passed into receivership in the hands of several corporate vice-presidents, some Negroes, and two or three hold-over members of the League's board. A Negro executive director from another part of the country was hired. The businessmen set about raising a budget for the League and re-establishing its respectability. The League was reopened and most of the businessmen withdrew from actual board membership, leaving two or three who represented important industrial areas. Projects were begun that would be attractive to moderate Negroes, such as "stay-in-school" campaigns and youth guidance efforts. At the same time — and this is of great importance in the understanding of the relations between white and Negro civic leaders in formal organizations such as the Urban League — the Negro executive director hired to rebuild the League was neither a lackey nor a conservative. He was an able man of advanced views, who quickly acquired a reputation in the Negro community as a rather militant leader.

After its reorganization, the League was able to endorse FEPC and issue a report critical of certain aspects of urban renewal, a program in which many white business and civic leaders had considerable interest. Although some white board members voted against these positions, their opposition was not carried beyond the vote. On the other hand, when the Negro executive made public statements asserting that Chicago "is the most segregated city in the nation," and when national circulation was given to these remarks, there were repercussions. No overt pressure was placed on him, but there were clear signs that important civic and political figures were disturbed by what they regarded as unwarranted assertions that adversely affected the reputation of the city. More important than what the Urban League in fact *does* is what it *says* or what it *seems* to do.

The interests of important white businesses are served by the Urban League, and the price of this service is a certain amount of educational and community organization work done by the League to promote race ends. This price will be paid so long as such work does not disturb the reputations of white civic and political leaders nor hamper the prosecution of important civic enterprises.

In the past white businessmen have acted to constrain the civic activities of Negroes in other areas. In the 1930's and 1940's, many Negro groups which felt the shortage of jobs engaged in programs to induce, by boycotts and picketing, white business-men to employ Negro labor. A slogan was developed: "Don't Buy Where You Can't Work." In part it was a genuine effort to expand Negro job opportunities; in part it was an effort of Negro businesses to attract more Negro customers by identifying Negro business with a race cause. A Negro newspaper was particularly active in the campaign. White businesses retaliated by withdraw-ing advertising and the paper soon went out of business. The memory of this is still fresh in the minds of Negro journalists, and although they deny that their editorial policy is dictated by ad-vertising, their remarks suggest rather clearly that such dictation is unnecessary because the limits of editorial discretion are known in advance. One editor said:

> We have an historical precedent for this. We had a paper here . . . which developed a campaign of that kind. "Don't Buy Where You Can't Work" was the slogan. Well, it put them out of business . . . . They couldn't get any advertising . . . . They had been doing well up to that point. So we don't subscribe to the baseball-bat policy of action. We don't try to engage in any campaign to destroy a business.

Negro real estate brokers are dependent to a great extent on white sources for property listings, financing, and insurance. Al-though few Negro real estate brokers are found among the ranks of the vigorous in civic affairs, all of them discover that they can be blocked at many points in their normal business activities by white interests which choose to do so. In an urban renewal plan sponsored by whites in a racially mixed neighborhood, Negro real estate agents who had sold and managed property in the area for Negro owners and tenants found that many of their sales were being taken out of their hands by large white organizations in order to gain control of the racial composition of the area. Another Negro real estate broker became very active on behalf of neighborhood conservation in the Negro community, and an organization in which he was a leading force acted vigorously to uncover and report building code violations as part of a general clean-up campaign. Such activities affected adversely the interests of large property-owners in the area, both white and Negro. A bank where the Negro real estate broker did much of his mortgage business reportedly advised him against pressing his civic activities as he would only jeopardize his standing with the bank. The Negro withdrew from the civic association. Even though most Negroes would not engage in such civic affairs even if there were no threat of reprisals, it only requires one such example to provide a convincing reason for refraining.

In many more instances there is no need at all for whites to resort to such tactics in order to restrain Negro civic leadership. As portions of the Negro community grow in wealth or position, they acquire a whole range of commitments and obligations which they are unwilling to risk for the sake of the intangible rewards of civic leadership. A Negro leader who had recently completed a new building observed that no one had attempted to influence him in civic matters, but that nonetheless he did not wish to be foolhardy:

I haven't felt any pressure . . . not at all. . . . Of course, now we have a lot more irons in the fire on this new building that makes me feel that we don't want to move so fast that we lose this. In getting this building, we had co-operation from [everybody] . . . . I'd hate to do anything that would harm our building program.

"White influence" on the Negro community increases, not so much because of the increased activity of influential whites, but more because the Negro community itself continues to grow in ways which render it more vulnerable and hence more sensitive to the economic implications of its own civic life. In a later chapter it will be pointed out that the pattern of ends sought by Negro leaders is changing and becoming more diversified, in part because of the increasing diversity and unequal desegregation of the Negro community. This argument can be anticipated here to suggest that as more Negroes enter into normal business relations with the larger community they become subject to new sets of constraints — ranging from attitudes to tangible risks — on civic leadership. Not all kinds of Negro civic action raise issues crucial to white interests, and a low level of Negro leadership here must be ascribed to many factors other than simply a fear of reprisals. The proposed Cook County hospital branch, for example, has been opposed by Negroes (and Negroes in the Urban League) without attracting retribution; this is an issue which can be more or less freely agitated. Negro support of FEPC conforms to the general pattern of expectations; no Negro runs any real risks by advocating the measure. On the other hand, Negro attempts to enter white neighborhoods clearly are a vital matter, and whites are quick to suspect such actions on the part of Negro organizations even when the financial capacity to engage in "blockbusting" does not exist. The Negro-supported ordinance to outlaw discrimination in publicly-assisted housing was opposed by the white business community whose spokesman was a realtor and civic leader who generally enjoys a reputation for comparative liberalism on race matters.

The position of the white businessman-civic leader in those areas where no clear business or organizational stake is involved is a complex and uncertain one. Influential whites, by and large, appear to desire peace and quiet on Chicago's South Side. A very few look for Negro leaders with whom they can talk to find out what is happening in the Negro community, what these people want, and how issues can be sold to them. "Where can I sit down with prominent Negro leaders," asked one white leader of importance, "and find out what they want and what the reasonable solutions could be?"[2] Such Negroes would have to be not only influential, but discreet. One Negro leader reported his discussion of this point with a white man:

[A very important white civic leader] once said in my presence that [X, a deceased Negro leader] was one Negro he could *talk* to. [He] could talk to him because he knew that it wouldn't get any further; [X] would respect his confidences. [He] couldn't do that with people like [Y] or [Z]. The next day it would be all over town.

Another Negro, a well-known prestige leader, who was asked what things whites seemed to want to discuss with him involving the Negro community, replied:

They ask me — the most important thing they ask me is — how can we get to the Negro community? How can we get to these Negroes to get them to give money and time to these projects?

Bringing Negroes into white voluntary associations is, to the white leader, a risky undertaking. Unless the association is of a character that clearly warrants it (the YMCA or the Community Fund or the Welfare Council), the entry of Negroes can brand the organization as "reformist" or "radical," dangerous epithets that can make the organization's tasks more difficult. An executive of a white civic voluntary association was asked if his organization took Negroes onto its board:

No, we haven't. There has been some discussion on that. There have been no Negro members. . . . Our membership is quite limited. And there has been some discussion on some groups which haven't been represented. . . . It's not because we are not anxious for their support. . . . But it is a matter of strategy. If there were too many people of that sort . . . people would say we were a reform organization . . . and we would lose our effectiveness.[3]

To the whites, this reluctance is particularly true given the organized constituencies many Negro leaders appear to have. An NAACP or labor union leader may not be able to deal with white groups effectively without losing his authority in the Negro group. The constraints that exist on an organization which has *members* (such as the NAACP) are not easily understood by a leader of an association which has no members but only contributing businesses. The elections to office in the NAACP are bitterly contested and are highly charged with ideological and emotional significance; elections of officers in, say, the State Street Council (an organization of downtown retail stores) are matters of form, disposed of in moments with no contest. Even conservative Negroes elected to office in the NAACP must respond in some measure to the demands of the more attentive —and usually more radical—members of the association.

Influential whites regard Negroes as a collective problem, but not as individually interesting phenomena. The presence of the Negroes is a fact; it must be dealt with when necessary, but few influential whites regard it as a condition which must or can be significantly altered. There have been efforts to bring the "Negro problem" before white civic leaders as a topic of discussion and thought, and there are a growing number who appear to be thinking of the long-range consequences of the glacier-like growth of the Negro community—consequences in terms of driving the whites to the suburbs, weakening the tax base of the city, and shifting the balance of political control. All admit that nothing is really being done about it. A corporate vice-president who had been active in the Urban League described his feelings on the matter:

I think that the town faces a long, difficult . . . problem. They'll elect their own people. . . . A Negro Mayor. . . Negro Council. . . . And I say, "All right, I don't want to live in any such community. . . . or even do business in any such community."[4]

In this most explosive area—housing and real estate—there has been little contact between Negroes and whites. Formal business organizations in the field, with the exception of certain voluntary associations, are by and large closed to Negroes. Many staff members of organizations like the Commission on Human Relations have sought to promote ad hoc meetings or conferences between influential persons, Negro and white, to discuss what can be done regarding difficulties such as mortgage financing and land availability for Negro home-owners. Such efforts have generally come to little. In 1957 a conference was arranged at a large hotel, one of the purposes of which was to discuss residential segregation in realistic terms. Unfortunately, a decision was made to hold it as a public meeting, rather than a private one. As a result, publicly-acceptable positions were taken and controversy was avoided. A Negro describes the tone of the conference:

It was designed to orient influential white business people to assume some of the responsibility in this field. . . . The trouble with that thing was that the Negro real estate people didn't show up. [X] was supposed to come . . . but he called me on the day of the meeting and said he couldn't make it. . . . [The same was true with] the top people from the Loop. . . . So the professional race relations people took over the meeting, and, hell, they don't count. They asked the usual questions.

In all cases, however, the white reaction to the real estate question is essentially a reaction to the felt presence of Negroes rather than a response to the civic actions or attempts at influence of Negro leaders. Indeed, it seems to be true that the greater the importance of any given race issue, the less important are the actions of Negro leaders. In part this is due to the fact that on less ramified issues—for example, getting welfare services or preventing race violence from spreading—Negroes can and do act or speak with a fair degree of unity, while with the larger issues, there is a falling-off of Negro support for any given position. In part it is also due to the fact that the simpler issues have fewer consequences for influential whites, and indeed may elicit white sympathy or at least involve whites whose goals are not incompatible with the goals of Negroes. On the larger issues—real estate and housing—the consequences are grave and far-reaching; here, whites are far less likely to be at all responsive to the demands of Negro leaders. Some white real estate leaders have explored possibilities of extending greater assistance to Negroes in securing mortgage financing and in obtaining vacant land; these efforts have thus far been highly tentative and uncertain. But what is important is that no Negro has induced them to act in this way by bringing to their attention in dramatic or persuasive form the problems of the present patterns of segregation. Action by whites, limited as it is, has been for the most part action at their own initiative. To the extent that Negroes have been brought into such matters at all, they appear to have been brought in as private advisers rather than as civic leaders.

Influential whites who enter into explicitly "race relations" associations such as the Catholic Interracial Council or the Urban League risk their prestige, and many receive phone calls and letters from people who wonder "what they are up to." At the same time, few Negroes are taken into explicitly white associations, although more today than in the past. One thoughtful Negro leader described what he felt to be the reasons for this:

It's a two-headed animal. First, civic efforts which have opportunities for Negro participation are limited. The Community Fund, the Red Cross, but not much else. . . . People [Negroes] don't offer to serve because they fear they won't be accepted. And no one asks them to serve because they don't know who to ask, and no one volunteers. . . . I only got on the Community Fund because I started asking the Fund why there were no Negroes on it, and, boom, they asked me. . . . Second, I think there is an even deeper reason. As a race, we haven't come to appreciate our responsibilities back to the community. . . . There is just beginning to emerge a leadership potential in the upper-income group. . . . But we don't have a heritage of service, like some of the . . . white families and companies do.

Because of these factors and others, the Negro seems to be in need of white allies, but forming such alliances, even with the best of intentions, is not as easy as it might seem.

The Negro and the White Ally

The attainment of race ends has been, generally, more conspicuous in New York, Philadelphia, and Detroit than in Chicago and it would perhaps be easier to assess those relationships of influence that make such attainment possible elsewhere than Chicago. Illinois has no FEPC law (New York, Michigan, Pennsylvania, Massachusetts, New Jersey, Wisconsin, and twelve other states do); Chicago has no open occupancy law (New York and Pittsburgh do); Chicago has fewer important interracial housing projects than New York and Philadelphia. An analysis of "how things get done" on behalf of Negroes in Chicago is made more difficult by the fact that so few things seem to get done at all.

Another problem imposes necessary qualifications upon statements about the processes of gaining concessions for Negroes. What is meant by "leadership"? Many groups contribute to efforts to gain concessions; what group or men are the strategic factors? Who, if anyone, is most effective, least dispensable? There is no real way to answer such questions conclusively. At the same time, it is not utterly meaningless to ask what groups have taken the initiative in raising issues; what groups have provided the professional and voluntary labor which have kept issues alive and in the foreground of attention of those who must deal with them; what groups have made the effective decisions as to how various issues would be treated, manipulated, compromised, or settled; and what groups have mobilized support—in terms of time, money, and popular demand—for these issues.

It appears clear that civic leadership on behalf of race ends has more often arisen, in Chicago, from white groups than from Negro groups. Whites, liberal or benevolent or self-interested, have raised issues, mobilized support, carried the battle to the decision-makers, and taken charge of the settlements or compromises. In almost all cases, they have had the co-operation, in

varying degrees of effectiveness, of organized groups in the Negro
community such as the NAACP or the Urban League. On occasion, the initiative has lain with the Negro association, and
sometimes an outspoken Negro leader has been able to create
the issue almost single-handedly by a well-timed application of
the race label to a matter which whites were endeavoring, consciously or unconsciously, to settle without regard to its racial
dimension. This was the case when Negroes suddenly and un-
expectedly objected to the proposed South Side branch of the
County Hospital. In other instances, Negro-led groups have la-
bored so long in a certain area of race interests that they have,
so to speak, set the stage for civic action: they have, by persistence and repetition, created an issue by refusing to let the forces
of the status quo remain undisturbed. In other cases, Negro
groups have been effective in winning some victories in those areas
of civic protest wherein Negro voluntary civic leadership can act
with unity and through established channels of access. This has
been true with regard to the legal defenses which have been
waged locally by the NAACP in the courts on behalf of Negroes
who have been the victims of restrictive covenants, racial violence,
or police mistreatment. Even in this area, however, Negro civic
action has not been directed to goals larger than individual grievances settled on a piecemeal basis. The most important single
series of Negro-led court actions focussed on general race ends
was the litigation concerning restrictive covenants which culmi-
nated in a United States Supreme Court case.[5] But here it was
not simply a question of voluntary civic action; lengthy and expensive court action could be sustained because the parties on
both sides were business and institutional interests with a stake
in the outcome—Negro life insurance and real estate companies
which had mortgage commitments in the area of contention, and
a university which sought to maintain racial barriers in that area.

A white group can often be found in the forefront of the battle
for the attainment of race ends. Agitation for a fair employment
practices act has in the past largely been led by certain Jewish
organizations. The campaign to build public housing on vacant
land sites in white areas and on an integrated basis was waged
largely by the Public Housing Association and related white
groups, while—with the exception of one or two Negroes profes-

sionally interested in the matter—the Negro leadership remained "relatively passive."[6] The only sustained and unequivocal opposition to those portions of the Hyde Park-Kenwood urban renewal plan that were alleged to be anti-Negro came from a spokesman for the Catholic Church. The management of efforts to integrate private hospital staffs was in the hands, as indicated in an earlier chapter, of the Chicago Commission on Human Relations. The efforts to promote conservation in a large section of the South Side Negro community were organized at the outset through the work of a Negro and a white businessman, but the maintenance of the organization soon fell most heavily on the more active white members.

The importance of city-wide, white-led voluntary associations is seen more clearly when Chicago is compared to New York City. In the latter case, these groups have won important victories in such matters as securing legislation against discrimination in public and private housing. The function of white liberal groups has been both to seek these ends and, at the same time, to stimulate and guide Negro civic action.

In New York City, in contrast to Chicago, a large number of voluntary associations have a vested interest in liberal causes. Most often these groups reflect the existence of a sizable bloc of Jewish citizens who tend to proliferate well-staffed organizations with a commitment to social equality and integration goals. New York is a city with a large number of Jews, and hence has a strong group of such associations as the Anti-Defamation League, the American Jewish Committee, the Jewish Labor Committee, the American Jewish Congress, and so on. It is also a city which is the site of the national headquarters of a host of liberal associations of all kinds. New York is, if anything, over-organized in proportion to its population. More voluntary associations are there than would exist if it were simply an equally-populous city but not a national headquarters. This is one of the factors that gives to civic life in New York a tone and rhetoric which is unlike that in any other northern city. The almost universal comment of white and Negro leaders in Manhattan is that "you can't be in favor of sin around here." It is difficult to oppose openly the goals of these groups. Opposition must be indirect and often aimed at means rather than ends. A series of past successes in campaigns for liberal causes has breached the dam. These past victories have established principles within public policies and laws which can later be appealed to in order to justify new policies and laws in related areas.

Voluntary associations endeavor to expand, or appear to expand, in order to continue to distribute the incentives that keep their supporters and members interested. These organizations seek new issues as a means of implementing their ideals, gaining allies, and justifying their budgets. The fight for an open occupancy ordinance in New York City was led by the New York State Committee Against Discrimination in Housing (NYSCADH), an organization of liberal civic associations. It was created largely at the instigation of the leading Jewish organizations in New York in 1949 after the failure of a court attack on the Stuyvesant Town anti-Negro policies. It began in 1950 to press through the state legislature a series of bills which would involve public authorities, in ever-increasing degrees, in the racial problems of private housing developments. Four major state laws and two New York City ordinances were passed in large part due to the efforts of this and related organizations. White (primarily Jewish) groups have been the most important single factor in the Committee. From the first, an effort was made to involve Negroes in its work, and a sizable number of prominent Negroes have played important roles and occupied top positions. Most of this Negro support has come from the ranks of Negro professionals who are officers or executives of other organizations (public and private) with an interest in the field of housing. This has included Negro officials of some large labor unions, the national NAACP, the Urban League, some churches, and various city agencies. In addition, some of these groups, such as the NAACP, have made financial contributions to the Committee.

Some important white leaders of the Committee, however, feel that the Negro masses ought to be involved in a campaign to correct anti-Negro practices in the housing market. They welcome the support of the Negro professionals, but wish in addition for Negro grass-roots support. Said one:

We didn't get much help from the Negroes — not on this or anything else, at least not as much as we'd like.... We didn't get any mass grass-roots support from them. We wanted them to write letters, hold meetings, and plague their Councilmen. But it was very hard for us to get these letters going. We never managed to send in more letters than those opposed to the law.... I guess it was because they [the Negro groups] lacked the staff and personnel.

The often repeated statement that New York Negroes are "more active" than those in other cities is properly placed in context by the history of the NYSCADH. Negroes were active in the sense that a large number of middle-class Negroes with a professional interest in matters such as housing could be found and recruited into the Committee. Further, the *national* offices of the two most important Negro voluntary associations were located in New York and their staff and financial resources (although not great) could be made available to such a campaign. But the organization of the Negro community itself was no more extensive than in, say, Chicago or Detroit. The crucial factor in the success of the Committee was the initiative and sustenance provided by white liberal civic associations.

Organized white liberalism appears to be less effective in obtaining concessions for Negroes in Chicago than it is in New York City. The obstacles seem to be greater and the resources fewer. One officer of the Chicago NAACP, observing that progress was slower here than in the East, felt that Chicago Negroes were in a difficult spot, they could not rely on the benevolence of the city as a whole, and they could not organize themselves to compel concessions:

In New York you have a city which is maybe one-third Jewish.... They will push for reforms like this. You can have a reform movement in New York without having to organize the Negroes. If you get the *Times* interested and the civic groups... the Jews... and the like, you can do it. Here, it's impossible. I don't think Chicago has ever had a reform movement. There is no real force you can get on your side to do the job. You have to organize the masses, the Negroes, and this is almost impossible.

The advantages white groups enjoy are not difficult to surmise. In any successful civic endeavor, time, money, and a paid staff are almost always necessary. Things are accomplished—issues raised and sustained, support mobilized, facts gathered, representations made—when people are hired to do these things. The moving forces of civic action are largely the organizations (such as businesses or institutions) which have a stake in a civic problem and the voluntary associations which thrive on civic issues and which have professional staffs to develop them. Such organizations and associations are scarce in the Negro community, and abundant in the white community. The Anti-Defamation League, for example, is a large and well-staffed association with generous financing which can bring to bear on racial or ethnic problems more time and energy than any comparable Negro association. Since any Negro cause is in need of broader support, there is usually a search for white allies. With the existing distribution of resources, white allies tend to become senior partners.

In addition, civic action requires access—the ability to deal with important city figures as equals and at ease. Negroes for the most part lack this access, and those who have it tend to be too anxious to maintain the access to jeopardize it by raising unpleasant subjects. White liberal groups can provide much of the access Negroes lack, and so again tend to be drawn into race issues in positions of predominance rather than mere support.

But it is not solely the logic of the situation that tends to place civic leadership for race ends in white hands. Negroes themselves are in part immobilized by certain constraints internal to the Negro community. The difference between the resources brought to bear by the Negro as compared to the white community on civic problems is not simply a function of the difference in total wealth. Negroes have fewer dollars upon which to draw, but it seems remarkable that a community of perhaps 750,000 people could raise in past years only about $35,000 for the NAACP and $10,000-$15,000 for the Urban League.[7] The fact that more is possible, given an adequate level of organization and leadership, is suggested by the sudden rise in both these figures after the Urban League had been reorganized and the NAACP placed under new leadership. In 1958-59, the NAACP raised about $70,000 and the League about $50,000 to $80,000. The only sizable professional staff consisting of Negroes and devoted to race problems is that of the Urban League, which relies in substantial part on the support of white business groups.

A final aspect of the relations between Negroes and white liberals is seen in the internal politics of the NAACP. To the extent that whites participate at all in the association, they usually do so as members of the more liberal, even left-wing faction. Campaigns to elect a more militant slate of officers in the Chicago branch have had, as a nucleus, a group of white liberals, trade unionists, and Socialists largely drawn from the university community. Although many Negroes are also associated with this group, the impression is often created that the organization's political alignments coincide with a Negro-white split. Some militants allege that the opposing, moderate faction is "anti-white." Many whites are aware of their somewhat difficult position in the NAACP and seek more and stronger Negro leaders to champion their cause. In the meantime, a situation exists in which, in a very real sense, whites constitute one important source of whatever radicalism is found among organized Chicago Negroes.

Interracial Attitudes

The most conspicuous single source of white liberal civic leadership in Chicago is the Jewish organizations. Negroes recognize this, and many give the Jews credit. Negro anti-Semitism, which at one time was so prevalent that it formed one of the major themes of the Negro press, seems to have diminished, particularly among the better educated and more cosmopolitan Negroes. During the Depression and war years, when Negroes were impoverished and harrassed to a greater extent than today, anti-Semitism was common, notably among Negro businessmen who felt keenly competition from those white businesses—which were in fact often Jewish—that operated in the Negro neighborhoods. The founder of the *Chicago Defender* was suspicious of Jews, and that paper in past years contained many uncomplimentary references to them. In the post-war years, when the Near East was in turmoil over the efforts of Arab states to resist the establishment of Israel, many prominent Negroes sided with the "colored" Arabs in their fight against "white" Jews.[8] Despite the decline in anti-Semitism, many Negro leaders, mostly older ones, still distrust or dislike Jews,[9] and even more Negro civic leaders see tactical problems in cooperating with Jewish organizations.

"The Jews have the South Side all tied up, completely," said a prominent Negro doctor. An important Negro politician exclaimed, "These Jews are sucking my people dry and not giving them anything in return." The standard lists of unfavorable Jewish attributes are recited by such Negro leaders as evidence for their charges—Jews are "clannish," "grasping," "pushy"; they "haven't learned to forget being a Jew." A well-known Negro civic leader admitted that there was a "higher kind of Jew" who is active in the B'nai B'rith and who contributes to Negro causes. But at the same time, most Jews in business in the Negro community are the "mercenary type of Jew who is merciless . . . and greedy . . . and who is out to milk [the Negro]."

Negroes who are free of these attitudes nevertheless feel that many Jews have been hypocritical in their interracial civic efforts. To them, Jewish efforts toward brotherhood in the civic sphere are more than offset by what appear to be their anti-Negro actions in the private sphere. Many Negroes were bitter about a leading Jewish builder who was very active nationally and locally in brotherhood movements but who, as an entrepreneur, built a suburban housing development that excluded Negroes. One said:

Look at [X]. He heads the B'nai B'rith which is supposed to be liberal and believe in brotherhood and all that, but he organized [a development] and made a boatload off of it. . . . But no Negro gets in. We can't let [them] continue to kid us.

Even some sophisticated Negroes who are professional staff members of organizations working in race relations are dubious of the extent of Jewish commitment to ends Negroes seek. Most Negroes at this level are happy to work with Jewish groups, but feel that lesser Negro leaders—ministers and labor leaders—are suspicious of Jewish control and Jewish motives and with some justification:

There are some grounds for this. The Jews have never made a community of interest with the Negroes. . . . For example, the Jews will back open occupancy legislation but they will sort of conceal the Jewish interest in it, for fear of making common cause with the Negroes and thus embarrassing themselves. They feel that they can get more as Jews than they can in association with Negroes. [X] felt this way. He felt that the Jews had enough problems which they had to fight themselves that they couldn't also fight for Negroes without alienating influential non-Jews. . . . They would help us privately but not so much in the open.

Many Negro leaders, particularly the politicians, are quick to

accuse Jews of outright hypocrisy. When a Jewish alderman proposed a city open occupancy ordinance to reduce residential
segregation, several Negro politicians—who were cool to the
idea—found that charges of such hypocrisy, made privately, were
one convenient way of disposing of the plan without dealing with
its merits. They announced to other Negroes that it was a typical
Jewish smokescreen of liberalism to cover up the alleged efforts
of the Jewish ward which the alderman represented to exclude
Negroes through urban renewal and land clearance plans. Another
Negro politician had similar feelings about an ordinance which
would have made racial discrimination in publicly assisted housing
projects unlawful. A Republican Negro alderman had introduced
the measure in the Council; he could not be publicly attacked by
other Negroes. But one of the witnesses who spoke in behalf of
the ordinance at the hearings was a Jew from New York, a prominent authority on minority-group housing. One Negro reported:

> In the hearings on that bill, one smooth-talking man from New
> York . . . came here to testify on it. They questioned him for two
> or three hours, and weren't getting anywhere. Finally they began to
> needle him, and then when he got a little mad he said, "This ordi-
> nance wasn't written by Negroes, it was written by the B'nai B'rith."
> It was a *Jewish* ordinance. . . . There's always a hidden reason for
> the public reason. . . . I suspect his motives.

Another facet of the Negro attitude toward Jews as civic allies
—a facet which has diminished with the abatement of the "red
scare" of the 1950's—was the fear that white liberals, particularly
Jews, were engaged in race relations work as part of a left-wing
movement. Most Negro leaders recoil at the least suggestion of
Communist or left-wing contacts. When the Council of Negro
Organizations was formed in Chicago in the 1930's, it was in part
intended to provide co-ordination of conservative and moderate
Negro civic leadership to offset the effect of the National Negro
Congress which had been organized as a movement of left-wing
Negro intellectuals. After World War II, when the question of
co-operating with white liberal groups arose, the Council of Negro
Organizations decided against it partly on the grounds that white
liberals, particularly Jews, were carriers of the Communist infec-
tion. One officer of the CNO said later:

> We didn't have any relationships at all with these other organiza-

tions. . . . You see, we weren't sure of their political ideologies, and we didn't want to be labelled as Communist or something. . . . There was a lot of labelling going on then. So we only worked with Negro organizations.

At the same time, whites have reservations about Negroes as civic partners in the struggle for racial equality. White liberal organizations which have worked with Negro groups in common causes often feel that Negroes are singularly hard to organize for civic ends. By white standards, Negroes seem to contribute less, work less, and provide less concerted, co-ordinated, and available sources of time, effort, and money. "You name it, they haven't got it," said one white at the end of a campaign in which he had tried to obtain Negro help for ends which he thought Negroes desired. "Co-ordination has always been lacking among Negro organizations. . . . I was in touch with all of them, but there was no real co-ordination at all." In a campaign to secure state legislation favorable to Negroes, a white who endeavored to mobilize Negro support despaired at the absence of response. An attempt was made to get some of the many Negro social clubs to contribute time and money to the campaign, and a Negro was hired to contact these groups. No contributions were forthcoming, and indeed the clubs refused to permit representatives of the civic group to address their memberships on the nature of the campaign. No advertising on behalf of the cause was permitted in the clubs, no speeches, and no open solicitation of funds. Finally, one club permitted the group to place a small container at the entrance into which members could drop contributions if they wished. The white liberal said at the end, "It was an utter flop. We never tried it again."

Other whites complain privately of the Negro's apparent lack of philanthropy. One observed:

Both Jews and Negroes have social strivers who try to gain prestige and status by organizing social affairs and the like. In the Jewish community this can be turned to the advantage of welfare and social action causes by making welfare solicitations a social occasion. For the Negroes, this doesn't seem to work. Negroes seem to have no tradition of giving and no goals beyond personal ones. I don't know why this is; I really don't. We [his organization] haven't been able to overcome it. Maybe it is just so hard for them to get enough to stay alive, or maybe it's because they've been without things for so long. I don't know.

Whites who join Negro organizations like the NAACP some-times—although by no means always—encounter barriers to full acceptance; what is more important, they become discouraged at what they feel is the excessively low level of Negro participation in such associations. One said:

When I joined I thought it was a wonderful thing, despite its weaknesses. . . . It was Negro-led . . . and only in a Negro-dominated organization do you get the feel, the shock of knowing the Negro plight. . . . But now I'm wondering if perhaps it shouldn't be re-organized . . . so we could get more membership participation.

Whites almost invariably have a fairly standardized set of hypotheses with which to explain the alleged deficiencies in Negro civic leadership. Not surprisingly, most thoughtful Negroes tend to agree with them. Both groups point to the slavery tradition, the lack of a "tradition of giving," the *nouveau riche* tendency of the Negro middle class, the accentuated class divisions in Negro society, the parochialism of a purely "racial" point of view, and so on. (Few people seem to account for "apathetic" behavior with the equally plausible hypothesis that many Negroes genuinely may not believe that the race ends are desirable or important. Resisting an explanation which discredits programs is not un-expected among people who are programmatically committed.) All of these explanations probably have some element of truth, and point in interesting directions; only a thorough inquiry into the ethos of the Negro at its most fundamental levels could provide any certain answers. What is important here is that these beliefs are widely held and condition action.

Several formalized efforts have been started to bring about Negro-white co-operation for race goals in Chicago. The most enduring of these—discussed elsewhere—has been the Urban League. Three others can be mentioned here, each of which rep-resents a different dimension of civic action. One, the Council Against Discrimination, was an organization of organizations, white and Negro, designed to co-ordinate, and on occasion ini-tiate, civic action against racial and religious injustices on a wide front. A second, the Illinois Committee for Fair Employment Practices, was a co-ordinating body which had a single racial end as its goal—the passage of FEPC legislation. The third, the

Mid-South Chicago Council, was a group organized to bring Negro and white businesses and neighborhood associations together in an effort to obtain an ostensibly tangible goal—area conservation. Each group failed—failed either to survive or to obtain its announced objective. Failure cannot in every case be explained in terms of organization weaknesses; for example, no organization of any kind could probably have obtained passage of an FEPC law so long as the Illinois State Senate was controlled by downstate Republicans.

The Council Against Discrimination (CAD) was a citizen's committee formed in the 1940's in Chicago as a "watchdog" group to make certain that the newly organized Commission on Human Relations would function in the city administration on a nonpolitical, professional basis. Secondarily, it hoped to co-ordinate the work of existing voluntary associations in the field of race relations. It survived for about fifteen years, finally expiring after a long period of relative inaction. The secondary purpose—to carry out its own program in race relations—soon became primary when the Commission on Human Relations began to function competently and without political interference. Although headed by a Unitarian minister, the CAD was largely financed and supported by various Jewish groups. A Negro labor leader was active from the first, and the NAACP and Urban League were brought in. In part, the organization existed to handle tasks single groups could not manage because of fears for their tax-exempt status, the attitude of their boards of directors, or lack of manpower. Its leader quickly became known as an outspoken and vigorous protest leader; so vigorous, indeed, that strains began to appear within the organization itself. Some member groups, such as conservative church federations, disliked the militant posture of the CAD. To have reduced the militancy of the CAD would have, on the other hand, displeased certain Jewish and labor groups, which felt it had been formed for this very purpose. The CAD became one more race relations association competing for the scarce race relations dollar; its budget had to be raised by appealing to the same groups to which organizations such as the NAACP and the Urban League and others appealed, and these member organizations began to feel that it was usurping their prior claims on these scanty resources.

Not only were dollars scarce but issues were scarce as well; when a really "hot" one came up, there was something of a scramble to see which organization would "take it."

An ideological split became evident in the CAD based on the affinity some members had for left-wing groups that had formed the rival Committee to End Mob Violence. Changes in leadership were unable to halt the loss of confidence in the CAD. The Negroes in this process were among the weakest supporters of the CAD. There was some Negro distrust of the CAD, and suspicion of its heavily Jewish backing; allegations of Jewish "dictatorship" were made. Negro representatives were divided as to the stance the organization should take. Apparently, a degree of Negro chauvinism was also involved. Organizations to aid Negroes should be led by Negroes, some thought. One Negro leader was lured away by another group which placed him in charge and gave him unlimited freedom to protest and agitate. Other Negroes began to lead their own associations in race relations activities independently of the CAD. Some insight into the malaise of the CAD can be gained by comparing the statements of two Negro leaders, one conservative and one militant, who were members of the organization at one time. The moderate Negro observed:

Take the FEPC campaign. The NAACP wouldn't join with us ... in that. ... They wanted to run an independent campaign, with the Packinghouse Workers. That was when the NAACP was run by the Reds. ... The NAACP wouldn't join [CAD] campaigns, and it weakened our case for FEPC to have them sending independent delegations down to Springfield and testifying on their own. ... I don't believe they really wanted the FEPC law anyway. It was just one of those issues on which they could grab a little publicity, and they took it. They were independent, so they wouldn't have to share the limelight. ...

The militant Negro had a different version:

There was this Council Against Discrimination we had for a while, but it degenerated into a debating society and when it finally folded it wasn't anything at all. I got disgusted with it; whenever an issue came up, nobody could agree on it. ... Every Negro group I approached would be with me, but the [Jewish and Catholic] groups, they wouldn't speak. They're pretty conservative.

The Illinois Committee for Fair Employment Practices has had a history which illustrates some of the same problems. Efforts to secure FEPC legislation have been made continually in Illinois since 1943. In 1949 and 1951 these efforts came within a few Senate votes of success. As it appeared to the leaders of the movement, however, this progress was made in spite of, rather than because of, Negro support. The Negro voluntary associations were in a state of disrepair—the NAACP had no staff and was torn by internal conflicts; the Urban League had a staff, but one which lacked the full confidence of the League's board. An effort to mobilize a grass roots campaign in the Negro community resulted in NAACP meetings attended by only twenty or thirty people to hear speakers on FEPC. Negro groups provided little money to the co-ordinating Illinois Committee. Some rivalry existed between the state NAACP conference and white groups as to which should organize the FEPC campaign; the competition for issue control was the inevitable starting point of the movement. Representatives of the many Negro social, business, labor, and community organizations rarely attended steering committee meetings of the co-ordinating agency or sent lobbyists to the state capital.[11] The Negro press did not give the issue heavy or dramatic coverage. The Negro politicians in the state legislature were, of course, in favor of the bill, but, with one or two exceptions, only went through the motions of pressing the issue. Most made one impassioned speech in its favor, appended their names as sponsors of the bill, and that was all. Few would labor steadily at the legislative politics required—committee work, personal contacts, and parliamentary maneuvers. At the last moment, when the bill seemed doomed to defeat by a narrow margin, a proposal was made that the FEPC bill be amended to provide for "local option" —that is, it would empower local communities (such as Chicago) to adopt a strong FEPC law—rather than impose a state law. Some Negro groups originally favored the plan as a possible means of getting "half a loaf" rather than none. At the last moment, however, most of the Negro groups—voluntary associations and labor unions—announced their opposition to local option. An NAACP officer active in the campaign described the reasons for this uncompromising stand:

There are many Negroes in East St. Louis and Peoria and places like that downstate. . . . If we had settled for local option, it would have been a case of deserting them. . . . There should not be any compromises on this. We have to think of them, too. . . . It would be like asking Congress to pass a bill just for the South. That wouldn't be fair. You can't be isolated, you have to think of everybody. We have to help all the people.

After these reverses, efforts in 1953-57 toward FEPC legislation were largely limited to biennial token campaigns simply to keep the issue alive. In 1959, a vigorous effort was once more made, and this one attracted substantial Negro co-operation. Improved Negro contributions were largely due to the strengthened and more stable positions of the Urban League and the NAACP.

The Mid-South Chicago Council encountered many obstacles in its brief career as an organization to promote neighborhood conservation in the Negro community. Some of the problems which beset it, including conflicts and uncertainties among Negro members, are discussed in another chapter. Another problem, relevant here, was a certain amount of suspicion among Negroes as to the motives and goals of the white business members. For over a year after the founding of the MSCC it was an all-Negro organization. An organization of white—predominantly Jewish—merchants and property-owners in the area offered to contribute time and money to the MSCC. The white organization was able to offer the Negro group the services of a paid executive, something the Negroes were unable to afford by themselves. These businessmen wanted to secure city approval for conservation plans in the area, and organized Negro support was essential for that purpose. In exchange for this support, they were prepared to offer the Negroes money and contacts.

None of the virulent kind of anti-Semitism was evident among the Negro businessmen and property-owners which might have been found among some of them during leaner years. But suspicions did arise, and seemed to be reinforced by the fact that the white businessmen were "absentee landlords"—they operated businesses in the Negro area, but did not live there. A Negro officer of the MSCC described at length the reactions of, and discussions among, the Negroes:

There was a long debate about this . . . at a luncheon and other meetings. People would get up and make the usual statements about not trusting the Jews, fears that the white man just wanted to use the Negro for his own purposes, or that the Jews would get in and then take over the organization and run it themselves. . . . They were suspicious of their motives. . . . But finally co-operation was agreed upon. . . . I think they [the Negroes] had reasonable suspicions unreasonably magnified. There was a lot of ignorance on the part of the Negro as to what was going on and what all this meant, and they were in part justified in thinking that the Jews wanted to use the Negroes to help them do something which would help the Jews.

Another Negro officer of the MSCC was less detached about the matter; he felt white businessmen took from the community and put nothing back:

The [white] businessmen on 47th Street, they don't contribute to *anything*. . . . There are some big persons there. . . . They could contribute. But the trouble is, their interests don't lie in this community. They get a living out of this community and live somewhere else.

Negro concern over "losing control" of the MSCC gained some ground when it became evident that the white members were far more active and contributed more money to the program than did the Negroes. Further, the whites seemed to be acting toward an agreed-upon goal with singleness of purpose and undivided attention, while the Negroes were only too aware of their own disagreements and uncertainties.

In general, these illustrations—with proper qualifications and modifications—seem to bear out the broad statement that the Negro's situation accentuates significantly the normal problems of civic action and co-operation. Resources for any civic enterprise are scarce, but for the Negroes they are critically so. The time and the money necessary for such ventures is either nonexistent or is allocated to other purposes. All civic associations compete for issues, but Negro associations seem to seek more urgently the exclusive control of "Negro" issues and the intangible stakes that such issues have. No white man, it is repeatedly said, can possibly understand—and therefore, by implication, lead or organize or control—Negroes. White civic leaders almost always enter race relations activities with paid staff; Negroes only rarely do so. Relationships between Negro and white allies often tend to be relationships between Negro volunteer leaders and white professional leaders, and the expectations of the latter are almost never fulfilled by the performance of the former. All civic leaders seeking concessions from authorities or other groups to which they do not have easy access tend to see those groups as unified blocs with common, and perhaps ulterior, motives; the Negro has so little access and has been disappointed so often in relationships with others that this perceived solidarity becomes racial mistrust and suspicion.[12]

Nevertheless, interracial co-operation is not completely lacking, and co-ordination is not utterly Utopian. After the failure of the Council Against Discrimination and similar organizations composed of other organizations, the professional staff executives of important race relations associations came together in an informal caucus which periodically met to discuss common problems and to talk over possible solutions. It is significant and revealing that the relative success and durability of this caucus seems to have stemmed from the fact that it is composed of professionals who act in these meetings informally and as individuals, with no commitments, no budget, and no publicity. Although disagreements occur, these conditions seem to reduce the disabilities which have characteristically hampered attempts at more formal interracial cooperation in the past.

The continued improvement in interracial co-operation will depend partly on the ability of the two major Negro organizations to maintain a stable pattern of leadership and a professional staff. White liberal organizations find the newer Negro group easier to work with than the Negroes active in the immediate post-war period. But complete co-ordination can never occur. The maintenance needs of the various Negro and white community-relations organizations are fundamentally different and will remain so, and as a result the constraints on the professionals will be dissimilar, particularly in situations where difficult decisions as to ends and tactics must be made.

PART THREE

THE CHARACTER OF
NEGRO PUBLIC LIFE

Chapter VIII

Goals of Negro Leaders

O NE of the most important constraints on effective leadership in the Negro community is lack of agreement among leaders as to what they want. Disagreement on ends, like any form of diversity, should not be a surprising phenomenon in a community—or collection of communities—numbering over 750,000 people. Yet, for a variety of reasons, it is often denied by Negroes themselves. Race relations operate in Chicago, as elsewhere, behind a double veil of secrecy. The first veil is that imposed, through common understanding, by the white civic leadership which prefers to keep "race" out of public issues, even at the expense of laborious circumlocution. Public issues should, where at all possible, be settled on nonracial or "aracial" grounds, even where Negroes clearly play an important part in the matter. Race is rarely discussed publicly by the white community except in the context of "brotherhood" organizations. In addition, the Negro community imposes its own veil of secrecy. As Drake and Cayton have indicated, "protective secrecy" was widely felt, by all classes of Negroes, to be a necessity.[1] Indeed, after the publication of their book, the authors were often criticized privately by Negroes for having divulged things about "Bronzeville" the white man should not know.

A second reason for the denial of diversity in goals is the evident fact that in the case of the most widely felt, generally discussed race issues there *is* a broad ground of agreement. These issues tend to be unifying, rather than divisive, and are experienced in similar fashion by all Negroes: white violence perpetrated on Negroes, specific instances of job discrimination, exclusion from public accommodations, and other clear instances of individual prejudice against Negroes are experienced by all. But the issues which are coming to the fore in Chicago race relations are no longer so simple, and it is on these issues which Negro leaders are being asked to act. The unifying issues tend more and more to be *national* issues—discrimination in the South, the actions of Governor Faubus, or proposals for national legislation. The *local* issues have become far less unifying, for reasons this chapter will attempt to develop.

A third reason is that there are among Negroes a number of widely shared "race values" on which a high degree of agreement can be found. These race values, however, exist at a level above, or apart from, the realm of specific end choices, and agreement on these values does not imply agreement on what to do in an actual case. Really two kinds of goals must be described: the race values, and the race ends.

Race Values

"Race values" are highly general, widely-shared images of desirable states of affairs in the Negro community. They can be found among both masses and leaders, upper class and lower class. A race value is a verbal expression of race consciousness; race, at some level of awareness, is an ever-present factor in the thought and action of Negroes of all strata of society. Drake and Cayton describe the prevalence of what they call "taking it out in talk" as a manifestation of the omnipresence of race,[2] and Riesman and his colleagues report on the "overwhelming" race focus of the responses of their interviewees in Harlem.[3] The fact of being a Negro, the inescapable impact of race, is the single most consistent theme in Negro discussion of civic issues. "Everybody knows," remark Drake and Cayton in a summary of the numerous anecdotes and illustrations they bring to bear on this point, "that no matter how high a Negro gets he's still just a Negro."[4]

One of the most successful Negro businessmen, a highly prestigious civic leader, spoke with evident feeling about the fact that "I'll never be anything but a Negro." After admitting his tendency to withdraw from race issues that did not concern him personally, he added:

A Negro never really escapes being a Negro. . . . Anywhere, any-time he will always be a Negro, I don't care how much recognition he gets from whites. A black man is a black man, anywhere you go. . . . I travelled in Europe this summer, and it's the same there. You can't escape it because you can't erase your skin color as easily as you can lose an accent. . . . So simple selfishness demands that you help Negroes because it's the only way you can help yourself. . . . There is no way a Negro can really get himself treated like a white man. No way.

This pervasiveness of color is borne out in the well-known color distinctions which exist within the Negro community itself.*[5] Occasionally, Negro leaders will employ color problems as an explanation for the behavior of others, usually behavior of which they do not approve. One dark-skinned Negro leader, himself a race moderate, spoke in this way of another, lighter-skinned Negro leader who was more militant and who had married a white woman:[6]

[He] has put himself in a bad position. . . . He married a woman who is not of his racial group. Now, I would defend his right to do this, you understand, but I'm not sure that a man in his position can afford this. . . . What does he do? He attacks everything in the

---

*5. *Ibid.,* pp. 495-506. Drake and Cayton conclude that skin color is of "lessening importance" in Bronzeville, although there is still widespread consciousness of it. Most younger Negroes interviewed for this study felt that light skin and regular features were no longer as important as they once were for attaining desirable social or professional positions. Color distinctions have by no means disappeared, however. Several respondents, notably older ones, spoke of the impact of their color on marriage prospects, recruitment into the professions, social relations, etc. Cf. G. Franklin Edwards, *The Negro Professional Class* (Glencoe, Ill.: The Free Press, 1959), pp. 104-113, for a statistical analysis of the color characteristics of a carefully drawn sample of three hundred male Negro professionals. My observations bear out Edwards' conclusions that most Negro professionals today are light brown in color, with more light than dark persons. Changes over time seem to be in the direction of decreasing the proportion of very light and very dark, while increasing the proportion in the middle color ranges. Interesting differences by occupation can be noted in Chicago. Politicians and Baptist ministers tend to be darker in color than lawyers, doctors, and ministers from Congregational and other "upper class" churches. More dark-skinned leaders are found in groups with a "mass base" (labor unions, Baptist churches, politics) than in groups with a "professional base."

city in an attempt to prove to Negroes that he hasn't sold out, that he is still a Negro.

A Negro editor interviewed a group of "upper crust male members of the Chicago Negro community" concerning a discussion they had held privately of a colleague who was in an important leadership position and who was about to marry a white woman. The majority disapproved of the marriage. Their reasons, as reported by the editor, were:

First, it was quite all right for a Negro in a leadership position to have an affair with a white woman. Second, under no circumstances should this gentleman marry a white woman, and finally, if he does marry one, he should be ostracized from upper crust social circles of color. . . . It would be very embarrassing to them for one of their "class," who would be in the forefront of public affairs, to have a white wife and it would be offensive to the white power structure in Chicago. Some also took the position that such a marriage was an insult to "Negro womanhood."[7]

The presence, the consciousness, of color, whether it be as a burden or as a weapon, is an overriding fact which touches almost all discussions of civic leadership and civic problems. The content and function of the race values which are the verbal expression of this consciousness are elusive. The most general beliefs and aspirations of any group of people are usually fragmentary, partially unspoken, and often inconsistent and disjointed. Simple appeals to "race pride" as a spur to action and unity are encountered with less and less frequency, particularly among younger leaders. Nonetheless, at some level the fact of being a Negro and the sense of collectivity which this implies are important and relevant to action. Apparent in interviews with a wide range of Negroes, but even more discernible in the statements of these leaders before Negro audiences, is a set of attitudes regarding what the race *as a whole* ought to do and believe. These attitudes often are expressed in the form of calls to action or duty. Four of these race values express themselves as appeals for unity, demands for leadership, fear of the "sell-out," and desire to eliminate the color bar. Negroes who embody these values are acting as "race men," which is a desirable although sometimes suspect posture. Some of these slogans are losing their force, and others are in tension with a set of contradictory values. Exploring the most general and most fundamental values of a group is a hazardous undertaking, but since (as will be argued later) these values have an impact on the course of civic leadership, it is essential that an effort be made to offer at least tentative statements of their nature.

Foremost among these is the value of race unity or race solidarity. The many remarks of the Negro rank-and-file cited in Drake and Cayton are paralleled by comparable remarks by Negro leaders.[8] "To get anything done in Chicago you must have a solid bloc," said one leader, "like the Italians, the Jews, and the Irish. They stick together and they get what they want." On the other hand, "the Negroes aren't solid, and they don't get what they want. They get nothing but the scraps." While race unity is seen as valuable, its absence is lamented. To one leader, the presence of so many Negro organizations is not welcome as a sign of a lack of apathy, but rather it is deplored as an indication of the presence of disunity. "We have too many organizations as it is. . . . People keep thinking up new angles to this race business and want to start a group working on it." Instead of combining forces, "we always seem to be seeking more diversity instead of less, even though what we need is more unity."

Race unity is virtually a slogan in the Negro community; the important thing, however, is that it is a purely instrumental slogan, devoid of specific content. Unity for what? That question is answered in a variety of ways, depending on the goals of the speaker — such as this one, in a public meeting:

> Let me say that there are some Negro people who have come to me to say that they disapprove of the NAACP getting on the complete integration kick. They say we'll dissipate our political strength fighting for complete integration. Well, I've learned race pride, I've learned race unity. . . . These people are handkerchief heads.

Even those Negroes who admit that disunity would be a more apt description for the facts of Negro life in the city are unhappy about it; problems seem to be common, and common problems should be solved by communal action. The Negro leaders who dominate public discussion of race issues, who provide the vocabulary for such discussion and who set its tone, are most usually the more militant leaders, and for them, appeals to race solidarity and race pride are important techniques of leadership. This notion of unity is not simply an abstract principle to which individuals happen to adhere because it appears plausible; it is rather an expression of a deeply-rooted sentiment springing from ghetto life. The resistance to stratification in the Negro community—the criticism of those who go "high hat" or "silk stocking" or "dicty"—seems to be more than a criticism of those who attain a position in which their interests are no longer identical with the interests of the race as a whole. It appears to be, in addition, a manifestation of the belief that life for the Negro, dominated by severe constraints enforced upon him by the white community, makes achievement or progress through individual ability or merit almost impossible; individual qualifications account for little because the larger world is organized on the principle that "all Negroes are alike." Therefore, there is no reason why *he* should advance while *I* am held back; his advancement must be due to other factors, and his rewards must be really undeserved. At the same time, the public literature of the Negroes points with pride to the achievements of Negroes in various walks of life; Negro accomplishment is supposed to increase race pride. Neither one sentiment nor the other is dominant; both exist side by side, competing for expression.

A second, equally strong race value refers to the importance of leadership while simultaneously deploring its absence. "Somebody ought to *do* something," is a representative statement, and Drake and Cayton describe the ceaseless process of "ritual condemnation" which proceeds at all levels. An ideal of selfless, effective Negro leadership is held up and then all would-be leaders are condemned for failing even to approximate the goal:[9]

Negro leadership in Chicago is more or less self-appointed leadership or people who have moved into a vocal position by certain circumstances. . . . We have no true absolute leadership in Chicago. Success in some field has shoved these people into a leadership position, a mythical leadership position, shall we say.

Leaders assail one another, just as they in turn are assailed by the Negro rank-and-file. So prevalent is the phenomenon that some Negro leaders search for explanations for it. "Sometimes I think," said one, "people don't really know what they want. They want someone to explain to them what they want and then get it." Many leaders, in a similar vein, sought reasons why the popular distrust of leadership was misplaced or inaccurate. "People look for a Moses," one said. "They look for a superhuman person to lift them out of their troubles. . . . When they can't find one, they say we have no leaders." Most Negro leaders will argue that there cannot be *a* leader, that the community is too diverse for that. Leadership must be defined in terms of specific problem areas. But at the same time, they cannot suppress a tendency to speak of great inspirational or popular Negro leaders elsewhere who have no counterparts in Chicago. Frequent reference is made to Adam Clayton Powell, A. Philip Randolph, or Martin Luther King as examples of the kind of Negro leader Chicago needs but does not have. Sometimes reference is made to Negro leaders who were in Chicago, but who have since died — men such as Oscar de Priest, Charles Jenkins, or Robert Taylor. Almost no one believed that there were any local, contemporary leaders of the stature of these. The quest for the exemplary or the inspirational leader underlines the significance attached to leadership itself. Spatial or temporal distance is required to elevate a leader's name to the rank of the great. "King is *the* great man, a really solid leader," said a conservative Negro. "Other churches are looking at this, and realizing that King makes them look silly in Chicago." When asked whom he most admired as Negro leaders, this man named two men who did not live in Chicago and one man who was dead.[10]

Another Negro, somewhat more militant, named King and Powell as the two Negro leaders he admired the most. When asked what Negroes in Chicago he admired, he responded:

> You know, I hate to say it, but it reminds me of a story about a minister who addressed his congregation one Sunday morning, "My friends . . . I would call you 'ladies and gentlemen,' but I know you too well for that." I have no knight in shining armor in Chicago. I see their weaknesses. I guess I am too close to them.[11]

The leadership which is so urgently called for by many Negroes will be inspirational. The ends are given; they need not be sought for. The problem of a leader is to select strategies and formulate the means to those ends. This is a technical function divorced from the creative one of determining what should be sought, what policy should be. The leadership desired is also to be inspirational in the sense that its task is to rally people to a cause, generate enthusiasm and support, demonstrate an exemplary selflessness and dedication, and maintain morale and purpose. The rank-and-file should be brought in; leadership should be drawn from the advantaged elite but have a base in the disadvantaged masses. It is this inspirational definition of leadership which accounts for the widespread feeling that there are "no leaders" in Chicago and gives meaning to the approbation with which such distant leaders as Martin Luther King are viewed.

The belief that there are few "real" local leaders appears to be related to the suspicion that any man who is given preference or elevated to a position of leadership is likely to "sell out." The sell-out is one of the most common charges brought against Negroes, and differences between leaders' attitudes and prevailing race attitudes on civic issues are usually ascribed to their having "sold out." Self-interest is always a suspect motive for civic action among any group, but it is particularly damning when "race interest" or "race pride" is postulated as the alternative.[12] Negroes are by no means convinced that desegregation is an indivisible benefit—i.e., a benefit which, although obtained by one, will be shared by all. Many feel that it is highly divisible—that the benefits one Negro earns, such as entry into a desirable job or neighborhood, will satisfy his aspirations, and the door will be slammed on those Negroes waiting to follow in his footsteps. And indeed, as will be discussed below, there is some justification for this fear. A Negro cannot take the "white man's side" on an issue on its merits; the assumption will inevitably be that he has done it for a price. Negroes distinguish between "Negro leaders" (i.e., those who owe their positions to whites or who are self-appointed leaders) and "leaders of Negroes" (i.e., those who have a genuine following).

The fourth race value is expressed in a variety of ways. "All we want is first-class citizenship." "Equal rights for all." "We are Americans, too." "Race prejudice must be destroyed." The common denominator is that color should not be held against a person; the color bar should be eliminated. Although this value is widely shared, it does not necessarily follow that Negro behavior on a specific issue will be based on principles deduced from it. In the concrete situation, the meaningful choices which must be made may or may not be facilitated by the application of the general rule. In many cases, the race value cannot alone decide the issue. Further, the belief that color should not be held against a person does not necessarily imply that every Negro desires, as his ultimate hope, to be "treated like a white man." Whether or not complete assimilation is a general goal among Negroes is a question which this study does not answer. We shall suggest, however, that many actions indicate a desire to retain in some part the advantages of Negro life and the segregated status quo. Notwithstanding these qualifications, there is no doubt that "discrimination"—however variously it may be defined from person to person—is generally condemned by these Negroes with genuine conviction. It is most clearly expressed in resentment against the maltreatment of Negroes by whites.

Some of the traditional race values, particularly the value of unity and race pride, seem to be slowly losing their force. Steadily, the demand for unity is giving ground to the increasingly evident diversity of the Negro community. It was never really possible to rally Negroes to patronize Negro businesses with a simple racial appeal, but today even the appeal is losing its plausibility. "Race pride," admiration for the "race leader," are not absent, but often—especially to younger Negroes—the phrases seem curiously worn and inapplicable. An editorial in the Negro newspaper, in a rare burst of self-appraisal, reflected on this change:

Race consciousness, race solidarity are no longer a rallying cry. They are words which have lost their luster and their places in our active vocabulary; they are obsolete. . . . We find no more compensation in race pride, in protective solidarity, in social protest.

At the same time, the author could not avoid making another appeal to these same values on behalf of certain community institutions which he feels are neglected — an appeal which he all but conceded will fall on deaf ears:

Negro business . . . as well as such protest and protective agencies as the Urban League and the NAACP . . . in the main depend on Negro patronage for survival. . . . We must stand together, support our own establishments in order that they might grow in strength sufficient enough to command recognition of our claim to un-hyphenated citizenship. Other racial minorities — like the Jews, the Italians — have done it; so can we.[13]

These race values are not merely elements of Negro discourse. They serve certain functions in the community and their impact is felt in the realm of civic action and leadership. They serve as criteria for evaluating civic action, as a means of defending the Negro community against criticism or attack, as an incentive to civic leadership, and as a constraint on that leadership and the public discussion of issues.

A race justification must be found for a public position taken on an issue. It is difficult for a civic leader to take a *public* stand that is contrary to what has been labelled as the "race" position. Race can be, and has been, used as the basis for an appeal for votes in an election,[14] or as the basis for an appeal for Negro patronage of Negro-owned business in such campaigns as those of the "Double-Duty Dollar" and "Don't Buy Where You Can't Work." A Chicago-based Negro insurance company was organized in an effort to take advantage of the Negro market to which white life insurance companies refused to sell. Faced with competition from larger, more efficient white firms, a frankly race appeal is one of the Negro company's few remaining selling points.[15]

Race is also used as a means of defending the Negro community against allegations of misconduct. When Congressman William L. Dawson was attacked by the Chicago metropolitan press in 1955 on the grounds of alleged links with criminal elements in the city, the Negro reaction was prompt and vigorous. The issue of guilt or innocence was immediately replaced with the question of black or white. The white man was attacking the Negro, and race pride required his defense. One Negro responded:

> They made the fatal mistake of attempting an all-out frontal campaign against Dawson on the grounds that he was a crook and had sold out the Negroes. I never saw in my life the Negro community here so unified, so solidified. Attacking Dawson is the one sure way of losing the Negro vote.

The Negro press regarded the charges against him as without merit, but their merit was secondary in any case. Said the *Chicago Defender:*

> The greatest Chicago crime is not the misdeeds of mobsters, gangsters, policy men, and petty thieves (which can and do take place

in any community), but the un-American crime of discrimination which keeps the Negro in the lowest economic brackets and with the poorest living conditions.[16]

Even after Negroes have fought bitterly among themselves, they may always unite, to their mutual benefit, in response to what can be construed as an anti-Negro act. Rep. Adam Clayton Powell, Jr., campaigned vehemently against another Negro politician, Manhattan Borough President Hulan Jack, in the September, 1959, struggle for supremacy in the Harlem section of Tammany Hall. Jack was called an "Uncle Tom" who worked on the "white boss's plantation." Shortly thereafter, Jack was called before a grand jury to answer allegations that he had improperly received benefits from a contractor who had done business with the city. Powell and most other Harlem leaders promptly issued a statement pledging their support to Jack. The clear implication of the statement was that Jack was being singled out by the city because he was a Negro. A Harlem politician who had opposed Jack in the September election told an interviewer during the investigation that he did not care whether the charges against Jack were true or not:

> But they were picking on him, and we will close ranks on that up here [in Harlem]. Jack is one of us, you know. Supporting him now will help all of us. Jack will get solid community backing, and Powell will be the spokesman for that community. . . . If they [whites] want to get after people, they had better start with some white politicians first.

A few months later, Powell publicly attacked the New York police for "permitting the white syndicate forces" to take over the Harlem numbers racket while driving Negroes from control.[17] This was almost identical to the charge Dawson had privately made against Chicago politicians and police a few years before.

Acquiring a reputation as a civic leader on behalf of Negroes—a race reputation—is an incentive for civic action which is responded to by some Negroes. It is not a uniformly attractive incentive for leaders, and few respond to it. Many Negroes are quite prepared to refuse without concern for their race reputation any call to volunteer action. One conservative Negro who tried to mobilize some lawyers for legal defense work noted that only three Negro lawyers (out of perhaps three hundred in the city) could be expected to contribute time. When asked if others were concerned over refusing, this person replied:

No, sir. Not a qualm. They will look at me as if *I* were the crazy one. They will tell me, "Don't burn yourself out messing around with that. . . . The important thing is to make money." No, they don't bat an eye.

But often, when a Negro is in a position of responsibility that is based on direct contact with the Negro masses, there are evident expectations that the leader will engage in some civic activity of benefit for the race. All Negro ministers agreed that this was essential if one hoped to become a "big" minister. One, highly regarded in the community, described these expectations and suggested the burdens they imposed and the rewards they held:

The minister in my position has to do these things. . . . I can't get to all the meetings people think I should. In fact, why should I go at all? Just to be a race man? Yes, for that reason I have to do it. . . . They expect me to. You can feel it. More than that, they *say* it. But it gets to be too much, I must say. . . . I have to do it, though. I have to appear to represent my race, even though I can't. No one can represent the race. . . . There is a widespread feeling that a man who has achieved something ought to *do* something. Nobody can escape it if you have made something out of your life at all. . . . They raise no objection to my outside activities. They expect me to do it. Just like they maintain a Cadillac car for me. Why? I don't know. It's expected. It's status. I like it, I admit I do. . . . I feel like a big man in that Cadillac. I don't know why. Maybe it makes up for the fact that I can't get into the restaurant downtown.

Sometimes these expectations can generate unwitting leaders. One Negro, who was involved in a civic issue involving proposed land clearance in a Negro neighborhood, and whose motives admittedly arose from a concern over the disposition of his own property, found himself becoming a "leader":

The last thing I wanted was to broaden the fight and take in more people or try to raise money from the churches and the unions. But the people, these lower-middle-class Negroes, kept pushing me. They'd bring me gifts on Christmas, like I was their preacher or something, and run to me for advice. . . . Hell, I didn't want to be a leader.

At the same time, the race values are an important constraint on leadership. Whatever is done privately, there can be public action which appears to contradict race values only at the expense

of criticism.[18] A relatively few Negro leaders are in a position
where they can afford this cost. The political leader, for example,
is strong enough to be able to engage in activities which bring
heavy criticism, and survive. But most leaders are in a more
precarious position and are more sensitive to the demands of the
race values. A Negro who was active in the campaign for a state
law to create a Fair Employment Practices Commission (FEPC)
discovered that the bill, drafted to extend an FEPC law throughout the state, was doomed to defeat in the legislature. When it
was suggested that it be amended to limit its coverage to Chicago
where most Negroes and other minority groups live, in order to
avoid the opposition of downstate legislators, the leader found
such a compromise could not be sold to the Negro groups supporting the bill:

> Of course nobody really talked about settling for less or for any
> compromises. They feared they would be accused of wanting to
> compromise, so people wouldn't bring this out into the open.

Race values can also affect issues in which Negroes are seeking tangible gains. A plan for the Negro insurance companies in
Chicago to pool their resources and invest in the Lake Meadows
apartment development fell through, in part because of anticipated
criticism. The project, sponsored by the New York Life Insurance
Company, was attacked by some Negroes who believed that it
represented an effort to "clear Negroes out" of valuable property
and to take Negro homes without fair compensation. The Negro
insurance companies felt they could not invest in such a project.
One of the principal reasons was the criticism. One executive
said:

> We went into it thinking it was a good thing for the community,
> but we did not realize the resistance that would develop. An awful
> lot of people we do business with thought we should not be in it
> and said that we could get a black eye in the community. So we
> dropped it.[19]

Many Negro businessmen were reluctant to become identified
with an effort to undertake a neighborhood conservation program
in a congested Negro area. Such a program would have involved
building code enforcement and some clearance of dilapidated
structures. Such measures were not popular in the Negro com-

munity. One ground for their reluctance was the possibility of repercussions in public opinion. A leader in the effort to launch the program observed:

> The Negro businessmen came to realize that it ... might lead to enforcement procedures or some clearance which would involve a lot of Negro people ... and they felt they couldn't, didn't dare benefit at the expense of the displacement of Negro people. . . . They feared being identified with efforts to displace Negroes which might have ramifications in terms of customers, the Negro press, clients, or business associates.

Where the race interest is even clearer, as in the case of, for example, the proposed open occupancy ordinance, almost all Negro leaders are agreed that, however a person might actually feel about it, public opposition to it would be foolhardy:

> If there are [any Negroes opposing it], it is an undercover operation. They can't do it above board. A Negro would be insane to oppose open occupancy publicly. He can't; he would lose everything. I mean that literally — any Negro who lets it be known that he favors the present pattern is a mental case, ready for the psychiatrist. And he'd soon be at the psychiatrist's, too.

A characteristic response to this constraint is to have both a public and a private position. One prominent Negro, who disliked a proposal to build low-income public housing near his home, observed:

> Strictly as a property owner, I am opposed to it. . . . But I wouldn't express this opinion, because I feel that Negroes need public housing, and so I can't oppose it even though I might want to. . . . I think it will lower the quality of the neighborhood.
> Q. Do you think most Negro civic leaders take public positions on this which differ from their private feelings?
> A. Yes, I think most, nearly all, of them do. They are alike on that. I have a tendency to be like that myself.

The constraints of the race position are not always inexorable. Some issues do not become labelled, and in other cases the spokesmen for the community make only a half-hearted attempt to define and assert a race position. The NAACP, for example, is ordinarily a powerful influence in the community because the causes it champions are causes from which few Negro leaders can publicly dissent. Not infrequently, however, the leadership of the NAACP will—for a variety of reasons—merely "go through the motions" on an issue and make the representations expected of it without much vigor. This is particularly true when an organization such as the NAACP is under moderate or conservative leadership—a leadership which may not be strongly committed to the role it is expected to play, and which is also associated, professionally and socially, with other moderate Negro leaders who prefer not to take a race position on a given issue. An illustration of this situation and the extent to which Negro leaders can sense when the NAACP is acting from conviction and when it is merely meeting the expectations of the community is contained in the history of Negro opposition to the Hyde Park-Kenwood urban renewal plan. The NAACP president issued statements posing objections to the plan on the grounds of its effects on Negro residents in the area. But many Negroes, including some who were in other leadership positions (as, for example, members of public and private agencies involved in the issue), preferred to see the plan adopted without change. They were not concerned about the NAACP position; in this case, they felt it was purely *pro forma.* "I didn't feel any pressure on that," said one of these leaders, as he explained the significance of the NAACP action:

I think [it] was just playing politics, myself. The NAACP, the branch, never took a strong stand on this. They never did. . . . I never thought the NAACP's stand was very strong. He [the president] was a smart politician. He heads a pressure group, a group fighting for certain legal rights. As the head he felt impelled to make a statement. But I never felt he said anything so strong that they couldn't compromise.

Another Negro, also a proponent of the plan, was even more confident that he did not have to fear for his reputation at the hands of the NAACP:

The NAACP people, I meet them at cocktail parties, and over highballs — they will tell you that they don't believe in public housing either, and they don't want it around here [in Hyde Park-Kenwood]. But they say their constituents won't let them say that. . . . So they have to print or say that they do.

Not all issues have a clearly defined "race position" which identifies the "correct" stance for a civic leader. Negroes can be found on both sides of many issues. Negro civic leaders, for example, have made public statements and joined organizational

efforts both for and against the proposed South Side branch of
the County Hospital. Negroes have been both for and against
various neighborhood conservation plans. Civic issues in the Negro community can be ranged along a continuum from those which
are complex, divisive, and with uncertain implications to those
which are relatively simple, unifying, and with clear consequences.
What is important is the high number of issues in the Negro
community which are either defined in terms of a "race position"
from the outset (reactions to interracial violence, for example)
or which, in the natural course of public controversy and agitation, become so defined in a fairly rigid fashion. Ideological constraints, such as are provided by the "race label," are far more
important in the Negro than in the white community because the
issues to which they refer are so much more salient. Some ideological constraints operate in both the Negro and white communities at the level of civic leadership, but in the white community,
they function at the periphery of action. Constraints which define
the opposition, for example, of a white businessman civic leader
to Communism, labor, or Negro agitators are not irrelevant to
his field of action, but they are not central. Few issues inescapably
raise such questions for him; they are remote, and taken for
granted. In the Negro community, ideological constraints are
highly relevant to action because the issues which form the subjects of civic action are those issues which raise ideological questions—the rights of Negroes and the injustices done them by
the white man. Ideology is at the center, not the periphery, of
action. Not all Negro leaders respond equally to ideological issues;
for some, who are temperamentally unprepared to accept ideological constraints, their operation is a psychological burden.

As the race values perform certain functions in the Negro community—serving as appeals, defenses, incentives, and constraints—they also create certain problems. As civic issues become more complex, the race values no longer provide an un-
ambiguous basis for the selection of concrete ends in specific
cases. The possibility of unfettered public discussion of alternatives is hampered by the power race labels exert. The problem
for many Negro leaders is how to win concessions of a tangible
character in civic issues and still avoid losing the symbolic struggle—how to get some Negroes into public housing projects in

certain areas while at the same time not publicly admitting to Negroes the fact that a quota system must be employed to achieve this. Such problems will emerge more clearly in a discussion of the ends of civic leaders and the conflicts and choices these ends often entail.

Race Ends

Of those activities which appear to have the benefit of the race or the Negro community as their object, two general categories of ends can be distinguished. For convenience, they can be called *welfare* ends as opposed to *status* ends. "Welfare" ends are those which look to the tangible improvement of the community or some individuals in it through the provision of better services, living conditions, or positions. Among welfare ends sought in the Chicago Negro community are the provision of better or more schools for Negro children, the construction of additional low-income public housing units, the location of a branch of the County Hospital in the Negro community, an increase in Negro political representation, and an increase in the supply of private housing available to Negro purchasers. "Status" ends are those which seek the integration of the Negro into all phases of community on the principle of equality—all Negroes will be granted the opportunity to obtain the services, positions, or material benefits of the community on the basis of principles other than race. Such principles include the ability to pay and personal achievement or qualification. Status ends which have been sought in the Chicago Negro community include the integration of all public schools, the opening of all-white public housing units to Negroes of comparable income, the desegregation of private hospitals, the equal treatment of Negroes in the allocation of public offices and honors, and the establishment of the principle of open occupancy in the real estate market.[20]

These distinctions are basically analytical, but their importance rests on the fact that issues arise in Chicago affairs in which choices are presented to Negro civic leaders requiring that they decide on the desirability of a *welfare* as contrasted with a *status* goal. The choice is not always, or even usually, a mutually-exclusive one—in many issues, it is possible to obtain some of both benefits, and the problem is how to reach an optimum balance. But the choice exists, and in many cases it is a hard one. Some of the more sophisticated Negro leaders recognize this choice. One used almost the same terms employed here to describe the difference between other leaders and himself:

> They have good hearts, but they don't see the basic issue. . . . You see, they're concerned with the welfare of the Negro, instead of with the status of the Negro. For the sake of welfare, they'll push for better housing, or better jobs, or more public services. But I'm working for the status of the Negro: equal opportunity, and no favors. The Negro won't be anything until he moves into the mainstream of human life.

Those who defend the choice of welfare ends in civic issues argue that the Negro is dispossessed and is in need of *things*— "here-and-now" needs are real and should not be postponed for the sake of more remote ends. Those who choose *status* ends argue that the Negro cannot justify seeking special treatment, but can only progress through vindicating the principle of social equality by being given equal or non-racial access to the life of the larger community. Moreover, they submit that improving material conditions in the Negro community can result in institutionalizing and perpetuating the pattern of segregated living and thus in the long run aggravating, rather than ameliorating, the lot of the Negro. Welfare and status ends are distinguished by, and defended in terms of, tangible versus intangible benefits, short-term versus long-term gains, and specific versus total solutions to the problems of the community. The differences between those who advocate welfare ends, or *things,* and those who urge status ends, or *principles,* are important and are developed in later chapters on political style and types of Negro leaders. For the present, it is useful to illustrate the character and consequences of this fundamental choice of ends through the examination of a few concrete issues that have arisen in the community.

Negro leaders almost universally pay tribute to the goal of integrated educational facilities. At the same time, they hope for an improvement in the quality and standards of existing and future facilities. No logical inconsistency exists between these goals, but reality occasionally forces a hard choice. Although there is no legally defined segregation in Chicago schools, school district lines tend to follow the lines of racial communities, and as a result, the great majority of all children attend schools which are racially homogeneous. This "de facto" segregation is opposed by such Negro groups as the NAACP, and demands are made that integration be achieved by redistricting or even by transporting Negro children in buses to all-white schools where vacancies exist. It is also urged that the building of new schools that would be, because of their location, all-Negro is wrong and should be resisted. New Negro schools would only perpetuate segregation and "take the pressure" off the efforts of Negroes to enter white schools in adjacent neighborhoods. Some Negro leaders are willing to pay a price for this. "At this stage in our national life," one wrote, "I believe that it is more important to put an end to segregation in our school system than it is to build more schools, if such a choice has to be made."[21] It is not easy to persuade the average Negro of this, however. An NAACP leader, asked what it was felt the rank-and-file wished, observed:

> Oh, most of them aren't really interested in redistricting. . . . They are interested in things like double shifts, getting good teachers, uncrowded classrooms. . . . They may favor redistricting if they believe it is a way to get these things. . . . I don't know.

Many leaders are more anxious to improve schools—to respond to the demands of their constituents—than to seek redistricting, which may not affect the quality of facilities in the short run. When an NAACP leader attempts to impart status goals to others, problems may result. For example:

> Until recently Negroes have been unaware and uninterested in this, but now they are reading our reports and are getting interested. . . . A group of Negro ladies, parents of school children in Englewood, were picketing City Hall or something to demand more school facilities for their children. They wanted a new school out there. . . . I talked to them and tried to point out to them that if they got a new school, it would be all-Negro, it would be segregated. . . . This confused the ladies; they didn't know what to do. But they were persuaded to take the NAACP's side of the matter and support some arrangement which would integrate the schools in the area without building a new Negro school. . . . But I don't think they will hold firm on this. They seem to want the school too badly, and I don't think we can count on their loyalty.

Low-income public housing, which in the past has generally attracted the support of Negro groups, is a goal which has entered an era of re-examination. Even among Negro leaders who have no personal stake in the issue, disagreement or uncertainty as to what should be the proper stance on this matter is growing. Some continue to feel there is a need for more shelter: "They are going to extend public housing down State Street, which I am for. I have long hoped to clean up State Street, and the good Lord has seen fit to do it." But a growing number feel that public housing—which, for political reasons, can only be built in Negro areas—is perpetuating segregation and is becoming stigmatized as "Negro housing" characterized by unattractive, high-rise buildings concentrated on a few sites. One Negro commented:

There was earlier an urgent need for shelter. The need was so great that no one considered the social implications of segregation. ...Now there is so much public housing on the South Side, and practically none on vacant sites [i.e., sites in white neighborhoods]. ...They ought to stop building public housing for the time being unless they are going to permit it in other areas besides the Black Belt.

But such a choice—to oppose further public housing and to work instead for desegregation that would permit it to be scattered—is a hard one, and most Negro leaders are not prepared to make it. Most hope that both ends can be served simultaneously, but if they cannot, then one must take what one can get:

If I had to make a choice, and I don't always think you do, between more public housing or putting it in integrated areas, I would favor putting up more housing.... There is a real need. I don't think, I hope the choice won't have to be made.

While most deny that such a difficult choice must be made, most admit by their actions that the issue has too many sides to permit them to take a clear and assertive stand. An editor of a Negro newspaper described his difficulties in this respect:

We think that public housing is wrong the way it's being handled. ...But on the other hand, we can't oppose it too much because we don't want to penalize people who need housing somewhere of some kind.... The whole thing is bad.... But if we come out against it hard, then they'll just not build it anywhere, and that would be worse. So what do we do? We just mumble about it.

Another issue which contains within it choices of a comparable order is the public controversy which has surrounded the proposal to construct a branch of the Cook County Hospital on the South Side in or near the Negro area. Several questions of policy are involved in the matter, but the ones which have caused one of the few *public* debates of an issue in the Negro community concern whether, or to what extent, building such a branch would result in an all-Negro or "Jim Crow" hospital and whether such a hospital is desirable as a means of providing added medical facilities for Negro patients. Involved are both an issue of *fact* (whether the hospital would be segregated, intentionally or unintentionally, as a result of the character of the neighborhood in which it would be located) and an issue of *value* (whether even an all-Negro hospital would be preferable to no hospital at all in the area). In reality, however, the factions have aligned themselves in such a way and the debate has proceeded in such a manner that the fact issue and the value issue have been collapsed into the single question of whether to build or not to build. Those in favor of the proposal will argue that the facts do not bear out the charge of "Jim Crowism"—"the proposed site . . . is not considered to be placed in a segregated area for the exclusive use of one racial or minority group;"[22] or "no responsible officials would try to develop a new hospital to further segregation;"[23] or "establishing a branch hospital for the . . . more adequate care of the indigent patient load, from the facts thus presented, does not represent Jim Crowism."[24] At the same time, these proponents argue that whatever the facts, the factual issue is secondary to the overriding consideration that "there is a here-and-now need for more hospital beds. . . . Integration may be the long-run goal, but in the short run we need more facilities." Some are even more explicit. While conceding that "the very location of such a branch would cause it to be peopled almost entirely by Negro patients and thus—a segregated institution would come into being," the same writer adds that it is a "badly-needed institution" for which he is "prepared to vote" because it will "relieve human suffering."[25]

The opponents of the proposal counter with the assertion of their version of the facts—it is "an attempt to build a segregated institution."[26] Those who support it, it is charged, "are those who basically are in favor of Jim Crow in general in the city, and particularly in medicine."[27] There is no need for such a branch, because the existing County Hospital is "not overcrowded with indigent patients." On the contrary, it has "an overflow of patients because it is receiving and supporting [Negro] patients who are able to pay."[28] Negroes go to the County Hospital, not because they are indigents who cannot afford to pay, but because private hospitals refuse to admit Negroes and as a result, all Negroes must go to the County Hospital. These facts are important to the opponents of the plan because the ends they seek are different from the ends of the proponents: they wish to oppose that branch hospital plan as a means of generating pressure on private hospitals to admit Negro doctors and patients on an equal basis. One says:

My big objection to the whole thing, the reason why I am going to make an all-out, last-ditch fight, is because it [the proposed branch] will disturb any progress in integration we are making. . . . The South Side branch will be a repository for Negro patients and a means for the preservation of the existing pattern of discrimination.

The disagreement on facts, in this case as in so many, reflects a more fundamental disagreement on the ends to be sought—here, a disagreement as to the priorities to be assigned welfare versus status ends. An interesting variant of this same choice is contained in the problem of Negro representation in public office and on public agencies and committees. Occasionally, in the course of an issue, the question arises as to whether Negroes are "entitled" to representation—or sometimes proportional representation—on some board or commission which will deal with the issue. A common view is that expressed by a writer in the Negro press:

There are 36 Municipal Court judges and of the 36 only two are Negro. There are 48 Circuit and Superior Court judges and of these 48 only one is a Negro. . . . We should have our proper share of elective offices as well as political jobs, both major and minor. . . . Since all other minorities seem to gain some sort of proportionate representation in our local government, it seems that the Negro should have the same right.[29]

It is not only the politicians who seek additional offices by such claims. When the Chicago Home Rule Commission issued its report on Chicago's government, it recommended a reduction in the number of aldermen from fifty to thirty-five, with the thirty-five divided between twenty-five elected from aldermanic districts and ten elected at large from the city.[30] The report conceded that a short-run consequence of such a plan would be a reduction in Negro representation.[31] The Negro member of the Commission, a highly-regarded civic leader, filed a minority opinion dissenting from this feature of the plan:

> I oppose the recommendation. . . . Under existing racial patterns in Chicago the application of the plan will be disadvantageous to minority groups, especially the Negro citizens. . . . A Negro candidate running for alderman at large would experience indifference and possibly hostility in making campaign appearances and appeals in certain sections of the city. . . . An undue [financial] burden would be imposed on candidates from minority groups. . . . The redistricting . . . could result in fragmentizing minority voters in such a manner that the number of successful minority-group candidates would be restricted.[32]

A factual argument is often made that Negro representation is necessary in order that the Negro's viewpoint be expressed in bodies where important decisions are made. But again, the factual argument usually reflects a more basic value—that Negro representation is essentially good. This is made evident when a comparison is made with the views of those Negro leaders who oppose representation for the sake of representation. Such opposition is based on the general "status" premise that the Negro should be treated equally, with no favors, and judged by the same standards as applied to others—even if this means no Negro is selected. One Negro leader applied this standard to the citizens' committee which officiated at the visit of the prime minister of Ghana to Chicago:

> Take Kwame Nkrumah's visit here. Instead of treating him like the head of any other foreign nation, the Mayor treated him like the head of a Negro nation. . . . Instead of inviting those people he would invite to see, say, the King of Sweden, the important people in the mainstream of the city's life, he invites about eighty Negroes who are prominent or who he thinks have influence. . . . The whole affair was a case of discrimination, of special treatment.
>
> *Q.* But wouldn't the Negroes have complained if they had not been invited, and alleged unfair treatment?
>
> *A.* Well, I don't know. Let 'em scream. All he has to do is show that he is picking important people in the city's life. . . . He doesn't have to cater to these people.

To such a leader, there is no reason for voting for a Negro for public office simply because he is a Negro:

I don't have to have a Negro in office to feel that I'm represented. I want the best man, even if he's white. . . . Now they want to take the Second Congressional District away from [a white man] as soon as there are 51 per cent Negroes in his district. That's terrible, he's a fine old man.

The distinction made here between more representation for Negroes and equal treatment of Negroes is a special case of the more general problem of the definition of *integration*. Does integration require the actual mixing of the races—the presence of Negroes in white areas—or merely the opportunity for such presence? Negro leaders show little unanimity on this, in part because of real disagreement and in part because the choice in any specific case is usually greatly complicated by other factors which keep this issue from being raised squarely. A Negro minister pointed to a case in which, to him, the issue seemed to be clear:

I was told that in all of Hyde Park . . . there isn't a single Negro minister running a church, even though there are lots of Negroes living there who go to church there. . . . To some Negro ministers, this means it isn't "integrated." Integration to them can only mean that there is a proportional number of Negro ministers in that area. But why should it? If you believe in equality, judging a man as an individual, why should there be any Negro ministers at all in there unless they are as well qualified as the whites?

In an urban renewal plan proposed for a Chicago neighborhood, large numbers of Negroes (as well as whites) were to be displaced by land clearance. The prices of the sale and rental housing to be constructed were high, and few Negroes—because of low incomes—would be able to return to the area, even though overt racial discrimination was not practiced. Some Negro leaders were content with this arrangement, and although they had objections to other parts of the plan, they felt the opportunity existed for Negro entry and hence there was no discrimination:

Hell, I don't care about the rentals. I don't know anyone stupid enough to pay them. But if there is some Negro that dumb, let him pay. The problem is opportunity, not whether there are actually Negroes in any given area.

To other Negro leaders, however, exclusion of Negroes in large numbers was a fact, even if it could be described as the impersonal effect of the market mechanism rather than as the effect of deliberate racial discrimination. To these, if race is an insufficient or immoral reason for excluding Negroes from an area, income is also an insufficient or improper reason for excluding people: "The thing is, the Negroes are being priced out of the Hyde Park area. It's partly racial, but the economics of it affects both white and Negro." The plan was described as a "well conceived scheme to clear Negroes out" and replace them with a "privileged class of rich patrons."[33]

Nowhere are choices of goals more complex or more difficult than in the area of housing and residential segregation. In no area are the issues so complicated by a host of economic and political factors; at the same time, in no other area are both welfare and status ends so conspicuously denied. There is an evident and great shortage of housing and a high degree of overcrowding, often in substandard units. Similarly, there is strong resistance, often enforced by violence, to the movement of Negroes into all-white areas. Few Negro leaders agree on what is the crux of the housing problem. To some it involves only the problem of eliminating the violence and other forms of resistance which now accompany the glacial expansion of the Negro area along its own periphery. To others it requires the elimination of obstacles to Negro penetration of white areas throughout the city, and not merely those at the periphery of the Black Belt. To yet others it involves the provision of new housing, either within established Negro areas or on vacant land sites in all-white areas. Little agreement exists on the causes of the present problem. Some find the root in the lack of vacant land for new construction; others see the shortage of mortgage financing as the strategic factor; still others see the issue simply as the result of a lack of firm police protection for Negro home buyers. There is, finally, little agreement as to what should be the desirable ultimate state of affairs. For some, it would be a completely interracial ecology, with whites and Negroes distributed throughout the city on the basis of income. To others, it would be nothing more than the ability of Negroes to buy or rent homes peacefully, even though the homes they do buy eventually become parts of all-Negro communities as whites flee to other areas.

So little progress has been made by the city in dealing with, or even thinking about, this subject that few real choices have had to be made by Negro leaders. Since what any leader wants emerges most clearly in those concrete cases where actual decisions must be made among competing alternatives, it is difficult to be precise in an area where so few decisions have been made and so few alternatives presented. One proposal which has received limited public discussion in Chicago, and one which illustrates the problems involved in this subject, is the question of quotas in housing. If one's goal is the attainment of interracial living patterns in residential areas, and if (as seems to be the case) whites tend to flee from those areas which have been entered by more than a relatively small percentage of Negro families, then it can be argued that it may be necessary to devise and enforce some form of quota that will fix the ratio of Negroes to whites in a given area in order to create and maintain an interracial pattern. If, on the other hand, one's goal is an increase in the housing supply available to Negroes, then all restrictions—including quotas—to the entry of Negroes into residential areas should be removed. Quotas operate to increase the chances of interracial communities at the expense of reducing, in that area, the amount of housing available to Negroes. A non-quota system, on the other hand, increases the housing supply available to Negroes at the cost of decreasing the possibilities of an interracial area being maintained.[34]

Those Negro leaders who are willing to endorse quotas have a two-fold problem: first, the question of its utility and propriety; and, second, the question of whether Negroes in general, who have in the past been victimized by quotas applied by those hostile to the race, can be induced to accept the quota system. As one leader phrased it:

I think you need a quota system to make open occupancy work in any area. . . . Now most Negroes are opposed to a quota system. "Quota" has had bad associations for them; it has usually meant ways to keep Negroes *out* of places. But I think that a quota system is needed to make change orderly.

Another leader who had publicly endorsed a quota system spoke of it in terms which clearly indicate his mixed feelings on the matter:

That's a funny thing. It makes you scratch your head when it comes up. . . . It's hard to know what is right. . . . I don't want permanent guarantees. What we should try to do is make it clear to people what we are after. . . . We are trying to build a democratic community. With the demand for Negro housing so severe, I suppose you have to have quotas of some sort for a while. It is a temporary necessity. . . . Then you get into the problem of who is a Negro. ———— went over his quota once because a person he sold to whom he thought was white turned out to be a Negro.

A "democratic community" is a somewhat abstract goal, reflecting a commitment to a definition of integration not shared by all leaders. Some have other definitions which place a greater emphasis on the material needs of Negroes for housing:

I have always objected to quotas. . . . I think it is . . . bad in housing. . . . You have to put first things first. The first thing, the most important thing, is to give people a roof over their heads, *not* integration. . . . If in the process of putting roofs over their heads, you see that the houses are all going to one race, then you just have to live with it.

To others, the problem rests solely with the whites who flee Negro-invaded neighborhoods.[35] The Negro should make no concession to this weakness:

Houses are commodities just like anything else, which Negroes should have the same right to buy in the market place like anyone else. . . . If all the whites stampede . . .the people to deal with are the whites, . . . not the Negroes. I can't see quotas.

The choice between proximate, tangible, welfare ends and ultimate, intangible, status ends can be seen in interesting detail in the disagreement between two officials of the Chicago Housing Authority, which administers public housing, on the question of a quota system in public housing units. A Negro, who opposed the quotas which were intended to make the units interracial, describes the conflict:

I felt that additional public housing units should be built on an open occupancy basis, even if they all go to Negroes. . . . I suppose that if you object to public housing being almost all Negro, I have to take some of the blame for that. Miss Wood tried to set up a system of quotas. . . . I opposed her. We had built [some] homes, about 900 units in all, and after we had four buildings finished and for about two months after, we didn't rent a single unit. Miss Wood wanted to get some white people to move in first, because she knew that if Negroes moved in first, the whites would never move in. . . . And, of course, there weren't any applications from white families. That was a crime — all those families out there suffering, and we were keeping them out of decent housing. I insisted we let the Negroes move in right away.

The growing importance of problems of housing and residential segregation will, it can be assumed, steadily bring welfare-status choices to the fore. In articulating and, in great part, *creating* these new demands, the role of the professional executive of race relations organizations and voluntary associations can scarcely be exaggerated. Further, the emerging issues centering around housing create new problems in the relations between leaders and followers, between the middle- and upper-class Negro who is in a position to take advantage of gains in this area and the lower-class Negro who generally is not. When the issue was interracial violence or job discrimination, gains won by leaders were of value for large numbers — perhaps all — Negroes, in terms of increased safety or justice. When the goals are ending the barriers to Negro home ownership in white neighborhoods, those Negroes who might benefit become a much smaller group. When so many Negroes continue to feel a need for material improvements, the leader who seeks status goals is becoming a member of a small and relatively detached vanguard. A professional staff man said:

There is no organized, expressed demand for integration. The Negroes are silent by and large, for fear of political reprisals, or for lack of understanding, or because of the naive feeling that money is everything. They want *things,* and integration comes second. They won't make a choice that puts integration first. People haven't thought about it, they don't know. Only the professional staff people have thought about it, but they have no influence.

The opportunity to benefit from integrated schools or from living in a changing or interracial neighborhood is an opportunity largely open only to middle- and upper-class Negroes. Only a relatively few Negroes can afford the luxury of entry into a desirable residential neighborhood that a collapse of racial barriers would permit. "How many Negroes," asked one Negro real estate broker, "are going to want to buy on the North Shore?" Perhaps

more important than economic ability is desire: how many Negroes value the opportunity for integrated living in areas outside
the Negro community? Only careful research of another kind
will indicate what the potential Negro market for residential
dispersion is, but it is interesting to note that the great majority
of Negro civic leaders disclaimed any desire to move outside the
Negro area. A remark of a well-educated and prosperous minister is typical:

> I could move out like Mister Charley does. I make that kind of
> money. I could have a maid and maybe a chauffeur. They pay me
> well enough here. But I don't. I bought a house across the street. . . .
> I feel more comfortable here. I only feel like half a man out there in
> Mister Charley's country. . . . You ought to try being black for six
> months. Unless you have a sense of humor, you'd go crazy.

For such people, the "housing problem" is in reality the
reduction of the housing shortage and the elimination of obstacles
to the expansion of the Black Belt—it is only theoretically a free
real estate market with Negroes moving unhampered throughout
the city in search of homes. The theoretical value—the value of
the status ends—is not insignificant to them, of course. A free
real estate market has an aspirational value which is important
to some:

> What we insist upon is that the doors of opportunity be open
> *at the top* so Negroes can move ahead. . . . That is the minimum. All
> Negroes can't be assimilated right away, but doors should be open
> at the top in housing, jobs, politics, and so on. . . . This will accelerate
> the acculturation process for the whole mass. But we don't even have
> that in Chicago. . . . Most people just refuse to come to grips with
> the problem. To them, it's just a matter of increasing the housing
> supply, that's all.

Some Negro leaders made efforts to have the builders of a
middle-class commuters' suburb several miles south of Chicago
open it to a few Negro families. The appeal was refused, but in
the course of the discussion the Negroes argued that the policy
they urged was not based on the demand of Negroes generally
for such suburban housing, but was based rather on the "precedent
value" such a policy would have. One leader said:

> I didn't think there would be much Negro demand for housing in
> [the suburb]. Most Negroes didn't have the money to afford houses

in that price range.... And [the suburb] was going to be quite
a ways from Chicago, too far for most Negroes. ... But I felt that as
a demonstration it would be a good thing to have six or twelve
Negroes living there. One Negro wouldn't want to go that far alone,
but six or twelve might.

Whatever aspirational or precedent value such programs might
have, the great bulk of Negroes continue to live, and will continue to live in the estimate of even the most sanguine Negro
leaders, in the densely-populated all-Negro areas of the south and
west sides of the city. Although housing is becoming the dominant
issue in Negro civic action, and "open occupancy" is becoming
the principal goal of such action, the vast and growing Negro
slums with all the social problems that seem to arise from such
congestion remain the refractory problem they have always been.
The same Negro leader who spoke of the value of open occupancy
conceded the irrelevance of that doctrine to much of the Negro's
plight:

Open occupancy won't do much to help the Black Belt, no. ... We
recognize that. There are 80,000 families in the Black Belt. Open
occupancy would take some of the pressure off, reduce deterioration
on the South Side, and create some vacancies. This would help to
retard deterioration. I don't think that open occupancy would desegregate the South Side. In fact, I can't think of anything that
would desegregate the South Side.

Occasionally, a Negro will admit that he is not altogether
certain he approves the actions of those Negroes who elect to leave
the Negro community to enter a remote white neighborhood.
Several civic leaders suggested the suspicion that surrounds such
efforts as those of a very prominent Negro who purchased an
expensive home in a white suburb:

Why does he want to move out there ...? The men will say that
he just wants to be whiter, and the women will ask, why does he
go somewhere where he's not wanted? Why does a man go out
and endanger his wife and children? They suspect him. Maybe later,
after he succeeds, and is accepted, then they run big magazine stories
about him and he is a big hero.

A well-educated civic leader, active in many race improvement
organizations, described his mixed feelings about those who leave:

You take men like Dr. Percy Julian or Dr. Falls. They have a
right to move out there ... and live in white neighborhoods. I would

help them to assert that right. . . . If they have the courage and the means, then more power to them. . . . But down deep inside my heart, I know what I'm really thinking. I'm thinking, why don't they stay here in the Negro community and build a beautiful home and keep it up and hire a maid and a chauffeur to drive them around in a Cadillac automobile? Why don't they? They could show people, white people, what Negroes can do and how they can live. . . . Why did they have to leave us?

Conflicts Among Goals

Not all, or even most, problems that arise in an effort to select goals for civic action emerge from competing versions of the public interest. There are in the Negro community, and among Negro civic leaders, conflicts of interest just as there are such conflicts in any community. It is difficult to assess the extent to which such conflicts block civic action for the same reason it is difficult to assess how the civic leaders view the public, or the race, interest—too few issues proceed to a point of decision where concrete choices and negotiation must take place. But, although a comprehensive picture of the nature and extent of interest conflicts cannot be drawn, enough issues are available to offer some suggestive insights into the kinds of problems which arise in an attempt to assert the community interest over private interests.[36]

One important dimension of civic life which affects the possibility of agreeing on community goals is the uneven impact of desegregation. Desegregation has proceeded to the point in Chicago, as in other northern cities, where some Negroes have benefited while others have not. This differential effect is seen in commerce, where some Negroes have established business relationships with whites and others have not. A second dimension of civic life is the general diversification which has occurred as the community grew from a handful of people to several hundred thousand—diversification of income, occupation, and education. Few civic issues will affect each group or strata equally; most issues, on the contrary, promise costs for some groups as the price of the benefits they hold out to others. A third dimension emerges from the fact, frequently commented upon, that the prolonged existence of segregation inevitably results in the creation of organizations which profit by segregation and which would be jeopardized by desegregation and dispersal. These organizations —businesses, institutions, and political arrangements—are said to have a "stake in the ghetto." All of these dimensions of conflict—unequal desegregation, natural diversity, and the stake in the ghetto—are spoken of freely in the abstract but are dealt with or pursued covertly, since their existence is a threat to the widely shared value of race unity. Some illustrations of the conflicts can be given, however.

When integration has proceeded unevenly, those organized forms of community life which are integrated and in part dependent on the support of white contributors are often embarrassed by the protest activities of all-Negro organizations. A campaign was launched in 1958 by a group called the Negro Labor Relations League to induce through picketing and boycott tactics white merchants to hire Negro workers. Although the NLRL had a bad reputation among many elements of the Negro community, it nevertheless had sufficient support to score a few early successes. Two of its targets—a bank and a food store—were members of a biracial business association, the Cosmopolitan Chamber of Commerce. The association, formerly the Negro Chamber of Commerce, had decided to "integrate" and to solicit white membership and support under predominantly Negro leadership. The picketing and threats of picketing were a clear source of embarrassment to the Chamber. A Negro officer of that association sought to explain the role of his group when race ends —hiring Negroes by all-white institutions—were sought against members of his group:

Q. Isn't ——— food store a member of the CCC?

A. Oh, yes.

Q. Have you played a part in the efforts to get ——— to hire Negroes? The NLRL [Negro Labor Relations League] was picketing them . . .

A. No.

Q. Why not?

A. Well, it was never brought to our attention.

Q. But you were aware of it?

A. Well, yes, we were aware of it. . . . Sometimes you can't do all you want to do. Frankly, if a chance comes along to avoid a little controversy, well, I'm inclined to take it. I mean, you know — but we should never dodge an issue if it were brought to us directly.

Q. But there's no sense in looking for trouble?
A. Well, you can't volunteer for everything that comes along. ... I find myself doing too much, anyway.... We just can't get involved in too much.

The Negro business community itself is sufficiently differentiated to permit conflicts of interest to arise within it. The Cosmopolitan Chamber of Commerce, if it promotes the business of some of its members, is in effect taking business away from other of its members. Similarly, when some civic leaders made efforts to sustain a Mid-South Chicago Council which would seek vigorous prosecution of laws, building codes, and city cleaning programs, they discovered they could not do so without exposing interest conflicts among Negro business members. Those Negro property owners who would benefit in terms of enhanced property values by a thorough neighborhood "clean-up campaign" found that such a campaign, involving citations for building code violations, worked against the interest of other Negro property owners who faced the possibility of answering those citations:

One or two guys in the Council started a stink. [X] and [Y], who had properties that were affected by these surveys, ... came to us and said, "Now, look, you've got to keep this thing under control." It wasn't couched in self-interest terms, of course, but more in terms of an appeal for the poor small Negro property owners.

Just as conflicts take place among Negro businesses that can block action, conflicts also arise between a Negro businessman's interests and what other Negro civic leaders hold to be the interests of the community. One problem that elicits this difference is the population loss of many Negro areas. Some Negro businessmen are concerned about this loss, as it means a lessening of customers and business. Proposals to rehabilitate these areas often involve plans for land clearance and housing code enforcement to reduce population densities even further. An officer of the Cosmopolitan Chamber of Commerce described the inability of his organization to take a clear stand on the matter:

The whole area around here is less congested than it was, and that means less business, of course.... It [code enforcement or clearance] will reduce business a bit more. It's one of those things. I, personally, if I have to make a choice, would decide for the people in this.... But I don't know how others would decide. There always seem to be these conflicts you have to deal with.

The Mid-South Chicago Council, an organization to deal with blight and conservation problems in the South Side Negro community, expired after two or three years of efforts. Among the many reasons for its demise was the fact that many Negro members—who were largely businessmen, real estate brokers, and property owners—grew cool to the idea of area conservation when they realized that building code enforcement would mean a reduction in population density and hence a shrinkage in their market. Neighborhood rehabilitation, they felt, was coming to mean either the introduction of competition from new white businesses brought into a redeveloped area or population losses or both.

An issue which is very controversial among Negroes, and in which class lines are drawn with relative clarity, is the question of public housing. In a study of the public housing issue in Chicago, Meyerson and Banfield describe in several places the Negro attitude toward such projects, and note that Negro leadership tended to speak, when it spoke at all, in opposition to public housing or at least public housing in its own neighborhoods.[37] When, as a feature of the Hyde Park-Kenwood urban renewal plan, certain groups proposed the inclusion of public housing units, the Negro civic leadership was once again divided. Hyde Park-Kenwood was a desirable residential neighborhood, and a large number of middle- and upper-class Negroes had homes or spacious apartments in the area. Few Negro leaders could be induced to take a public stand on the issue of public housing. Those that did fell into three more or less distinct groups. First were the ardent proponents of extensive public housing—as many as six hundred units—for the area. These were largely leaders of labor unions with large Negro memberships. Second were Negro civic leaders from business and professional groups who occupied offices in voluntary associations such as the NAACP and who felt constrained, by the demands of such offices, to speak on behalf of public housing which presumably would house many Negroes being displaced from their homes. These men spoke with a marked lack of conviction. Finally were a group of Negroes, residents of the area in desirable homes, who vigorously, though privately, opposed any public housing at all. Among these were the two Negro members of the Community Conservation Council who voted with the majority of the Council to exclude public housing from the renewal plan they were recommending to the city. One prominent Negro, with a home in the area, said:

When you get people living together whose actions and culture are far apart, then you are bound to have dissatisfactions arise, race notwithstanding. . . . You get some people who want to raise chickens or goats in their backyard. . . . Other people shouldn't have to suffer for that. It is better to have in one neighborhood people of like thinking and tastes.

Another Negro civic leader, who also lived in the area, made his class interest explicit:

I think [we] would take the same position as a white man of similar class and status would. It's a class question, really. . . . I didn't want any public housing here, but I was willing to go along with them [some white liberals who did] for the record. . . . You can't create a homogeneous community out of heterogeneous elements. . . . You have to have a homogeneous community, educationally and economically, if it is to be a stable community.

On occasion, there is a confrontation between Negro leaders of different classes on an issue such as this. The gulf that separates them is described graphically by a participant at such a meeting:

I was called to a meeting . . . [about the neighborhood]. There was [X, a voluntary association officer], [Y, a Negro businessman and civic leader] and [Z, a Negro labor leader] and some others. [Z] got up, in his bluff workingman's way, and said that he lived in [the neighborhood] and that he had a sister with seven kids who lived in the Black Belt. His sister's apartment caught fire and burned down, when she and the kids were outside by chance. So [Z] brought them down to his home and moved them in. . . . I looked around at this point, and boy, you should have seen the faces in that room. Brrrrr. The thought of these seven Negro kids prancing around in front of [his] home was too much for those people. Poor [Z]. By his standards, he thought he was doing the right thing. But these people, the other Negroes there, were aghast; they don't want a lot of lower-class Negro kids in every block. . . . He and [Y] will never really be able to talk to each other.

The race values resist the normal operation of the processes of social stratification in the Negro community. Negro civic leaders whose personal interests run counter to what others have defined as a race interest devise a variety of solutions to the problem of what public position they may take. One person, an officer of a Negro newspaper, felt the urban renewal plan should be adopted, but at the same time felt obligated to contribute to the newspaper's vigorous editorial campaign against it. Another civic leader, an officer of the NAACP, managed to shift the position of that association so as to retain a symbolic position in favor of low-income housing without insisting on the actual construction of such housing in a particular neighborhood. A local unit of the NAACP had demanded, in an early statement, that six hundred units of public housing be built in the Hyde Park-Kenwood area as part of the renewal plan. Three months later, in a formal statement to a City Council committee, the NAACP president left the amount of such public housing "to the judgment of persons more expert than we" and its location to the judgment of city officials who were asked only to "inventory vacant land sites . . . in Hyde Park-Kenwood and throughout the city." When questioned by a councilman about his statement, the Negro leader said that the "public housing need not be in Hyde Park-Kenwood as long as it is in low-density, non-segregated areas. . . . These may or may not be in Hyde Park-Kenwood."

Segregation has its own vested interests, as many writers have observed. These are the so-called "advantages of the disadvantages"—the benefits that accrue to some from the fact of segregation. The creation of Negro organizations or associations in response to exclusion from white organizations leads to the development of commitments, attitudes, and incentives which tend to perpetuate the Negro organization and which lead it to resist re-entry into white institutions. The extent of this phenomenon is difficult to assess with accuracy, for each element in the Negro community accuses other elements of benefiting from, or having a stake in, the segregated status quo. Ministers accuse Negro real estate brokers of profiteering through scare selling of homes in transitional areas, while the real estate brokers deny it and instead accuse the ministers of exploiting a captive audience of Negro parishioners for their own ends. Both groups accuse the Negro politician of being dependent on segregation to maintain the all-Negro wards and constituencies which elect him to office and resisting efforts to disperse these constituencies through civic improvements. The politicians accuse Negro teachers of fearing white competition in integrated school systems. Gunnar Myrdal elevates these problems to the status of a "dilemma" which afflicts the entire Negro middle and upper class,[38] and E. Franklin Frazier bases much of his polemic against the so-called "black bourgeoisie" on the feelings of insecurity that are revealed in the fear of white competition.[39]

These strictures should not always be taken at face value, however. In many cases where Negroes can be found opposing the presumed interests of the race, simpler—and often more correct—explanations can be discovered. Integration might pose two kinds of threats to a Negro's position. The first kind is that which would result from the break-up of the ghetto and the complete dispersal of Negroes throughout the county on the basis of some principle other than race. This would end the residential concentration of Negroes and undermine the position of those Negroes whose business, profession, or organization depends upon the existence of such concentration. This threat is not yet a real one in Chicago. Even the most optimistic reformers see little immediate prospect for such dispersal. In time, it may come; today, it is not significant. Although Negro leaders may oppose race issues out of self-interest, that self-interest does not as yet arise from a fear that the issue will lead to complete integration. More commonly, their opposition reflects an unwillingness to submit one's reputation and esteem to the stresses of controversy, the constraints imposed by an organization (such as a political party) of which one is a member, a desire to protect property values and the character of a neighborhood, or the need to meet the demands of constituents. Decisions are made within the constraints of a specific situation where a choice exists; it is rare that the choice is between preserving one's position through retaining segregation and losing all through massive integration.[40] The prospects of achieving Negro dispersal have not reached the point where Negro leaders who benefit from Negro concentration see a threat to their positions arising from efforts to reduce this concentration. The Negro politicians in Chicago, for example, greeted coolly and with obvious reluctance the proposal for the enactment of an open occupancy ordinance which had as its goal the removal of barriers to free entry by Negroes into white neighborhoods. It was widely believed in the city that the politicians' opposition stemmed from a realization that open occupancy would mean the end of the Negro wards which elect them. Ending the

Negro wards by legislative enactment is hardly an imminent possibility. A candid Negro alderman explained his indifference to open occupancy on that score:

What it comes down to is this: It won't happen in my life time. This condition [Negro concentration] will be with us for a very long time, no matter what I do. . . . Negroes won't be living just anywhere, and no whites are going to move in here. You couldn't pay a white family enough to move into this ward. I know.

Other factors account for the undeniable lack of enthusiasm with which the Negro aldermen approached the proposed open occupancy ordinance—the constraints posed by party loyalty to an organization which clearly did not want either residential segregation weakened or a bitter intraparty fight to determine whether it should be weakened; the suspicions and rivalries aroused by what seemed to them to be the publicity-seeking tactics of the sponsors of the ordinance; and a simple disagreement as to the merits and feasibility of the law. In any case, the Negro politician does not pursue a career which is to any great degree dependent on bartering in civic issues, so long as he is not known for any obvious opposition to defined Negro interests. As a Negro alderman said:

If I got up in a meeting and spoke out in opposition to open occupancy, for instance, I would be badly hurt. . . . But I don't have to make any statements on it. If I were a talking politician instead of a doing politician, if I went around making speeches, and was a great orator, that might be true. But the point is, I don't have to make speeches or statements about open occupancy to stay in this office. I stay in this office by doing other things, by rendering services for my people, and the issue of open occupancy just doesn't come up.

Much the same argument can be made to counter the stake in the ghetto imputed to other Negro organizations—the newspaper which sells to a ghetto market, the insurance company which attracts only Negro clients, the hospital which serves Negroes with a Negro staff, or even the NAACP which (by similar logic) could be described as an association which would be put out of business by complete integration. Logically, a stake exists; empirically, no issues as yet threaten it. A Negro doctor on the staff of the Negro hospital, who favored building a county hospital in the same area to handle Negro patients, expressed no concern about the impact of such competition:

Provident wouldn't really feel that kind of competition from the County Hospital. There will always be a need for a Provident Hospital in Chicago. . . . We will always have patients who insist on going to Provident. Maybe in fifty or sixty years there will be so much integration that we will feel the competition, but not in five or six years.

The second kind of threat to Negro leaders arising out of the prospect of integration is much more real. That is the threat to specific organizations or institutions which would result from the ending of discriminatory practices. Here there is a real stake in segregation. In these areas, organizations exist which sustain large numbers of Negro office-holders, and the status and power which office confers is not an advantage to be lightly surrendered for the sake of an abstract goal such as integration. Furthermore, many Negroes do not seek or value white contacts and prefer all-Negro organizations.

An example might be a nation-wide association of Negro church congregations. It claims several million members. A Negro minister describes its character and its leadership opportunities:

These people are [mostly] from the deep South and they tend to be clannish. . . . They have very little education. Things are changing a bit now, but it is still a case of fear and suspicion of the other racial group. . . . Also, they have a personal, selfish interest in . . . the status and authority which offices in the Convention can give them. . . . They would lose office and lose all this status if they merged with another group. . . . They would be swallowed up by it.

An officer of the association was asked about his feelings concerning a merger between his organization and the comparable white association in order to further integration. His guarded reply suggests his lack of enthusiasm for the idea:

There is little in our denomination which you can point to regarding the need for or expediency of a merger. . . . It would be fine, I suppose, as a thing to have, but the initiative would have to come from the white groups. We shouldn't approach them. I think the whole matter of integration has been misinterpreted in this country. . . . I have little interest in any effort to actually require people to associate. I would encourage people to go ahead with what is distinctively theirs. . . . You can have a democratic nation with people still practicing segregation in religion. . . . We ought not to impose integration where we don't have it.

Opportunities for status are not abundant in the Negro community, and when a Negro organization does provide such opportunities, it becomes valuable. The heated, often bitter, contests for office in such organizations as this church association suggest the value which attaches to it and the unrealism of expecting its leaders to will it out of existence through integrative mergers. A Negro leader describes an intellectual society of which he was a member when confronted by such a problem:

I'm in a society of Negro intellectuals who are studying Africa, part of an international organization started in France. . . . We were faced with a problem because some thought that we shouldn't keep whites out, that it might give us a bad name in some quarters — particularly when we were getting money from [them]. . . . I got up to speak and . . . I defended keeping votes away from whites because we needed an organization we could control. . . . They went wild and applauded. I could have gone on for ten minutes rabble rousing on that theme. And these were intellectuals, mind you.

The Chicago Medical Society, the local affiliate of the American Medical Association, admits Negro physicians without discrimination. Nevertheless, there persists an all-Negro medical group, the Cook County Physicians Association. Although some Negro doctors feel that the CCPA is slowly disappearing, others told an interviewer that the CCPA is needed because it keeps Negro doctors from being "gobbled up" by integrated groups and enables Negro doctors to hold positions of prestige and voice their own opinions.[4]

Not only do Negro organizations provide opportunities that integrated groups would not, but in addition, the existence of a Negro organization — such as an all-Negro hospital — drains off energy and ambition which might otherwise be directed into efforts to gain admission into white organizations on an equal basis. A survey of hospital discrimination in important American cities found that all-Negro hospitals did not exist in the six cities which had the highest degree of integration; all the most segregated cities, on the other hand, had all-Negro hospitals.[42] Chicago has both an all-Negro hospital and a "comparative lack of pressure by Chicago's Negro physicians" on white hospitals for entry.[43] A Negro doctor described how the Negro hospital becomes a focus for self-segregation and a deterrent to action seeking admission to white hospital staffs:

The idea of segregated medical facilities is so entrenched that most [Negro] doctors take the attitude of "I can't help. . . . Why try? . . . We've done that before and lost so many times." Then, others would like integration but feel that it [is] for the people behind them, the young people, not for themselves. If you get to be senior attending surgeon at Provident Hospital, you are not anxious to apply for a staff position at a white hospital. You couldn't go in with the equivalent rank, of course, and naturally you don't feel like starting at the bottom all over again in a white hospital.

Some Negroes also feel a degree of dislike for, and suspicion of, whites. This can overlay a self-interest in the status quo with a disinterested reason for questioning the value of efforts toward integration. These suspicions rarely appear verbally in discussions with civic leaders, but evidence of their operation is not absent. One civic leader, active in an attempt to further integration in public schools, related a typical story:

A woman called me the other day, indignant over the changes I had proposed in a speech about the Chicago public schools. She said she didn't want her kids in a white school. She had gone to a Negro school, and so would they.

Many Negroes in positions of leadership genuinely feel that Negroes will be treated fairly only by members of their own race. Efforts were made to place Negroes in managerial positions in public housing projects and to secure Negro-controlled co-operative housing located within the Negro area.[44]

All of these constraints on the desire or readiness of Negro civic leaders to seek integration goals operate under the general need to cloak self-interest in the guise of race interest in order to avoid the sanctions the Negro community imposes on those who *openly* flaunt race values. Some reflective leaders will discuss these limitations, and muse over the possibility that the defined race goals — such as open occupancy and free Negro movement in the city — may be wrong. Negro politicians, while conceding that they dare not publicly oppose open occupancy despite the fact that it is harmful to party harmony, go on to suggest on occasion that Negro political strength, which they believe has emerged with the growth of solid blocs of Negro voters, is being unwisely jeopardized in favor of integration. To them, political strength is a sure and effective tool. Even though it is not threatened today by open occupancy, should it not be protected against future contingencies? One politician said:

There's no question but what open occupancy would hurt the politicians. . . . But it would be politically disastrous to the Negro people. . . . But you have to go along with the times. Times change, and progress can't be blocked, even if you want to. I think open occupancy would be a sociological advantage to the Negroes, but a political disadvantage. . . . It doesn't make any difference what I would like to do. . . . You have to go along with the times. It's the coming thing. But I can remember when we had just one Negro alderman, and now we have six. Isn't that worth something?

There has been a general decline in pressure for the more blatant and self-serving kinds of welfare ends. Fewer and fewer "Buy Black" campaigns are observed, and when they do appear, responsible Negro leaders are often quick to disavow them and to work — privately — to still them. Some elements of the Negro community in all cities will, on occasion, attempt to organize such campaigns. This occurs most often in connection with the various "black nationalism" movements, including the remnants of the old Garvey group and the more numerous followers of Elijah Muhammed. In New York, however, when it appeared that the local NAACP was giving some support to an effort to induce liquor stores to buy only from Negro salesmen in Harlem, the NAACP's *national* Negro leaders moved quickly to "clarify" the situation and to insist that, while inequities existed and should be combatted, the *integration* of the labor force in that industry was their principal objective. Similarly, Negroes in Los Angeles were divided for a time as to whether certain wine companies should be boycotted to compel them to hire more Negro workers. More conservative Negro leaders were sharply attacked by one Negro newspaper for stating that no real evidence of discrimination could be found in the company. An effort in Chicago to organize a Negro boycott of stores handling certain products produced by a company which allegedly did not hire Negro workers never really came alive. In most of these cities, relatively little psychic energy is available to be mobilized for such movements. Negro leaders usually are dubious as to both the merits and the motives of the sponsors of such campaigns, and feel that such tactics are somehow outdated. The boycotting drives of the 1930's are no longer so evident; prosperity has lessened the tensions that produced them and given new and different opportunities for advancement and success to those who would lead them.

The split between welfare and status ends still persists, however, and in many places seems to be becoming more evident. In New York, the Urban League and the NAACP opposed the building of a new public housing project in Harlem on the grounds that it would institutionalize and solidify residential segregation in that area by being almost all-Negro. The Negro political leaders and (originally) the Negro press disagreed, and pressed for the project, claiming that it filled a material need for more decent shelter. The Housing Authority succeeded in winning approval for the project, capitalizing on the divided opinion among Negroes.

Conflicts of interest exist in other cities as well as Chicago. The question of how private charitable funds should be distributed among hospitals in Detroit, for example, raised the problem of a Negro private hospital operated by prominent Negro doctors. The Negro press and other groups protested giving funds to an all-Negro institution, arguing that integration of Negroes into white private hospitals would be hindered by such a move. The NAACP, which included among its directors some of the Negro doctors involved, was immobilized by the conflict — unable to take a positive stand and pursue it with vigor. In the end, this made little difference. The existence of any controversy among a large group of potential beneficiaries about how the funds were to be divided meant that the donors, acting on the principle that such gifts should promote good-will rather than ill-will and that controversy would "taint" the cause, decided not to give any money at all to Negro hospitals. Thus, the goal of those seeking status ends was served in this case by *not* being able to unify the Negro community but by creating controversy instead.

Issues in the Negro communities of various cities often tend to unfold in a comparable fashion. Many of the themes of this chapter can be brought together by describing an issue in New York City which involved a conflict between welfare and status ends and in which, as a result, the Negro community could not speak with one voice despite a great concern on all sides with the general problem at stake.

Negro mothers in New York on more than one occasion picketed schools in Harlem to protest the inadequacy of the facilities. A lawyer instituted legal proceedings on their behalf. These acts created difficulties for Negro civic agencies. They are often caught up by the problem of how to press for school integration, rather than school improvement, without alienating Negro opinion (which sees improvement as the more evident and immediate problem). Organized civic action has recently been focussed on a plan to have the school system transport, by bus, Negro children from over-crowded schools in Negro areas (such as Bedford-Stuyvesant) to all-white schools in Glendale (Queens). The NAACP has given little support to boycott and picketing efforts directed at substandard schools within Harlem, although it has announced it will defend a lower-court decision (being appealed by the Board of Education) critical of the Board's policy in Harlem schools.[45]

This issue was characteristic of much of Negro civic action: Strong, often exaggerated and over-simplified charges are made by a Negro acting for people seeking certain welfare ends. There is a reluctance by the established civic agencies to endorse the charges without reserve, in part because they see complexities which the rhetoric of the agitator has obscured and in part because they have access to important centers of influence which they do not wish to jeopardize by name-calling and a rigid attitude. The Negro press, attracted by issues which have drama and a grass-roots appeal, engages in unbridled attacks on the offending system. Soon a position is reached in which Negro civic groups can no longer stand aside without paying heavy costs in terms of Negro criticism, and they are compelled to take sides. The issue of what *ought* to be done, what are the ends to be served, becomes muddied. Not only is there a conflict between welfare goals ("give us better schools") and status goals ("let us into white schools on an equal basis"), but many issues such as the worth of "progressive" education and teaching techniques, having nothing to do with race, become buried in the rhetoric of race issues and values. Means and ends are steadily interacting: general or loosely-defined ends are sought, and means are selected to attain them. But the means selected have consequences in terms of mobilizing or alienating support and inflaming followers. These consequences react upon the ends chosen, narrowing them to those most appealing for the organization being created and making more rigid the position taken on those ends. Given the existence of latent but strong attitudes (such as race feelings) in a community, civic leaders can rarely be deliberate in their choice of means. Means tend to have an "end-component' and flexibility in the selection of means is reduced.[46]

Chapter IX

Political Styles

Two political styles emerge more or less clearly from a study of Negro civic leadership — the *militant* and the *moderate*. Negroes disagree both about ends and means, and the conflict over means typically takes the form of a dispute as to which political style is most appropriate for civic action. A description of these two styles can be obtained by assembling under these labels observations about the characteristic ways in which Negro leaders approach the world about them — how they see it, feel about it, describe it, and act toward it. No "pure" examples of such styles can, of course, be given, but so many close approximations exist among real leaders that it is useful to describe the artificially-polarized ideal types.*

The modes of thinking, speaking, and acting characteristic of these two styles can be described, for the sake of convenience, along a few simple axes: how the leader perceives and describes (1) the nature of the issues confronting him and the values he

---

*These labels are used with the greatest misgivings. In order to avoid the tendency to read content into these words apart from the specific, substantive material for which they are mere rubrics, I was tempted to term these two syles simply "A" and "B." But that would be even more confusing to the reader than the names selected. It must be stressed, however, that these labels have no normative implications. Nor do they have any connection with the kinds of leaders mentioned by other authors writing on Negro leadership — for example, Myrdal's "protest" and "accommodation" leaders. Myrdal's typology and mine were devised for different purposes. Cf. Gunnar Myrdal, *An American Dilemma* (New York: Harper & Bros.), pp. 720ff.

brings to bear on them; (2) the ends or goals he deems it appropriate to seek in the realm of civic action; (3) the means he employs in seeking these ends; and (4) the motives, goals, and attributes of the other actors, white and Negro, whom he sees in the world about him.

The Militant Style

Issues and Values

The "militant" or "protest" style is often clearly revealed in the extent to which the leader sees the issues confronting the race and the community in simplified form. In those cases where information is shared on an approximately equal basis, the protester will see simplicities where the moderate sees complexities. A vigorous NAACP officer, with experience as chairman of its Housing Committee, brings the problem of residential segregation within the compass of a single paragraph:

> This whole housing problem could be solved in a few months. . . . All you have to do is find some decent white people and some decent Negroes who want to buy homes and get them together in a friendly way. . . . There won't be any trouble if they are properly brought in. . . . Then when the bullies start throwing the bombs, the community will be against them.

The consequences of an abrupt and radical change in the racial pattern of residence in the city are never considered to be serious by the great majority of these leaders. In almost every case, the questions raised by others regarding the impact of open occupancy on the movement of whites from the city to the suburbs, the possibilities of open violence, and the legal questions involved are regarded by the militant as a "smokescreen" purposely created by whites to confuse the issue and block action. And in the event some of these predicted consequences should come to pass, these leaders are prepared. The person quoted above continued:

> Why should the city be saved? I mean, if these people leave it, what difference does it make? . . . It only makes a difference to those who remain. They are happy out there, let them go. . . .

Not only do issues tend to be seen in simplified terms, but often many issues are brought together or agglomerated into a single general issue which should be considered and dealt with as

a whole rather than in parts. Speaking of the problem of segregation in health facilities, one active voluntary association leader in
a public address exemplified this tendency when he asked:

What are the possible remedies? We can't tackle the problem piecemeal. We've got to hit all at once. It's no good to try to improve . . .
these things.

A militant typically will present a maximum number of demands
to a public agency for solution. This tendency to agglomerate
issues rather than to deal with them singly is illustrated in the
shift which occurred between the statement to the Chicago Board
of Education in 1957 made by an NAACP militant leader and the
statement made one year later by an NAACP leader who was a
moderate. Where the former listed over ten demands, covering
all aspects of school board policy, the latter made only three
recommendations which focussed on a single facet of school board
policy — the work of its Human Relations Committee.

In describing the issues in civic affairs, the protester utilizes a
vocabulary that invests his goals with moral principle. He tends to
speak of these matters in terms of their ultimate rationale, rather
than in relation to immediate needs, and justifies his demands with
an appeal to an elaborate and highly general set of values and
rights.[1] A characteristic remark is one made by a vigorous lay
civic leader who complains of the decline of this moral fervor
in the work of professional staff members of voluntary associations:

Now in human relations you have to "consider" the other fellow.
It used to be a question of principle, of rights. . . . We didn't care
what the other guy thought. . . . We have the *right* to do this. Man,
I believe, is a child of God, and God created everything he has on
earth. The Constitution of the United States guarantees me these
rights, and I don't have to ask the other citizen whether I can enjoy
them. . . . There wouldn't be any point to it anyway, because they
probably would object. . . .

The militant ascribes civic reputation to other leaders on the
basis of both their civic posture and their rhetoric, and this rhetoric
is most highly valued when it embodies a clearly moral attitude
toward race issues:

They wouldn't quarrel with him on the basis of right and principle.
He was usually on the right side, and it was hard to argue with

him. . . . They couldn't deny or oppose, on moral grounds, the fight for the complete liberation of the Negro people.

This high degree of commitment to goals of a general, morally rationalized character often leads the protester to adopt a flexible attitude toward means and the roles of voluntary associations working in the field. He possesses a firm image of those ends to which means and organizational roles should be adapted; the struggle for some goal should not be deflected or abandoned simply because it does not comport with the defined mission of the active organization. This is most clearly illustrated in the relative indifference of the protester to the distinctions which others make as to the proper function of the NAACP in contrast to the Urban League. He sees the Urban League's less militant role not as a strength but as a weakness, and a faint pallor of moral stigma clouds the fact that its maintenance needs require it to attract white business support through a more moderate approach.

The militant sees the world as it should be, and is therefore very conscious of its shortcomings and the obstacles to progress.* This attribute, which parallels in many ways what Karl Mannheim described as "utopian thinking"[2] as well as some of the qualities Eric Hoffer found adhering to the "true believer,"[3] cuts across many of the other traits under discussion here. The tendencies, mentioned below, to see the opposition as not only powerful but also consciously co-ordinated into something akin to a conspiracy or at least a united front, the reliance on negative rather than positive inducements, the tendency to seek general, all-inclusive reforms rather than narrow, specific ones — these all may reflect an absorption in the extent to which the real world falls short of the desired world and the magnitude of the obstacles to progress.

At the same time, the protest leader is not an ideological isolate; in general, he shares the values of the white liberal or radical, with the exception that race is placed in a position of pre-eminence. Militants from the Negro community are characteristically found

---

*"Militancy" was defined by a militant leader in these terms: "Militancy means mass meetings, and having interracial ball games in tense areas to prove you have a right to be there, and going out into Trumbull Park, and talking to the Mayor with the gloves off. . . . We've always had the hards and the softs in the NAACP. . . . The softs don't want to rock the boat. They would rather play the game. . . . Try to bring about changes pleasantly."

to be active members of a wide range of liberal causes and associations. One of the most militant NAACP leaders, twice a candidate for branch president, was also a vice-chairman of the Independent Voters of Illinois, the local affiliate of the liberal Americans for Democratic Action. In a more radical vein, a former staff member of the Urban League noted for his militancy was the chairman of the left-wing "Committee to End Mob Violence." He was not openly disturbed by the character of his associates in the organization.

> The Committee to End Mob Violence had an assortment of people in it, including the left-wing labor unions. . . . They [his opponents] painted me with a red brush because of that. The red scare was on then in full force. . . . I said that I didn't make any political distinctions as to who came into the Committee; I was interested in the community problem, not in people's politics.

Ends

The Negro militant tends to seek what we have called "status" ends in distinction to "welfare" ends. His position is advanced: integration is the general goal, and the improvement of the welfare of the Negro is of secondary importance. Indeed, welfare measures are often seen as steps away from integration, for often — as in the case of the County Hospital branch or the extension of public housing in the Negro area — they reinforce the existing pattern of segregation and "take the pressure" off other areas of the city to admit Negroes on an equal basis. The protest leader will typically be found speaking and acting vigorously in favor of integrating schools through redistricting rather than merely seeking new or better schools in Negro areas; in favor of open occupancy legislation; in favor of checking the expansion of public housing in the Black Belt; and in favor of equal treatment of Negroes even at the expense of proportional representation in public agencies and affairs.

The militant is aware that these measures often do not touch the masses of Negroes as closely or as surely as do many welfare issues, but he is confident that the more subtle issues are the more important in the long run. Speaking of Negro reluctance to generate pressure on behalf of school redistricting, a former NAACP leader described his problem:

This is an intangible factor, a psychological factor. . . . How do you make the masses of people understand this?. . . . It's easy for them to see the problem when their teachers get paid less, or they are on double shift, or less money is spent on Negro schools. . . . But when you have this feeling, that is harder to make them see — that education, if it is segregated, can do harm that nothing can undo. Modern psychological fact has proven that. . . . So we are trying to do this: make Negroes aware of the problem. . . . To meet this would take courage on the part of political leaders.

When a difficult choice must be made between welfare improvement now and integration gains later, the militant will press for the latter at the expense of the former and accept the cost in terms of immediate deprivations or even personal suffering. For him, results have a price. It is often a price which they, because of superior income or higher status or unique opportunities, would not have to pay personally, but this fact should not detract from the evident sincerity of their convictions.

A Negro leader in the cause of desegregating private hospital staffs in Chicago conceded that some Negro doctors felt they might lose Negro patients to white doctors if integration were a fact, but discounted the importance of their fears, adding that in any case "you have to be prepared to accept a temporary period of suffering if you are going to gain anything in the long run."

Another Negro leader, fighting the construction of a South Side branch to the County Hospital, urged in a public meeting that the Negro masses should be prepared to accept even a reduction in available medical care as a necessary cost of continued integration:

I don't think it is brutal to say that there must be some suffering for a few for the good of the many. Look at Montgomery, Alabama. There people had to suffer in order to kill Jim Crow on their busses. If people hadn't walked to work and lost their jobs and given up their credit and lost their cars and their mortgages on their homes, they would be riding those Jim Crow busses today. But I doubt that we in Chicago could get people to put up such a fight in Chicago. Piecemeal solutions won't do.

Occasionally a Negro, in such a public meeting, will question whether the cost is not too high or whether in fact such a choice must be made. At an NAACP meeting, a speaker had urged, in impassioned tones, Negroes to carry the fight for a free housing market into the suburbs by buying in white areas and defending their purchases even if it involved "getting hurt." A Negro doctor rose to question the price the protest leader was asking them to pay:

[Doctor:] We have enough laws. It's a question of enforcing them. It's all very well to talk about courage, but you can't expect a man to endanger his wife and children. That's not courage. You have to have police protection. . . .

[Speaker:] Anyone who thinks more of life than of rights hasn't got any rights. Nobody is going to bother you if they know they are going to get hurt trying. You ought to be willing to die defending your home.*

[Doctor:] That's not the question. What if I'm away at my office and come home and find my wife and children injured? That's not courage. It's not cowardice to say that you don't want that to happen. . . .

Almost without exception, the militant will select as the most important issue involving race relations, and therefore, of course, the most important issue generally, the question of housing and residential segregation. "Housing," a Negro labor leader remarked, "is the central problem. It not only affects people, but it also affects planning in the city. Real estate affects so many civic developments; nothing can happen, almost, that does not involve real estate." But more than its implications for city planning are the myriad other race relations problems that seem to arise out of housing. A young Negro doctor felt that not only was it desirable to collect a variety of race issues into a single package, but that in addition they could best be solved in this way:

It all comes back to residential segregation. You can't get around it. They can segregate schools and hospitals by putting them in Negro areas, and then say, well, they are open to anybody, but of course only Negroes go there. . . . It shows up in education, where the school board is very flexible about adjusting school district lines to keep it all-Negro. . . . Residential segregation is the big problem that must be answered first. Residential segregation is the thing that creates the void, that destroys Negro-white communication. The people don't know the problems of the other group.

---

*The speaker here, it should be noted, was displaying a *public* protest style. In private discussion, he showed no trace of this style. Interestingly enough, he himself had no intention of attempting to invade a white suburb; his home was located in the center of the Negro area, where, he said, he planned to remain.

The belief that housing is *the* race issue is not of long standing. In the past, particularly before and during World War II, jobs and employment discrimination were the major pre-occupation of both whites and Negroes working in race relations areas. But when jobs became relatively plentiful, and access to jobs became somewhat easier — although by no means free — owing to the great demand for labor, particularly in the North, attention shifted to the problem of housing. But this shift has not, by any means, proceeded uniformly among Negro civic leaders. The primacy of housing as the race issue has been advocated by the professional staff of race relations associations and agencies, but it is principally among the militant leaders that the notion has found its quickest acceptance.

Means

In keeping with the tendency to agglomerate issues and to present a maximum number of demands, the protest leader seeks inclusive solutions of a public nature. In this respect, he has a greater confidence in politico-legal solutions (the passing of a law, the enforcement of a regulation or rule) and virtually no confidence in politicians (those who might pass or enforce the law). In most of the civic issues examined, the militant leader almost invariably called for the adoption of new legislation (an FEPC law, an open occupancy ordinance, a hospital integration ordinance) as the proper and definitive "solution" to the matter.

The tension between the demand for political solutions to race issues and the antipathy toward politicians was examined in an earlier chapter. The roots of both of these phenomena are easily visible. The Negro has a long history of progress through the enforcement of law, and a reasonably firm conviction that in the last analysis, the laws of the land or the Constitution and the principles of morality from which they derive their power and effect are on his side. But a demand for legal solutions is not simply a function of past victories or accurate hopes, for the Negro community itself is divided on the efficacy of laws. Rather, the effort to "politicize" the race question seems to be another attribute of style, representing the urge for the quick, the decisive, the comprehensive, and the permanent. A new law can cut through laborious bargaining or the need to educate or induce;

it can be sweeping in its scope, and it will endure. For all these reasons, it is attractive to the protest leader.

Americans distrust politicians, but mere distrust is an inadequate description of the keen dislike Negro militants feel for Negro politicians. To the protester, machine politics as practiced in Chicago is bad even when it is benevolent; that is, it is to be opposed regardless of whatever benefits it might distribute to some people who seek aid. Personal benevolence — the distribution of individual favors — is not a legitimate goal of collective action. Collective action, such as politics, must have communal goals. According to one militant:

> The political machines are the worst feature of modern life.... They are a disgrace, even if they are benevolent to some. I've never heard of Dawson being benevolent, or Hague, or Crump, or Tammany. But even if they are, it doesn't make it right.

The tendency to seek politico-legal solutions to race problems may be merely a special case of a general disposition to favor compulsion or force in handling problems. The attitude of Negroes toward the value of compulsion can be ranged along a continuum extending from general agreement among all types and styles of leaders as to its efficacy in quelling race violence to considerably reduced agreement, generally limited to militants, as to its value in dealing with residential segregation.

One militant views compulsion in this way:

> The Negro intrudes himself into these all-white areas. He is doing it now. The only way for the Negro to enter is to forcefully intrude himself. . . . There is this open occupancy ordinance. That is another method of intruding. You have to do the intruding, with or without the law, but the law can help by making more force available to the Negro who wants it.

That protest leader was relating force generally to the merits of a legislative solution to the housing problem. Another militant finds value in an approach involving compulsion where no law at all is at stake:

> One way [to handle the housing problem] is for the Chicago Negro real estate brokers to show these people in the Chicago Real Estate Board [an all-white organization] up as fascists who keep the Negro people segregated. . . . Break into the CREB by any means. Call them names just like you call a Faubus a fascist.

The NAACP in Chicago, under militant leadership, reacted to the notorious Emmett Till case (a Mississippi lynching of a Negro boy in a particularly brutal manner) by passing a resolution calling upon the federal government to occupy Mississippi with federal troops, withdraw its electoral franchise, and suspend its Congressional representation until it had made amends.[4] The same leadership considered filing perjury suits against certain Illinois public school officials who had sworn that there was no segregation in Illinois schools.

The militant feels that he can justify his use of force because of the failure of other means in the past, as in the effort to integrate private hospitals:

> We tried the religious appeal first, since most of these hospitals have a religious connection.... That fell flat on its face, I must say. ... The appeal that is most effective is the threat of state action. They have a morbid fear of socialized medicine, and any form of state action appears to them a step toward socialized medicine.

In selecting means appropriate to their ends, protest leaders display a preference for mass action and mass participation, not solely, one suspects, because it is one of the few forms of compulsion at the disposal of Negro leaders, but also because of the inherent worth of mass action. A former voluntary association staff member had a note of excitement and high adventure in his voice when he described his plans for producing an FEPC law:

> On the FEPC bill, we really wanted to put some pressure on the Governor to get the bill through. Pressure in the form of great throngs of people to be sent from all parts of the state down to Springfield to dramatize the issue. Like they did in New York. ... We talked to people like [X] and others, and they wouldn't do it.... They said we shouldn't embarrass our friends.

No great throngs were sent, and it is doubtful whether in fact they could have been mobilized; nevertheless, the same leader felt that approach would have been the right one because he favored "more direct people's action" as opposed to "this political maneuvering."

In the attempt to integrate private hospitals, Negroes expressed clearly opposed views as to how best to proceed — whether to compel or persuade "at the top" through meetings with administrators, or to generate pressure "from below":

My technique was to reach the interns and the residents and the nurses and work upwards. Start at the bottom where the patient contacts the hospital at the lowest level. . . . The Commission on Human Relations couldn't see this at all. But the grass-roots approach won the battle in the end. . . . We got support that way you couldn't get working at the top.

This preference for mass or "grass-roots" action is reinforced by or is perhaps a reflection of the distaste of the militant for the constraints which seem to control the behavior of those who elect to deal with civic problems through access to "the top" or by working within the organization whose policies are being challenged. The militant leader values protest over access. Since protest is usually on behalf of ends which are felt to have a moral justification, this statement could be enlarged to argue that the protester values principle over position. Other ends — the retention of position and power or the maintenance of some organization — are simply morally inferior to the larger civic ends. The protest leader considers the switch of the Negro political leader from one party to another in the 1930's as conclusive evidence of an indifference to civic or racial goals:

Dawson had been a militant Republican with a group of supporters around him. They were just politicians; they had no principles. If they had had any principles, they wouldn't have been able to change parties overnight.

The proper means for Negro politicians to adopt are to assert themselves publicly and to draw attention to, rather than conceal, the differences between the goals of the party and the goals of the race:

Those people he [Dawson] has under him now are just slaves to the machine. They won't rock the boat if the word comes down that the Mayor or the Governor don't want the boat rocked. . . . Every Negro alderman should be in there fighting all the time, saying, *carthago delenda est.* He should hold people up to ridicule who won't go along, and keep agitating.

This attraction for mass action and the stress placed on the desirability of agitation, even at the expense of alienating the people one seeks to move, suggests that the militant finds agitation to be intrinsically worthwhile, apart from all considerations as to the immediate results of such effort. The costs of agitation can often be discounted by the value of the agitation itself:

[B], the union man on the board, can make some crucifying statements to those people. He's all for integration, and he tells them so.
It probably hurts him, because he alienates some people who, if he
took a more moderate line, would make some concessions. . . . But I
think we have to have his type; I'm for him. Somebody has to speak
out.

The protest leader's dedication to his own political style is not
always left to justify itself on the basis of its inherent worth, of
course. Not all militants would agree that it is always preferable
to agitate when by a display of some self-restraint concrete gains
could be registered. Further, and perhaps even more important,
agitation serves ends other than those immediately related to
public policy and civic issues. Agitation may be a means to maintain an organization (such as the NAACP) even at the expense
of access to other organizations (such as the Board of Education).
Or, agitation may serve to create a sense of awareness and morale
among followers which, over the long run, would be more important as a source of permanent strength for the protest leaders than
some concession from a city government:[5]

Even if you couldn't get things changed, there was still a reason
for doing this. Negroes have a feeling of inferiority. They will deny
it, but you take them into a cafe that doesn't cater to Negroes, and
ask them if they feel confident, if they feel as sure of themselves as they
usually do. They are not even aware of this most of the time. . . . It's
hard to make people understand this, because what it comes down to
is that you are telling them in effect there's something wrong with
them. . . . So we had to make the Negroes aroused.

The militant displays an unwillingness to perform those administrative tasks which are necessary to operate an organization.
Probably the skills of the agitator and the skills of the administrator (there are some Negro leaders in Chicago who display both
sets of skills), are not incompatible, but few men can do both
well. A former executive of a voluntary association was criticized
in a report of the parent national organization for precisely this
failing. After conceding that the association's "public standing
seems good," and that its annual meeting "drew the largest crowd
in its history" with a program which attracted "extremely favorable comment on all sides," the report went on to observe that
the executive was ineffective as an administrator. Despite his
"tremendous energy" he seemed to have "no stomach" for ad-

ministrative details. His protest activities led him into too many outside committee assignments, and he spent too little time at his own desk. Although always vocal, he was late to meetings and left early, and seemed to be unable to delegate tasks to his staff. This report on the consequences of hiring a highly vocal protest leader as executive for an organization which was not a protest association concluded ruefully that "he is anything but inconspicuous" and "he always feels called upon to enter the discussion."[6]

Other Actors

Empirically, it is often the case that the militant is at the greatest social distance from those influential whites who affect the course of events in the city most directly and surely. This is usually true either because the protester lacks status, or is considered to be "too radical," or occasionally because of a process of self-exile whereby he chooses not to approach, even up to the limits set for him, the larger community's influential persons.

One of the immediate consequences of this distance from white decision-makers for the leader's political style is that the Negro protest leader sees the white "power structure" as an undifferentiated bloc of corporate and political leaders who act largely in unison toward agreed goals out of essentially identical motives. These goals, of course, are seen to be contrary to the interests of the Negroes. A Negro protester expressed disbelief at the interviewers's suggestion that the white community leadership was thoroughly fractionalized and often in conflict with itself:

I think it's easier to represent the white community in the city. . . . There is more consensus there. You have wealth concentrated in a few organizations like the Chamber of Commerce and all. . . . It is centralized, and they know what they want. They all agree on not wanting to upset the status quo.

By contrast, the same leader sees the Negro community of which he is a member and of whose activities he is an acute observer as hopelessly divided:

On the other hand, Negroes vary all the way from the completely crushed and apathetic Negro who doesn't know what he wants to the upper-middle-class Negroes who are striving for acceptance and recognition in the community.

Often, this perceived solidarity in the white leadership of the city proceeds to the point where it ceases being merely a unity and becomes instead a conspiracy. A speaker at a Negro meeting struck a responsive chord in his audience when, as a latter-day Zola, he said, "I accuse . . . the mortgage bankers of this city of a deliberate conspiracy to crush the Negro in his efforts to buy decent housing." A Negro columnist writing in his paper referred to the "Lords of the Loop" who "have bags of money and other hirelings who know how to intimidate and threaten politicians." It was widely believed, he said, that they have "entered into a conspiracy" to "rule Chicago like the Commissars rule Moscow."[7]

The rhetoric of private discussion follows similar lines. The white business leaders "are all parties to the scheme"; Chicago has an "invisible government" which seeks ends hostile to the Negro community. The housing shortage in Chicago "is maintained by the real estate interests in order to gouge us on rents."

The militant tends to seek a racial explanation for apparently anti-Negro actions on the part of others; given two or three alternative explanations, the protester will choose that which implies the operation of racial discrimination and bias. Since the ends of the protest leader are so infrequently attained, he finds it necessary to explain the reasons for failure. In the search for such explanations, he is led frequently to a concern for the motives of the other person. When one has ordered his life along the axis of race, it becomes difficult to think of nonracial explanations for the seemingly anti-racial actions of others. Perhaps it is also true that the importance to the protester of ideas suggests to him the equal importance of beliefs and motives. The militant is uniquely a person for whom ideas strongly influence action; if it is so for him, it is likely, he believes, that ideas — other ideas, wrong ideas — influence the behavior of others.

One leader felt that whatever contribution whites might make to an organization such as the Urban League, it could not be taken at face value nor regarded as anything but a form of self-serving:

> Those people make me sick. . . . The so-called white Christians who sit in their front pew at church every Sunday and prate about their Christianity and then give us a few crumbs. . . . They're in the Urban League purely for self-interest.

In describing this world of organized opposition, the militant leader typically uses a rhetoric that pictures his relationships to it in terms of a "battle," an "attack," or a "fight." Others are "enemies," and the object is to "defeat" or overcome them. This battle rhetoric emerges in both public and private discussion. An example of the former, in which are combined many elements of the protest style, can be drawn from the following exchange between an NAACP officer and Negro members of his audience at a meeting of an NAACP neighborhood unit which was discussing the alleged refusal of a community organization to admit a Negro boy. The organization derives some support from the Community Fund, and the NAACP leader urged that the campaign be carried to it:

[*Chairman:*] We have to carry the fight to the Community Fund. . . . We have to compel the Fund to use its contribution as a lever to force the [organization] to admit this Negro, any Negro. We have to retaliate. And if the Community Fund won't go along, then the NAACP should organize a city-wide campaign against it. A principle is at stake here, even though it's only one boy. . . .

[*First member:*] The NAACP can't take on the Community Fund. . . . It's too big. What if we lose? Shouldn't we just take on the [organization] by itself?

[*Chairman:*] We can fight the Community Fund. We've got some labor unions lined up to support a fight like that.

[*Second member:*] We should attack these people if they won't help us, all right.

[*Third member:*] It's a matter of principle. We've got to force the Fund to see the light. . . .

[*Chairman:*] The NAACP, let me say, has to fight injustice against individuals. We can't put any faith in those so-called statistics which are supposed to show progress. Every person dies a little within himself in these things, and even one case invokes the principle.

[*Fourth member:*] But is an attack on the Community Fund likely to be successful? I mean, after all, it's pretty big, and it does some good, too.

[*First member:*] Yes, we might just be cutting off our noses to spite our face.

[*Fifth member:*] But let's get this straight. The principle of this thing is important. We can decide what to do about the Community Fund later.

A speaker at another NAACP public meeting admonished a Negro civil servant for his timidity when he expressed doubts of the existence of decent housing which he, as a Negro, could buy in the suburbs:

What it takes is people with *guts* to break into [that suburb]. You want to live in [that suburb]? We can fight for you, but we can't go in with bare hands. You have to apply first. Then we'll fight for you. You have to fight, like that Negro fellow did in Levittown.

One facet of the battle rhetoric is a refusal to co-operate with organizations which represent the "enemy," at least in the initial stages of an issue. The proper role of the militant is to put pressure on such organizations, not to bargain with them. These organizations can even include public agencies whose ostensible purpose, like the Chicago Commission on Human Relations, is to assist the Negro in improving his lot. A Negro militant criticized another Negro leader for suggesting that a body such as the CCHR hold a conference on residential segregation:

We wanted to plan a city-wide conference on this. [But] he didn't want this.... What he did was to send a letter to [X] urging the Commission on Human Relations to put on a conference on open occupancy. This was unprecedented. We have never called upon an agency like that, which is the creature of the city administration we were attacking, to do something we could do more effectively.

In evaluating the leadership of the Negro community in its fight against the forces which control the city, the militant, more than any other Negro leader, defines leadership in terms of the *posture* of the leader. A leader is not one who has achieved something in other areas of life, nor is he one who merely has a generally favorable civic reputation; a leader is only one who is outspokenly militant, who assumes a posture of protest and agitation, regardless of whether any tangible results accrue to such activity. When asked to name effective Negro leaders, the protester will name only those who generally share his style. Since few race ends are attained anyway, the question of accomplishment is of secondary importance in imputing reputation to a person:

[X] would be one leader. He is independent, and has never been afraid to speak his mind. ... As to what he has actually accomplished, that's hard to say.... He is aggressive and uncompromising in the stands he takes.

Another Negro militant mentioned the same person favorably because "he has been in a lot of fights." Far more protest leaders, needless to say, are favorably impressed by Adam Clayton Powell — not because they find accomplishments which other Negroes fail to detect, but because of the inherent value of his posture:

> Although he is disposed to be flamboyant, he has served a purpose.
> . . . He has communicated a flavor that has helped in a period of
> change. . . . Some say that he has not accomplished much, but his
> manner, his style have been of use.

It is important to reiterate a point made earlier: that in a realm
of civic action where ends are largely unattainable, *means* become
all-important, and form the basis — particularly for the protester,
who is most conscious of the obstacles to progress and most
vigorous in attacking them — for reputation, for distinctions, and
for evaluating programs. Politics ceases to be pragmatic, and
becomes instead rhetorical or even ideological. The rhetoric itself
has value:

> Adam Powell, well, no, he hasn't done much in terms of personal
> accomplishment. . . . But then I maintain that no Negro can accom-
> plish anything in the United States by himself. He has to make a
> long, loud, vocal protest to prick the conscience of the white liberals,
> the white civic leaders, the ministers. . . . Adam Powell has added
> to that protest.

Where posture is of overriding importance, it is not surprising
that the Negro protest leader believes that there are very few
"true" Negro leaders in the community. Other, less militant
Negroes might typically name many more leaders — usually
five or six, and sometimes as many as ten or a dozen, whom
they felt were distinguished. The protester embodies most
thoroughly the race value which both assigns great importance to
the need for leadership and laments the lack of it.[8]

The Moderate Style

The political style which we have chosen to call, for want of
a better term, "moderate" is much more in evidence in the
Chicago Negro community than the militant style. Negroes in a
position of prominence, or who are consulted about or participate
in an issue, are typically those who exhibit aspects of the moderate or "bargainer" style.

Issues and Values

The moderate perceives race and community issues as ones to
which there are no easy solutions, if indeed there are solutions

at all. He speaks much more frequently about how the other fellow will feel about a proposed solution:

I try to put myself in the place of the property owners; for example, the people in those little red bungalows along East Garfield Boulevard. A [Negro] person gets turned down when he tries to buy [a home] there. Can you prove it was because of race or religion? I don't know, I don't know. . . . And if you can't prove it, you are creating trouble. . . . Chicago would erupt over a thing like this.

Very frequently, Negroes who share this style are lawyers and they often speak of the legal difficulties in the way of a solution to a problem in race relations. One lawyer, a former NAACP officer, was dubious of a proposed open occupancy ordinance governing sales and rentals in private housing:

This is a constitutional problem. There is an equal protection problem here, and whether it is fair to classify this way I don't know. . . . The court might not see it. After all, the law is so amorphous on this point, and it looks like you are putting a premium on poverty.

The bargainer-lawyer's tendency to see complexities partly reflects the fact that most race issues revolve around questions of legislation and legal action in which lawyers are trained to see distinctions, difficulties, and the need for caution, but it also very likely reflects a general conservatism and pessimism about race progress through radical or compulsory means and a convenient rationale for not exerting oneself vigorously in behalf of such causes. Another moderate, also a lawyer and NAACP officer, could bring concern for the complexities of the problem to the point of opposition to the proposed measure — again, the open occupancy ordinance:

I was opposed to the NAACP passing a motion to support open occupancy. . . . Not because I'm against the principle of it, you understand, but for procedural reasons. . . . I think we have all that we can do without getting involved in private housing. . . . It is ridiculous to go into private housing now. . . . You've got the enforcement problems. . . . How do you know when discrimination has been practiced? . . . Then, you know, you are telling people how they can dispose of their private property. There is a very serious constitutional question there for me.

But is not only in the area of advanced integration goals where the bargainer sees problems. Even in the usually unifying case of race violence, some are hard put to find an easy solution:

In a thing like that [the Calumet Park race violence] there are a lot of problems. . . . The prosecution . . . had very little to work with . . . no witnesses. . . . Well, I sympathize with the lawyers and the judges in a case like that. I can't blame the courts . . . as some do just because there aren't more convictions.

Similarly, the moderates speak most often in terms of specific, concrete problems, rather than long-range, inclusive issues with many facets. The bargainer, unlike the militant, feels most comfortable in discussing an issue when it is limited in scope and when the solution proposed would be relatively simple and free from side effects.

The term "gradualism" has, in recent years, acquired an emotion-laden meaning among Negroes as a term — usually of opprobrium — used to denote an attitude toward integration. Without entering into the merits of that controversy, it is nonetheless true that Negro civic leaders can be distinguished by their differing attitudes toward time. Just as the moderate sees issues as complex and resists agglomerating them into omnibus problems, he also tends to place them in a longer time perspective than does the militant. A long, but illuminating, illustration of this occurs in the following remark, made by a prominent Negro concerning the progress of integration in employment. Time is seen, not only as a necessary perspective from which to view race issues, but also as an inevitable component of progress, a vaguely real agent of change:

These problems all go back in time to the 1930's or even earlier. . . . It's a continuing proposition. You can't ever really tell why it happens. It just suddenly happens when the time is right, and then time marches on. The stage has to be set. These things work slowly. . . . Job integration is the product now of ideas sown twenty years ago and earlier. . . . Back on those days, we didn't even have the words, the concepts, to describe these things. . . . FEPC wasn't even a phrase. Integration didn't mean anything, except maybe in chemistry. . . . Human relations as a field of work wasn't even heard of. . . . Slowly the stage has been set through giving these words currency and talking and visiting. . . . But I don't know why [a certain firm] changed. I wouldn't want to pinpoint it.

Not only is time an inevitable element of change, it is also a desirable one:

> Yes, creeping integration, that's right. . . . But I think it is moving along quickly enough, quickly enough. Any faster and we would outdistance the readiness of the Negro to accept integration and measure up to it.

A reason for not acting is carried in all these remarks: problems are complex, and only time can sort out the complexities and prepare the solution. Active protest is not, to the bargainer, superfluous, but it does tend to be quixotic.

The moderate, unlike the militant, rarely asserts race. Rather, he responds to race; it is a background issue. One can interview such a person for over an hour without hearing race raised as an issue by the interviewee. This is quite often a conscious process. Negroes, in their business and professional dealings with whites, will often go out of their way to avoid raising the race issue, or indeed any controversial issue that would detract from other matters or destroy a relationship. One moderate remarked:

> I'm not ashamed of my position, but I will avoid talking about it if I can. But if I do talk about it, I won't retreat on it. . . . I don't think these men would respect me if I backtracked once the subject was raised.

Sometimes a Negro will profess that he was unaware of certain forms or areas of discrimination until it was brought forcefully to his attention. A Negro labor leader from a politically conservative union described a recent experience:

> I just came back from Peoria where I was at a convention where a surprising thing happened. Three motels cancelled our reservations on us when they found out that all but one man in our delegation was colored. . . . I had no idea of this.

As the Negro militant tends to share the general political value scale of the white liberal, with race elevated to a place of pre-eminence, so the Negro moderate tends to share the political value system of the white conservative, again with race displaced to a higher — but not always the highest — point. This rather simple fact accounts for a great deal. It means that one should not assume that because a Negro feels strongly about racial injustice, he will be inevitably liberal on other issues as well. Race can be kept independent of other values, such as one's attitude toward labor unions, free enterprise, communism, and so on. This independence can and often does lead to suspicion between militants and moderates. One Negro voluntary association staff member condemned Negro-led opposition to a civic proposal because the union which provided the leadership was "Commie from top to bottom." Another Negro was alarmed by the politics of those who volunteered themselves as his allies on an issue:

> You know, on a lot of these things I kept finding myself surrounded by Communists. . . . On that bill to outlaw segregation in public housing, they were all around me. . . . Boy, I stayed out of things after that. I don't want no part of those reds.

This fear of a Communist identification is quite real on the part of many Negroes, and has been commented upon extensively in a book by Wilson Record.[9] Nor do business and professional Negroes always feel kindly toward labor unions, even those which work toward some race ends. A Negro doctor commented:

> I have never been convinced that labor organizations have a particular advantage. . . . They are an unstable foundation on which to do any constructive work. The present labor ethics seem to be to kick people around.

The moderate tends to see the world "as it is," and to accept the existing constraints on action without pressing for far-reaching or unprecedented charges. Moderates usually are recruited from business and the professions, men who are accustomed to working within the limits of the status quo. Even where — as is often the case — they have no personal stake in matters relating to race goals, they are nevertheless predisposed to move in customary ways and avoid the unusual, the disturbing, the Utopian.

In the same vein, a Negro moderate will typically have a relatively clear image of what constitutes appropriate means to civic goals and of the proper roles of voluntary associations, and he will resist sacrificing or altering those means and roles in favor of some general goal. The bargainer is not as highly committed to specific ends as is the militant, and is correspondingly less willing to alter the mission of an organization to strike out at a target of opportunity not previously agreed upon as being within its purview. To do so would mean a sacrifice in other goals — such as friendly relations with supporters:

The Urban League was taking over the functions of the NAACP and . . . it was abandoning its traditional function of an approach based on understanding and good will. It was moving in the direction of legal action and boycotting and introducing Negroes into white blocks. . . . This was irritating the people downtown, and I can understand why.

That view was stated even more forcefully by a prominent Negro lawyer who observed, after the League had been reorganized to remedy the problem spoken of above:

Frankly, I think the Urban League has just about worked itself out of a job. It's getting into things it's not qualified to handle. All that policy and stuff. . . . It should leave it to the NAACP.

The Urban League itself, in a report on its Chicago organization, felt that the maintenance of the association should take precedence over the pursuit of attractive ends, even where that pursuit had brought it some popular acclaim:

It should be repeated here that [although] these actions on the part of the Executive have had favorable and popular results, the . . . "right thing was done the wrong way."

The executive was criticized for "civil rights pursuits not in the Urban League purview" and admonished against "joint action with actionist groups" which "confuses the role of the organization in the community."

Ends

The moderate, in contrast to the militant, tends to seek welfare rather than status ends. This distinction cannot be driven too far, for *any* goal which has been firmly and publicly labelled as a "race" end is one which will elicit at least verbal agreement from almost all Negro civic leaders. But in those areas of civic life where the moderates contribute their own energies, they are far more often to be found on the side of immediate, tangible, specific, welfare-type goals. They are more likely to choose the welfare aspects of issues where such a choice is necessary, and they are the leaders responsible for those statements, cited previously, endorsing better schools, more public housing, a branch hospital, more Negro representation, and more private housing in preference to the more remote status ends. Some bargainers do seek status ends (although few protesters seek welfare ends at the expense of integration), but they tend to be exceptions. More typical is the Negro who remarked:

> As I see it, there is a *need*. . . . If I'm dying for lack of medical care, lying on a slab, I don't want to hear them arguing about integration. I want medical care now. Of course, the ideal would be integration in all hospitals, but if we can't have the ideal, I want to meet the need now.

The racial moderate will be most aroused by clear cases of abuse directed at Negroes that are the direct result of illegalities, maltreatment, or violence, and will support race efforts to counter them; he is less clearly aroused by cases that involve less apparent inequities that are the mediate result of patterns of segregation and discrimination. He will occasionally seek welfare ends even at the cost of postponing integration, provided always that such activity will not cause him to be publicly labelled as a betrayer of the race. More often, he will confine himself to expressing verbally his predisposition toward welfare ends: "There are many areas where we have to deal with the immediate problems today, now, and let integration wait until tomorrow."

In his response to a question asking him to name the single most important issue facing the Negro community, the moderate would often cite the problem of jobs and employment whereas the militant invariably cited housing and residential segregation. A moderate thinks

> . . . the job business is more important than housing. . . . If a Negro has the job and the money, then his housing will follow.

Several possible explanations for this discrepancy between the moderate and the militant in their selection of ends are possible. In part, the difference can be accounted for by a simple time lag in the spread of convictions from the racially *avant-garde* to the racially moderate. In some few cases, it might be the result of a stake in the ghetto. But in most cases this discrepancy appears to be the product of strongly-held convictions about self-improvement, about the value of progressing through one's own efforts and resources, and of a preoccupation with the economic axis along which the lives of ambitious businessmen are often oriented. Further, it may well reflect the fact that the money of some Negro leaders has enabled them to aquire in spite of restrictions what others seek through laws which will remove those restrictions. One very prominent Negro, who was a self-made man financially and who had acquired properties through clever use of his wealth stated this:

> I think that number one, you have to have more economic buying power for the Negro, in terms of jobs and education and money. . . . Jobs and education are probably first in order. I think that there's a way to move into any neighborhood if you have the money and the knowledge and a little imagination.

The Negro protest leader, or advocate of status ends, has not been able to persuade many moderates that the ability to acquire housing personally does not solve the problem created by the general pattern of a spreading all-Negro ghetto and, indeed, may aggravate it.

Where the militant was prepared to accept suffering as the price of mediate, even remote, intangible goals, the moderate will accept such deprivation only for proximate, tangible goals. Speaking of a Negro doctor's advocacy of blocking the proposed branch hospital even at the cost of some sacrifice, another Negro said:

> Yeah, but it won't be [X] that suffers. . . . He's not going to die for lack of medical care. . . . This is the same sort of question that was raised with the riders to the federal aid to edcuation bills [the Powell Amendment]. Whether to have integrated schools as a goal and no federal aid, or federal aid without integration. I don't see how you could deny that . . . some schools, even segregated, were better than no schools at all.

On the other hand, when a Negro businessman's property values in a certain residential area were to be enhanced by a renewal program that would displace many Negro families from their homes in the area, he observed:

> You can't expect to change economic laws. . . . Somebody is always going to get hurt in these things, but that can't be avoided. . . . I think the good would overbalance the objections.

When challenged by militants that Negro business is in conflict with race ends, the moderate — himself usually a businessman — will deny this. Good business is good race relations. A Negro businessman said:

I think that it's important to have demonstrations of the fact that the Negroes have the ability to succeed, and that this demonstration of success is a form of race relations.

He reflected for a moment on the problem, and after observing that he couldn't meet the demands on his time made by a voluntary association of which he was a board member, added:

This is particularly important when I realize that the [organization] only wants me because I *am* a businessman with money. If I don't succeed in that, they have no use for me. . . . If I can build a successful business, this would gain respect for Negroes, and this in turn would help the [organization]. They could point to it.

Means

The moderate, in seeking means to deal with race problems such as residential segregation, displays less confidence in the efficacy of legislative solutions than does the militant. Although few will permit themselves to be understood as opposing such legislation as an open occupancy ordinance, they are far from enthusiastic about its merits:

I would rather that Chicago people would see their folly in what they are doing. . . . A law might help, but whether it will change things, I don't know. . . . I wish people would have a change of heart.

Such a person will concede privately that he has strong reservations about legislative solutions — "I think the industry could do it more quickly and easily . . . legislation [is not] the best way to handle it" — but in public discussion the same person can be placed by more militant Negroes in a position in which he feels obliged to endorse it:

[*Militant:*] I want to ask Mr. [X] whether he wouldn't agree that we still need an open occupancy law? You said laws wouldn't do the job, but . . . we must have an open occupancy law. . . .
[*Moderate:*] I support it. But the solution requires more. I mean, the law will show the rank-and-file the problem. . . . But don't mistake me. I'll walk the picket line for an open occupancy law.
[*Militant:*] I want to make it clear that there is no one here who opposes the open occupancy law. There is no difference of opinion on that.

Although a moderate is reluctant to endorse the legislative

solutions of the Negro protest leader, he is at the same time less critical of the Negro politician than is the militant. Where the protester presses for laws and distrusts law makers, the bargainer is skeptical of laws and less critical of those who enact them. In part, the begrudging respect for Negro politicians may reflect the view that, whatever else may be said of them, the successful Negro politician has achieved position and status, and achievement is a quality that can be admired in itself. Such a Negro leader, with no connections with the political machine, was quite explicit:

> If you're looking for dirt about Dawson, you won't find it here from me. . . . Dawson represents something for the Negro people: achievement, status, the power of the ballot. . . . Attacking Dawson is one sure way of losing the Negro vote.

This leader believes the above is true even if the allegations concerning corruption in Negro politics are also true:

> Politicians are necessary. Politics takes money. The government doesn't provide that money, and there aren't many fat cats in the Negro community to provide it. So the politician, like Dawson, gets his money where he can find it. If he takes a little from policy, or from dope or from gambling, I'll be the last to criticize him. . . .

More usually, however, the bargainer will doubt or deny that Negro politics is as corrupt as either the white critics or the Negro militants claim it is:

> Well, I think Dawson has done a good job despite the things they try to lay at his feet. . . . I don't know whether it's true; I've never seen any evidence. I don't think he's guilty of all those things they say he does.

The lack of enthusiasm for legislative solutions evidenced by the bargainer does not extend to *legal* solutions — i.e., court action and litigation. On the contrary, the race moderate often sees the role of Negro protest organizations as properly confined to bringing suit on behalf of Negroes deprived of rights guaranteed by law.[10] A Negro lawyer, a former officer of the local NAACP branch, was clear on this point:

Q. What should be the tactics of the NAACP?
A. It has always focussed on legal fights, and I've always believed that the organization does that best. It should utilize the courts and

the law. . . . It has . . . and should stress the instrument of law suits.

Q.   What kind of activities did you pursue as an officer?

A.   They were, of course, all legal cases.

The alternative to a legislative solution, in an area in which laws do not exist to provide the basis for a court defense, is seen by the moderate to be a negotiated settlement in which one deals with people "at the top." Such means are most often urged in dealing with the more complex race issues, such as housing. This view, expressed by a Negro businessman, was also shared by a moderate Negro labor leader:

I happen to believe that the Mayor can't do it [deal with residential segregation] by force or by an ordinance, even if he wanted to. . . . It will have to be solved by the people who make the decisions in this town getting together and deciding that they will permit a peaceful solution to this problem.

But occasionally a moderate will see negotiation as the proper way to handle even those race issues wherein law enforcement could be used. A Negro alderman hoped such a solution might be possible for the rash of violent incidents between whites and Negroes around his ward:

I'd like to sit down with the aldermen from the adjoining wards and reason this out with them. It's possible to reach some sort of sensible conclusion. . . . Here's what I could do: I'd be willing to tell him, if he had a trouble spot, I'd tell my people not to move into that house or block for a stated period of time — say, two years. That would give him a chance to handle the situation and cool people off. But do you think I can find any white people from over there who will make such an agreement? Not on your life.

Few Negro leaders who share the bargaining style would be willing to carry negotiations this far. Equally few are those who espouse negotiation and yet see clearly its possible pitfalls, which they are consciously prepared to accept. A Negro leader spoke of the tactics he adopted to work for the entry of Negroes into certain exclusive hotels in the city in order that they might be accommodated for a scheduled conference, tactics involving the use of an influential white intermediary:

We gave a list [of hotels which discriminated] to Mr. [X] and he is going to pull it out of his pocket some evening after dinner with Mayor Daley, and go over it with him. Of course the Mayor will be very angry about the hotels; they are embarrassing the city, and hurting a convention, and the Mayor wants Chicago to be a big convention city. So he will undoubtedly put the screws on them. . . . The NAACP, of course, would have picketed the City Hall or something and made Daley mad at them instead of at the hotels.

But there was a problem with this tactic, a price to be paid. He continued:

The problem with our approach, of course, is that we may end up with some sort of compromise where one hotel lets us in for just this one time. Of course, I don't want that. I want a policy change that affects all the hotels permanently. But when you deal this way, you have to be prepared to compromise, I guess.

Mass tactics — solutions begun at the grass roots — not only are believed to be not as effective as working "at the top," but (as suggested in the comparison to the NAACP quoted above) they are thought to diminish the possibility of a solution at the top. But even where — as in many, if not most cases — success does not reward the efforts of the Negro moderate in his attempts to move the influential, mass tactics remain under a cloud simply, it would seem, owing to the personal, temperamental distaste a Negro businessman or professional holds for what he considers to be vulgar. A conservative former NAACP president said:

I have never been impressed by the virtue of mass activity. . . . Somehow, I can't express it too well, it seems to me that you will never change political problems like you tear down walls. . . . I will never believe that you can accomplish much acting like a battering ram. . . . There is something silly to me about a picket line. You get somebody picketing something, and then somebody else usually pickets the pickets. [Laughter] It's the characteristic way labor unions act. They always want to get out the masses.

The moderates place considerably more confidence in the value of persuasion and education than do the militants. To believe in the merit of persuasion, one has to believe in the amenability of others to argument:

You can work with most people on the basis of fairness. . . . You can bring fairness out of people if you talk to them sensibly. I believe that there is a lot of fairness in the American white men.

Often the problems which a Negro bargainer discusses with an influential white are not problems that involve the self-interest

gainer, sees the white businessman as similarly a bargainer, and of the white man. Thus, a Negro's conviction that it is possible to persuade whites may reflect little more than the Negro's experience with a series of congenial discussions about lesser issues — an experience that is carried forward and applied to problems, such as real estate, where a deep economic stake is involved:

> I would do my best, if I were the Mayor, to halt the migration of people to the suburbs and I would endeavor to educate people in how to live together peaceably.

Not infrequently, the Negro leader will recognize that persuasion has become a suspect word in the eyes of more militant leaders, and will attempt to justify his preference:

> I hate to say this, because it sounds so trite. . . . But it seems to me it will have to be a process of education. It's an abused term, I know, and it has been used to hamper the Negro. . . . But I think . . . that the political situation will cause some education. The exodus of the whites to the suburbs is giving the Negro more and more political power in the city. That will cause concern sooner or later.

It is only infrequently that a Negro leader will press an argument against legislation and on behalf of persuasion to the point of opposing such popular events as the NAACP efforts to place Negro children in the Little Rock high school. But one well-known Negro minister felt this was a case that illustrated the wrong approach:

> I think the NAACP was wrong the way they handled the Little Rock school case. . . . They fought those people, and made them mad when they didn't have to. You can't get things done by making people mad at you. . . . When the Supreme Court announced its decision, the NAACP started bragging about it and said that now we'd show them. . . . But all you have to do is talk to these people. If you are nice about it, . . . it could be worked out. There's no need to parade around and shout at them. You can't legislate morality, and you can't legislate integration.

A more characteristic opinion is that law, while not a solution, is a useful means to further an educational process: "I believe in laws . . . they have an educational value in themselves." But, "even if you have the law, you still have the education job to do." Further, the NAACP is something a Negro can rarely afford to attack. To those who are active in other kinds of associations employing different political styles, the NAACP remains as a useful alternative and complementary strategy: "I'm a member of the NAACP . . . but I'm not active in its program because I don't agree with how they operate, although I *do* like to see them do this thing."

A moderate is concerned with the value of access to white influentials, and is reluctant to sacrifice access to protest or policy. An NAACP officer justified his program of restraining agitation against the city administration because his militant predecessor had carried it to the point where he could no longer gain entry to the offices of responsible officials:

> The important thing is that I can talk to [the city official]. Before, with [X] in, he couldn't even talk to him. They didn't speak to each other.

Another voluntary association official described his dislike for tactics that would jeopardize his access to the Mayor:

> A lot of people yell for his scalp when a race incident occurs and they try to get us to join them in a delegation to go to Daley and protest. We don't operate that way; you'll never find us in a delegation in Daley's outer office. . . . We can pick up the phone and talk to him. We don't have to run around in delegations, shouting.

The fact that persuasion reaches only a few, while a law compels thousands, is not, to the bargainer, an argument against persuasion. It is met by citing the exemplary value of a pioneer effort, a pilot project:

> I'm sure there are many people besides myself who, if given the choice between an FEPC law and the hiring of qualified Negroes in certain good jobs at the First National Bank or at Continental, would choose the second. This is because the power of the First or Continental is infinitely greater than the combined power of Springfield and Chicago law enforcement — because the First stands high in the business leadership of this city or indeed of the world.

The protester tends to rely on negative inducements: compulsion, the threat of sanctions or deprivations, and so on. The bargainer, less convinced of or less aware of any real malevolence on the part of white influentials, typically speaks more frequently in terms of positive inducements: rewards, more attractive alternatives, or promises of gain. A Negro businessman, often a bar-

therefore a man who will respond impartially to a favorable market situation, with no real regard for social policy.

The question of styles is, of course, cross-cut by many other dimensions of civic action. One of those other dimensions — of skills — is relevant at this juncture. One kind of skill is the ability to perceive accurately the interests of the other person, and to make pragmatically correct judgments as to what will best move the other person to act in accordance with one's intentions. Few Negroes — because of social distance from the white leaders they wish to move, lack of entrepreneurial experience, or other reasons — exhibit a high degree of such a skill. When that skill appears, it seems to appear more frequently as part of the equipment of the moderate rather than the militant. Certain other kinds of skills, of course, are more frequently encountered among militants, but these are not relevant here. A Negro lawyer, with extensive white contacts, was a strikingly keen judge of the requirements for successful bargaining with whites on some issues, and this led him to search for positive inducements:

> You can't persuade the mortgage bankers to make money available to people just because they're poor Negroes without any place to live. Mortgage people are in this to make a customary return on investments, regardless of their personal feelings. . . . A good example of what can be done is Lake Meadows. . . . New York Life Insurance Company didn't go into this to make it interracial. They were forced to make it interracial by the facts of the market. . . . The New York Life board couldn't give a damn whether this is socially desirable or not; all they know is that they had to do it that way and it worked. . . . The important thing is that no matter what you do, you [have to] do it so that the natural market incentives are designed to promote or produce the social objective you want.

Among some Negro leaders who share this predisposition, this can lead to a frustrating search for such incentives — frustrating because the Negro is in no position to provide them himself or out of the resources he controls. But some continue, nevertheless, to speculate on how the housing market, for example, could be altered to induce white real estate, mortgage finance, and building firms to provide interracial or at least Negro housing on a par with that offered white buyers. One said:

> I would try to talk very quietly with the mortgage bankers and the various . . . groups in Chicago. . . . I would say, "Here is a good

housing market of first-class risks. Why pass it up . . .?" I would try to . . . reduce some of the risks. . . . The builder wants an incentive in the form of some means whereby he can get his money out of the project as soon as possible. . . . Another one [is] land. . . . What can we give a community like Maywood to get it to take an interracial community in its neighborhood? It's hard. . . . You have to give the whites an opportunity to renew [their mortgages and insurance] to reduce their tendency to run away.

In any case, the moderate, whatever means are selected, values results over effort. To the extent that the constraints of the race values make it possible, he is somewhat more prepared to yield symbolic ground in hopes of making tangible gains — i.e., to lose the ideological conflict (e.g., the vindication of one's position, the assertion of race values, and the sustaining of morale) in favor of some other goals (continued access, a compromise settlement, etc.) A conservative NAACP officer said:

We had to make a choice between being propaganda-centered or being, let us say, solution-centered. . . . Our goal was to obtain a broader base of support by more moderate action. . . . In the sense that we are no longer propaganda-centered, we are conservative . . . but . . . I would suggest the term solution-centered instead to describe our approach. . . . You notice, and I admit, that we are frequently not in the vanguard. It takes time . . . but slowly we are getting things done.

Both desire broad support, but the militant is less willing to purchase it at the cost of a decrease in militancy. This conflict is, at its core, a dispute over how best to maintain an organization. Protest is not inherently valuable to the bargainer; indeed, he may feel it is positively harmful. A Negro politician speaks of his views on the proper way to seek legislation to reduce hospital discrimination:

[A protest leader] wanted to speak for it. I told them to keep him out. . . . I didn't want any rabble rousing in there. There were no public hearings, which is what some of these people wanted. But they weren't necessary. . . . You can see what would have happened with public hearings. It would have caused a lot of excitement and attracted more opposition than we got.

Where the militant meets obstacles with a call for militant action, the bargainer meets it with a call for delay and, very often, studies, reports, and more facts. The desire for "facts" reflects not merely a desire for certainty or precision, but more likely a wish to avoid opposition and to reduce conflict. The display of facts is a means of persuasion to which no one can reasonably object:

> You want to get the thinking of people who have made a study of this problem. . . . Find out what solutions they have to offer. . . . We don't want to impose our views on anyone. Then develop a solid-front program, . . . based on hard facts.

Another Negro leader is critical of a voluntary association executive for overly-aggressive behavior:

> You should gather the facts first and analyze them carefully to be sure of what you are talking about, and then present them in such a way that you don't antagonize people. . . . I object to [X] putting a map under my nose and saying, "Now, there are seven Negro families living here, and no Negro families living over here; that means they discriminate over here against Negroes" — without ever telling me whether or not Negroes tried to move in over here, whether they could afford to, and what the economics of the situation were, whether they were good credit risks.

Other Actors

The moderate leader will accept a racial explanation for white behavior on civic issues only after other possibilities have been at least considered. More than the militant, the bargainer sees causes other than racial bias for what appears to be anti-Negro action — causes such as the impersonal market or the behavior of Negroes. This tendency is brought out, perhaps in exaggerated form, in an interview with one Negro lawyer in a discussion of public housing and segregation. Non-racial (or non-bias) explanations were repeatedly offered and defended against those who asserted bias as the cause of the behavior in question.

> *Q.* Why has public housing become largely "Negro housing"?
> *A.* It is a fact that whites don't want to live in Negro areas, and it's not all for racial reasons, either.
> *Q.* What other reasons would there be?
> *A.* If you are a Presbyterian or a Unitarian, and if you have always sent your children to white schools, you would naturally prefer to go to a church and send your children to school in an all-white area. That is understandable.
> Now, a lot of people don't want the expansion of public housing as a matter of basic philosophy. . . . They fear government ownership and control. . . . I can see their position.

Q. How do you feel about a South Side branch of the County Hospital . . .?

A. I was opposed to the . . . branch . . . then and I am now because I have never been sold on socialized medicine. I am afraid of it. . . . I think that it is one method of genocide, or at least that's a possibility if it gets in the wrong hands. . . .

Q. What about . . . the charge that it is a question of racial discrimination?

A. Many Negro doctors are not interested in qualifying for appointment to hospital staffs. Now, I won't say there is no discrimination. . . . But I do say that a lot of Negro doctors are not qualified, either. Now, I know I might get my throat cut for saying that.

The ability to be satisfied with non-racial explanations of white behavior is typically accompanied by a rhetoric which describes the larger community, not in terms of a battle or an attack, but in terms of dealings, relationships, negotiations. Other people are not "adversaries," but "counterparts," and they are counterparts who work under constraints. For example, the Mayor is seen as follows:

We'd be worse off without Daley. He runs the show now, but he couldn't do it . . . without informal power. . . . And he has to keep the power with votes from the Back of the Yards and elsewhere. . . . So he has to work the middle of the road. . . . We need his power . . . so we have to be satisfied with what we can get.

The bargainer professes to see the other fellow's point of view, and understand his difficulties, even when the other fellow acts in opposition to the Negro leader's ends. An open occupancy ordinance might be ill-timed, for

there is a lot of racial tension here. . . . With this tension, even aldermen who are fairly liberal-minded would have to vote against it. They couldn't vote for it with the people aroused and excited. And you can't blame them for it, either. Why should they light the fuse in their own wards?

Negro leaders are nominated much more frequently by moderates than by militants. This is probably a function of both a differing conception of leadership and the bargainers' desire not to alienate associates. The bargainer tends to define a leader in terms of accomplishment, often non-racial (for example, business success), rather than in terms of militancy. A "good" Negro leader is often a distinguished Negro who reflects credit on the

race. When asked who were the most effective Negro leaders in
Chicago, a young Negro businessman, personally very active civically, said:

> [X] . . . he has a business that's good; he's trying to build his
> publishing company; and has become a pretty big man. . . . [Y] has
> tried to think of the total market. . . . He wants to build a general
> interest newspaper, not one that's restricted to Negroes alone.

More often, however, some community service is required for
one who is economically successful to be considered a leader, but
it may be of an innocuous nature:

> Number one, I guess, would have to be [X]. He's done the most
> to . . . give us unselfish leadership. . . . One example comes to mind.
> When Morris was elevated to the national board of the YMCA, [X]
> sent a letter around to 75 or 80 of us at his own expense and called
> us all to a dinner for Morris.

Moderates ascribe the divisions among Negro leaders to differences over means but not to differences over goals. More commonly than others, the bargaining-style leader sees general
agreement on ends:

> There are always Negro radicals, like there are radicals in every
> group. But that's because Negroes don't always agree on *how* to get
> things, although they almost all agree on *what* to get.

The importance attached to achievement by the moderate in
evaluating men carries over into a more general approval of the
worth of self-improvement and individual effort in areas where a
protest leader might call for collective action. A rather systematic
illustration of this is a survey made in 1958 of the seventeen
Chicago Negro doctors who had successfully gained appointments
to white private hospitals. When asked what factors were responsible for their success, the two most frequent answers given were
that they had worked "as an individual" to "develop personal
contacts with key men on hospital staffs" and had become "well
qualified." Only a few mentioned group efforts to apply pressure
on the hospital or suggested that such group efforts should be
supported. In a private interview, one such Negro doctor discounted the value of Negro organizations which sought to induce
hospitals to make appointments:

I have felt that if you will find well-trained, qualified individuals and if they are adamant and work at it themselves, that they can get into a hospital on a staff. . . . It is a competitive situation, and you might as well recognize it.

An even stronger statement strikes a Darwinian note:

I have always believed that only the fittest can survive. If you're not fit, you die. . . . A man has to fight his way into this world if he is going to be a man. . . . The conditions of the world demand that a man be fit or die, that's all.

This concern for self-reliance seems to be connected with the frequent remarks made by moderates regarding the shortcomings of other Negroes. The criticisms they have of Negro behavior run the gamut of comments on habits, criminal tendencies, and attitudes. Other Negro leaders may see such shortcomings also, but they infrequently volunteer to talk about them and never phrase them in such strong terms as one occasionally hears from bargainers:

You can't expect to bring a pig into your house, no matter how much you say you like him, and not get your floor dirty. You've got to clean up these people. It's not a one-way street. Negroes complain about Hyde Park-Kenwood, but at least those people out there are doing something about their own neighborhood. But out at Robbins, and Phoenix, and Chicago Heights, you never hear those Negroes say, "Let's clean this up. . . ." They just go on living like pigs.

To more Negro leaders than one would suspect, judging only from their public statements, race relations is a "Negro problem" as well as a "white problem." For instance:

Negroes right now are a real threat in housing. They can cause a neighborhood to go down. Look at Hyde Park; it went down when Negroes moved in. . . . People convert to multifamily units and kitchenettes, and the behavior patterns of the Negroes that move in are bad. . . . So with things like this, you can't scream for open occupancy.

Similar remarks are encountered concerning Negro crime ("Some of these niggers come up here, six months away from a Mississippi farm, they're like an animal, a wild beast loose in the city"), tastes ("These people buy what they want and beg what they need"), attitudes ("A lot of good would happen if they would . . . take the chips off their shoulders"), and community consciousness ("Too many persons of our race appear to be too much concerned about their own careers and too little about the masses").

Patterns in Style

Differences in style can often be explained in terms of the willingness or unwillingness to act. The militant style is conducive to action. The simplification of issues, a firm commitment to ends, an acceptance of deprivation, the value placed on effort, the battle rhetoric — all assume a predisposition to act. The moderate style, conversely, provides reasons for not acting — the viewing of issue complexity, a concern over the propriety of means, the value of persuasion, and the desire to maintain access and good relations. The desire or lack of desire to act may be a product of different goals, such as a wish to gain stature in the Negro community as against a wish to gain stature in the white community, or a wish to advance racial as opposed to personal interests.

The most general source of differences in political style springs from the differing organizational positions of leaders and the differing sets of constraints those organizations enforce upon the leaders. Most differences in style have situational explanations. An official of the Urban League, which is supported in part by white businessmen, is under a set of constraints different from those facing the executive of the NAACP. A self-employed Negro businessman whose resources or market are not dependent upon white favor has a set of opportunities different from those of a Negro bureaucrat employed by the city administration. One kind of civic leader must retain access to white leaders, and can only do so through moderation. Another leader must maintain a Negro mass organization, and uses race appeals conservatively; a rival leader may challenge him by attracting the support of the more militant Negroes.

Each leader must maintain the loyalty of his supporters by different kinds of appeals, and hence through different political styles. This can be seen most clearly when two leaders compete for power within a single organization. In competition with one another, the differences between the two leaders' styles will be reduced *if each feels he must gain support from among the ranks of the other's followers.* In recent NAACP elections, however, neither side has felt such proselyting was necessary. Each was convinced that his followers were in the majority *if they could be mobilized.* Thus, radically different kinds of civic leadership styles co-exist in the Chicago NAACP because each leader is confident he has a majority. To mobilize that majority, each leader exhibits (and even exaggerates) his political style without making concessions to the alternative. In one sense, a "two-party system" exists within the NAACP, but it is a two-party system which does not produce the moderation and "center-seeking" tendencies supposedly characteristic of most such systems. In part, this is due to the nature of the ends which the organization hopes to serve, but in great part it reflects the polarization of the electorate. Each leader remains convinced that he can win if only he can mobilize all his followers. He is able to believe in his ultimate majority because of the low level of participation of the membership in the NAACP. When such a small percentage of the membership (5 to 10 per cent) appears at annual elections, neither leader feels the need to appeal to uncommitted members or followers of the opponent. Each simply tries to increase his share of the turn-out.

But organizational considerations of this kind cannot account for all differences in political style. The impact of the situation is not always uniform or predictable. There are strong differences in style among people in comparable situations, differences which must be ascribed — for lack of more complete knowledge — simply to temperament. The temperamental difference between Negro leaders in comparable situations can perhaps be most exactly stated by observing that whereas the temperamentally militant leader will feel the constraints of the situation as *constraints* and be restless under them, the temperamentally moderate leader will accept such constraints as in some sense "natural" and not test them by action. There are two Chicago Negro leaders, both employed by the Federal government and both serving therefore under the Hatch Act limiting political and community action. One described his attitude toward this situation as follows:

The only deterrent [to expressing my views more vigorously] is the fact that I work for the Federal government. My boss reminds me that people won't distinguish between what I say . . . and what I say as a representative of the Federal government. . . . But it is hard to keep quiet.

The other Negro does not press, even verbally, against such constraints:

> I wouldn't engage in anything with a political atmosphere. I can't, under the law. . . . But I'll go farther than that. I wouldn't get too far out there in a protest organization like the NAACP. . . . I support it, but I can't get too vigorous about it. . . . We can get more people to help us than we could . . . if we had a chip on our shoulder.

The importance of these differences in style can best be seen in those cases where Negroes of a certain temperament are placed in organizational roles which are defined in a way that makes the roles partially incompatible with the character of the occupant. Negro businessmen, for example, usually favor a moderate style. Office in the NAACP, on the other hand, is typically defined by attentive Negroes, and even more by whites, as a militant role. The tension between person and position is frequently evident. One businessman-NAACP officer desired to do something about residential segregation. He conceived the proper approach to be essentially a moderate one, in this case calling a conference under NAACP auspices of representatives from all-white villages and suburbs around the city to discuss peaceful means of facilitating the entry of Negroes into these areas. He quickly found himself caught between conflicting groups and encumbered by attitudes toward his role which he did not share. The whites saw the NAACP as a radical protest group, possibly interested in "block-busting." They were either reluctant, or refused, to have anything to do with a conference on such a delicate matter under the aegis of an organization which they defined as the "enemy." That the Negro leader was himself anything but a radical was either overlooked by or unimportant to the whites. On the other hand, certain Negro activists were dismayed that the NAACP leader should "pussy-foot" on an important race issue by conferring with the "enemy" — in this case, the white suburbanites. The NAACP leader was expected to lead an "attack" rather than to attempt to bargain.

Differences in political style seem to be emerging more clearly in the Chicago Negro community as the issues with which the leadership must deal are becoming less unifying and more divisive because of their differential impact on the community and their dissimilar effect on various Negro leaders themselves. Stylistic differences are at most subtle when Negroes are responding to a case of physical violence perpetrated by whites against Negroes; such differences, on the other hand, emerge much more clearly when the issue is the question of how best to end residential segregation or hospital discrimination. The latter, more divisive kind of issue, is, as has been stated in an earlier chapter, more and more becoming the dominant kind in Chicago race relations and, indeed, in most of the North. These issues tend to compel choices of political style in a way that the older, less complex issues did not. Still, it must be reiterated that style is not an either-or affair; Negro leadership can only be categorically divided into moderates and militants for the sake of analysis. Many Negro leaders serve in capacities where their work is largely "issue free" and where choices are unnecessary; others partake of both styles, depending on the situation, the ends sought, and whether they are speaking and acting in a public or private context.

In Chicago, far more persons tend to be moderates than tend to be militants. This seems natural enough, considering the relative absence of rewards for militant civic action. But the influence of the militants and the protest organizations on the character of civic action among Negroes is greater than their numbers would indicate. By asserting, and in some sense embodying, race values, the protester can and does set the tone of public discussion of race issues. Issues, as others have noted,[11] have a natural history which progresses from weak commitments and unclear divisions between sides, to strong commitments and sharp divisions between factions. Linking a given issue or end to a race value tends to accelerate the process of factional alignment, and although it may not unify the Negro leadership or induce it to vigorous action, it can and does narrow the permissible latitude of public discussion about the issue. Such a tendency can be observed in the development of open occupancy as a race position, rather than as merely one of many alternative ways for dealing with the housing problem for Negroes. A similar pattern can be detected in the Negro attitude toward urban renewal and redevelopment, which began with a relative lack of ideological race protest at the time

of the Lake Meadows clearance project, rose to the level of
sporadic outbursts by the time the Hyde Park-Kenwood project
was proposed, and swelled to a relatively high pitch of intensity
as Hyde Park-Kenwood neared adoption by the city. As protest
rose, the ability of other Negroes to admit approval of the plan
declined, and by the end of the process, most (but not all) racial
differences had been driven underground, although the differences
themselves persisted.

Chapter X

Types of Negro Civic Leaders

NOT only do Negro leaders have different political styles; they also do different things. Negro civic leaders, like leaders of any kind, perform a variety of functions.[1] In order to indicate the diversity that lies concealed in the single label, "leader," it is useful to discuss three or four of the most characteristic functions of leadership in the Chicago Negro community and to describe the kinds of men who perform these functions. These leadership "types" are not purely formal or analytical categories, but in fact represent actual empirical clusters of men, all of whom are regarded by one another as "leaders" and all of whom participate in work of civic organizations and the activity involved in the raising and settling of community issues.

These leaders, of course, do not always wear one hat, invariably labeled as a certain "type." But to a marked degree, they are consistent in the things they do — the kinds of organizations they support and lead, the kinds of issues which attract their interest, and the kinds of contributions they make (or fail to make).*

In this chapter, only *volunteer* Negro civic leaders will be discussed. Politicians, bureaucrats, and paid voluntary association staff members are not discussed, for their functions in civic life are largely the product of their formal position. The lay leader,

---

*The term "role" is deliberately avoided here. The variety of meanings which attach to it poses a problem I do not intend to unravel. Many Negro leaders refer to one another in terms which suggest strongly that the "types" are more or less clearly recognized among them, and are not simply logical constructs.

although his leadership may be conditioned by his formal position, has several choices open to him: to contribute or not to contribute, to select one organization or issue over another, to take the initiative or merely to respond. We are interested here in the patterns that emerge from these choices.

Three kinds of Negro leaders will be discussed here — the prestige leader, the token leader, and the organizer — and some variants will be noted.

The Prestige Leader

Eleven or twelve prominent Negroes are frequently cited by other Negroes as leaders with particularly high prestige. More important than this evaluation is the fact that they do comparable things and have comparable attributes in the civic life of the community. They invariably represent high — for the Negro community — personal achievement, achievement that usually flows from success in business or professional life. At least seven are in business, and five of these are businesses which they themselves organized and built. Four are professional men — doctors, lawyers, and ministers. In a real sense, most of them are self-made men. Regardless of what advantages they may have started with, and they usually started with little, they have attained a great deal. Almost all of them are financially comfortable by any standards, athough not really wealthy by white standards. Above this, they have respectability. Their respectability is not, however, of the same character as the stature of the social leader. Leadership in society and leadership in civic affairs are not identical, although they overlap to some extent. When asked to name Negro leaders, they consistently name one another and few other people. But at the same time, other kinds of leaders often name them, although sometimes with a slightly disparaging remark to the effect that they are "big men" who "do little."

In their civic activities, prestige leaders' most common characteristic is that they tend to avoid controversy. In the past, they may have been active on the boards of the NAACP or the Urban League, but now they have risen above that: junior members of their organizations do the work in these associations, and prestige leaders confine their efforts largely to noncontroversial civic enterprises, such as settlement houses, the Red Cross or Community

Fund, the United Negro College Fund, the Joint Negro Appeal, or the Board of Trustees of Roosevelt University. In cases in which they continue to be associated with race relations work, it is characteristically at the national, rather than the local, level. Of course, they still make monetary contributions to local race organizations, but their names are conspicuously lent most often to the national boards of the NAACP, the Urban League, church groups, or welfare associations. The prestige leader usually stays out of active politics, although there are interesting exceptions — consisting principally of some ministers who are closely identified with one party or another and who sometimes speak on its behalf.

Such leaders' prestige is attested to by the eagerness and persistence with which their names are sought for display on the letterheads of organizations seeking stature in the community. Often, these organizations get the letterhead name only; this causes a certain amount of disparagement by those who feel these leaders should be more active.

Prestige leaders are cited most often by other Negro leaders as having the "best" or the most "extensive" contacts with influential white leaders. To some extent this is true; these Negroes have been in the Association of Commerce and Industry the longest, and two of them are the first Negroes to sit on its board of directors. White political leaders often solicit their advice or backing for civic undertakings. The prestige leader is consulted on an ad hoc basis, or because of his membership in well-regarded welfare or professional associations which he shares with influential whites.

Furthermore, these white contacts are often irrelevant to race or civic issues — they are contacts made in noncontroversial areas of business or welfare work. They will share membership on the board of the United Negro College Fund, on the Board of Trustees of Roosevelt University, or in the Association of Commerce and Industry. Only infrequently are such contacts a channel through which a specific race issue is raised, negotiated, or settled.

The prestige leader, to the extent that he participates in civic issues, exhibits almost without exception the moderate style. He is publicly immune, because of his non-involvement and his prestige, from an "Uncle Tom" charge. In discussing race issues, the prestige leader will display a strong sense of general race values, but will often be vague on specific ends and means. This reflects, not necessarily a disinterest in the matter, but a lack of knowledge resulting from an absence of issue involvement and voluntary association participation.

Truman K. Gibson, Sr., the chairman of the board of the Supreme Liberty Life Insurance Co., is a frequently-named prestige leader. He is *"the* grand old man" among Chicago Negroes, according to a militant race leader, but "he's not really a leader per se . . .; he's sort of a tribal leader." A graduate of Harvard University, Gibson was the founder of the Supreme Life and Casualty Company of Columbus, Ohio, in 1921. In 1929 it merged with two other Negro insurance companies and moved its headquarters to Chicago. Gibson served as chairman of the board and (after 1943) as president until 1955 when, at the age of 73, he relinquished the presidency to a somewhat younger man. The company has been, for several years, a principal source of Negro civic leadership, including among its officers a past president of the Urban League, a president of the local NAACP, and a number of members of various public agencies in the city and state governments.

Gibson's name is rarely mentioned in connection with any civic issue, but it is mentioned innumerable times in connection with public-spirited endeavors involving a minimum of controversy. Active on behalf of war bond drives, fund-raising campaigns for Roosevelt University, the United Negro College Fund, and the Citizens of Greater Chicago, Gibson has touched almost all phases of the welfare and educational associations in the community. In race organizations, however, Gibson has been a supporter but not an active participant. Although on the Urban League board for a period, he has never held office in the NAACP. "I have never had any disposition to disfavor the names of these groups," he remarks, "but I have never felt that I should be an active leader." The firm contributes regularly to such organizations, but in amount, it tends to favor the YMCA and the Negro hospital over the NAACP. Although some of his associates have been politically active in a highly partisan fashion, Gibson lists himself as an "independent" in politics and never participates personally:

I have never felt any personal urge to go into politics. . . . I like to be able to give my best efforts to the insurance business. . . . And also, I have always wanted to cultivate all groups of people, Democrats, Republicans, all of them. . . . I have lots of friends in all sections, and I would hate to give any of them up.

His firm makes financial contributions to political candidates: "most all of us give something to both the Democrats and the Republicans. . . . We have many friends who are policy holders, in both parties, and we like to spread our contributions around."

Gibson's firm encourages its officers to participate in civic affairs, and such participation, it is believed, creates a favorable public image of the company:

This sort of thing gets you a favorable reaction in the city; your officers are noticed more. It gives us a good name. People who get interested in us are all possible policy holders. . . . It's not all self-interest at all, though. We are entitled, I think, to some of the friends we have.

Gibson was honored at a testimonial banquet for his contribution to the Joint Negro Appeal, an association which raises funds for Negro welfare organizations. A plaque was presented, and the Mayor spoke in glowing terms of his friend, "Truman." Gibson can number among his acquaintances some important officers of downtown banks, a powerful civic leader who is head of a title insurance company, the president of a large retail chain, and a wealthy member of the McCormick family.

Among Negro businessmen and prestigious civic leaders, Truman Gibson is highly regarded. He helps other Negro businesses as well as civic causes. He organizes testimonial dinners for other Negroes who have attained some honor or succeeded in some enterprise.

What function does a prestige leader such as Gibson serve in the race organizations and race issues? His prestige is viewed as something that is transferable, and hence his name can be used to legitimize or lend respectability to civic endeavors. "If Gibson's name is attached to the list," another Negro leader remarked, "it is respected and accepted." He also represents a source of money. "He has business acumen. You can always go to him for help, and he can get money and things." Not even the most militant Negro protest leader can despise a man with this attribute.

As one said, "he is always able to galvanize the financial boys into action . . . [and] he is in good with the boys downtown." To many protest leaders, however, Gibson is "just a businessman." Conservative Negro leaders, however, approve of him for just this reason. Not only does he have money and prestige, but Gibson is liked for his style: "I believe that a man like T. K. Gibson is more effective . . . negotiating with important people from a position of respect and achievement . . . [than] the agitator."

Other Negroes who can be loosely grouped together under the rubric of "prestige leader" share most of the attributes discussed above, but some differ in interesting ways. Not all Negroes possess a background so generally free of controversy. One is a former politician, a vigorous political militant on race issues who suffered ultimate defeat at the hands of the Negro political machine. But time has intervened to dull to some extent the edge of contention that once surrounded his name, and his field of activity has shifted to national, rather than local, organizations in the area of race relations. The fact that he is no longer associated with local issues, and that he has been successful in his businesses, has given him a certain status, but the memory of controversy lingers on: he "has the prestige and status, but he's too controversial — he's been in politics, and people haven't forgotten that." Being "controversial" reduces the number of times he is nominated as an important leader by other prestige leaders, and increases the number of times he is nominated by protest-style leaders. For the militant, it is to his credit that "he has been in a lot of fights . . . [he] is the local Thurgood Marshall."

Two prestige leaders wield an additional form of influence — control of important sources of publicity. "People cater to him," said one Negro leader of a head of a publishing house, "in hopes of either getting a good write-up or in order to avoid getting a bad one." The publisher himself admitted that this was "quite common," although he denied that such catering was successful.

Two Negro prestige leaders retain their prestige, although not without some grumbling, even though they have largely disengaged themselves from local affairs and given their resources to voluntary work both in other parts of the country and among other ethnic groups. Although some disparage the direction their efforts take, few can deny the evident recognition the larger community has bestowed upon them.

The Token Leader

The "token leader" is the Negro selected, most often by whites, to "represent" the Negro community in civic activities and on public agencies where it is felt such representation is required. He lacks the status of the prestige leader, and the scope of his contacts with the white community tends to be narrower and more focussed. To the white civic leader, he is a man chosen because a Negro is "needed" in order to legitimate whatever decisions are to be made by the agency.

Although prominent Negroes are often consulted about such choices, the advice given may or may not be followed. Those choices made by the Mayor, the former "reform" Mayor or the present "organization" Mayor, tend to reflect the requirements or wishes of the white civic leaders of the city who have an interest in the agency.

Such a Negro does not represent the more outspoken elements in the Negro community, nor is he a spokesman for those Negro groups which are contending with the agency on some specific issue. The organizations which wish to influence the public agency do not choose to utilize the Negro member as a channel for such influence; to them, he has the "agency viewpoint." Often the Negro member is reviled by Negro leaders, particularly militant leaders, for his failure to "speak up" on behalf of what they take to be Negro interests. Such criticism is only very rarely a matter for public discussion. The "Uncle Tom" label is often used, but only in private discussion or at least all-Negro discussion. This produces the interesting phenomenon of strong, often shrill public criticism by Negroes of the decisions of such bodies as the Board of Education, the Land Clearance Commission, the Community Conservation Board, or the Civil Service Commission but an absence of public criticism of the Negro members who often shared in those decisions. For example, the Hyde Park-Kenwood urban renewal plan was bitterly attacked in the Negro press. This plan was under the legal control of the Community Conservation Board, but the Negro member of that board, Robert Landrum, was never publicly mentioned, let alone criticized even though he had explicitly endorsed the plan in a public statement before a committee of the City Council.[2] The Board of Education was excoriated by the Negro press for what it regarded as a weak statement on human relations, but no mention was made of the Negro member of the board committee which drafted the statement.[3] The failure of the city administration to promote more Negroes in the fire and police departments to high-ranking positions has been a constant theme of Negro public attack, but the Negro member of the Civil Service Commission which exercises some influence over such promotions is seldom mentioned.[4] But in private discussion, Negro militants refer to token leaders with such phrases as "a caricature of an Uncle Tom," an "Uncle Tom with an advanced degree," "they look out for themselves," "he is hated by the Negro people," "hopeless," and "he doesn't know anything."

Such *private* criticism of token leaders and even of some prestige leaders is not uncommon. Occasionally it becomes formally organized. A club which is composed of many of the Negro business and professional men in Chicago has, from time to time, been the scene of bitter criticism of certain Negro leaders who, it was felt, had defaulted in their obligations to the race and the community. On one occasion, a leader was hailed before it and asked to explain his actions in a matter that was then pending before the city government.

These criticisms must be understood in the light of the possibility that, in terms of some reasonable conception of the public interest, the decision of an agency to which its Negro member adheres may be the proper one, and his Negro critics may be engaged in self-pleading or parochial protest. Public silence on the personal qualifications of these Negro members of public agencies probably can be most simply explained in terms of a desire to maintain the image of racial unity, to which the Negro press contributes by defending, rather than controlling, the Negro community. In addition, however, some cases of personal and political influence sometimes prevent press criticism. One Negro member of a public agency was placed there at the urging of an important official on a Negro newspaper because of a long-standing personal friendship. Other, comparable relationships undoubtedly exist, and, where no tangible stake in involved in an issue that would dictate the actions of a Negro press critic, these intangible, personal considerations often are controlling.

Rarely is the token leader assertive on race issues in his capacity as a member of the public agency, and rarely does he take a position in opposition to the public agency on some matter of presumed concern to the race. The token leader justifies his actions by arguing that he was selected for his position not so much because of his race but because of his qualifications, that the problems with which it deals are too complex to be judged solely on the basis of racial factors, and that a wider perspective than race is necessary to discharge one's duties in a manner that will contribute to the public interest. One such Negro, who had been criticized by some Negro militants for what they felt to be a lack of assertiveness, described his position in these terms:

> I haven't felt a loss of stature in the community. I get more requests for speaking engagements than I can handle. . . . I have gained acceptance on LaSalle Street and on State Street, but I never raise the race issue. I never raise race except in situations like this, talking to you. I am firmly convinced that if we try to do what is best for the people, *all* of the people, of Chicago, then we will do the right thing.

These Negro representatives are typically drawn from the ranks of professional and business people — lawyers, businessmen, bureaucrats, and an occasional labor leader from a conservative union. Only very infrequently are they nominated as leaders by either Negro prestige leaders or protest leaders. They lack the economic and civic stature for nomination by the former, and the militancy for nomination by the latter. With only rare exceptions, the token leaders are only slightly active in race organizations. They are usually not connected with either the NAACP or the Urban League, although they may be (and, indeed, often are) members of interracial business organizations (such as the Association of Commerce and Industry or the Bar Association), welfare and benevolent organizations, or civic improvement organizations such as the Citizens of Greater Chicago. None of the ten persons considered here to be token leaders was either an officer or board member of the NAACP or the Urban League at the time he was interviewed, although several had held some position in one or both of these organizations in the past. Indeed, given the differences which separate these associations from the public agencies whose decisions these associations attack or protest, it would be most hazardous — probably impossible — for a Negro to serve in both capacities.

The token leader invariably has a moderate political style, and undoubtedly this is one of the reasons for his selection for his position. Some are selected because they have had business, professional, or civic contacts with influential whites, and they are known by these whites to be "reasonable." Occasionally, although not often, the leader is urged upon the city by the Negro political organization and owes his appointment to its influence with the Mayor. In several cases, the appointee owes his selection in part to the recommendation of his Negro predecessor on the agency, and in one case, two successive members were brothers. Sometimes, prestigious Negroes in prominent positions in their community — such as publishers — are consulted about an acceptable appointee, but such recommendations as they might choose to make are not always followed.

Sydney P. Brown, a successful Negro lawyer, is one of the best-known of the Negroes who have served for a long period of time as representatives of the Negro community on a public body, and of all the leaders considered under this label, he has perhaps the greatest prestige. A graduate of Howard University and the Northwestern University law school, Brown established a legal practice as the general counsel for a Negro insurance company located in Chicago and later became a director and general counsel for a Negro savings and loan association. A life-long Republican, he held a political position as early as 1927 when, under a Republican administration, he was appointed an assistant state's attorney for Cook County. His appointments to important public agencies, however, were all made by Democratic mayors of the city of Chicago. He served during the war as a member of the Selective Service Board, and in 1946 Mayor Kelly appointed him to the Chicago Board of Education. He was reappointed by the "reform" Democratic Mayor, Martin Kennelly, and again by the "organization" Democratic Mayor, Richard Daley.

His first appointment to the school board came after he had made himself known among white civic leaders through his work on the Metropolitan Planning and Housing Council, a civic group interested in problems of real estate and housing improvements, and in the Boy Scout movement. In searching for an appropriate Negro member of the Board, a prominent Negro municipal official was asked for a recommendation, and nominated Brown, a fellow Republican. Brown became a member of the Board of Education and in time he was elected its vice-president.

His nearly twelve years of service on the Board of Education earned for him a certain renown, and endowed his name with some prestige. Upon his retirement for reasons of health, the Mayor and City Council presented him with a medal, and complimentary editorials were written in both the white and Negro press. But during his service there, he was often the subject of considerable controversy. Until his appointment to the Board, Brown was active in a number of Negro and interracial civic organizations — the Boy Scouts, a community house, the YMCA, the Urban League, the NAACP, and other organizations. But shortly after appointment to the Board, he resigned from most of these associations, pleading a lack of time. The controversies arose over such issues as upon what site, in the Negro area, to build a new vocational school; the question of hiring more Negro teachers in white school areas; the issue of redistricting schools to achieve integration, and related matters. On each of these issues, the Negro proponents — usually voluntary associations, but sometimes politicians or civic leaders — were convinced that Brown could be counted on to uphold the "Board viewpoint" rather than what they defined as the interests of the race. "Sydney Brown never did much," said one NAACP official. "He would always say, 'well, bring me the facts about an actual case [of race discrimination], and I'll see what I can do.' I think he just went along with them." Disagreement on matters of this kind often leads militant Negroes to impute bad faith or improper motives to the token leader, usually without justification. Militants reveal a desire to find some explanatory motive, other than a simple disagreement over ends, to account for someone's taking a position contrary to their demands. A common explanation was in terms of social and prestige rewards — the privilege of access and acceptance:

Sydney Brown is a smart man, and he wasn't inactive. But he never helped us. I think he succumbed to the pressures that white people put on Negroes in that kind of job. . . . Syd Brown just became

another smart lawyer who decided to play the game, that's all. . . .
The white people want you to be a regular guy, and put your head
in the sand, and work hard.

Race issues are not the only pressures a token leader feels,
however. As a Negro on an agency of importance to the community, it is widely assumed that he is, or should be, in a position
to do concrete favors for individuals in terms of jobs, preferment,
salary, or certification. People who seek such favors often mis-
conceive the function of the agency. Usually a Negro member is
not in a position to influence greatly the distribution of these
benefits. One politician, unsuccessful in his efforts to get Brown
to take an interest in past cases, ceased trying, and described his
relationship with Brown with this anecdote:

> When I told Syd about my problems with the Board, he said, "Why
> didn't you come to see me?" I told him, "Why should I, Syd? You've
> never done any favors for anybody."

Brown concedes that there has been criticism of his actions from
Negro sources, but defends his position by pointing out what he
considers to be the appropriate style for dealing with issues in
this context:

> I don't have any grief about my service with the Board of Educa-
> tion. . . . I found that I could sit down with white people, and I
> generally knew that they would be fair. It was a matter of laying our
> cards on the table and talking. Fussing and hollering, I probably
> wouldn't have gotten anything.

Accused by certain protest leaders of what they considered a
lack of militancy in pressing for a program of redistributing Negro
students into white schools, Brown responded by criticizing the
protesters in the NAACP.

> We weren't in bad faith. . . . No single organization can have all
> the facts. And these people, they had no plan. It always is easier to
> talk than to do. But what are you going to do with the children?
> Ship them around the city in busses, looking for vacant classrooms?
> . . . That Uncle Tom statement didn't affect me in the least. . . . I was
> doing what I thought was right. I didn't dance to their tune, and so
> I made a lot of enemies.

Other token Negro leaders do not dismiss these considerations
so easily. Some are acutely aware of the conflicting pressures

upon them. "I can't stick my neck out on this," said one. "It's loaded with dynamite. Look at me . . . I have to watch every word I say. There are many forces working on me, all the time." Another Negro, in a similar position, talked at great length about what were felt to be the injustices one suffers at the hands of Negro critics. "My critics hate me, they're always after me," said this person in words which suggested real feelings of persecution. "They showed real hostility to me. . . . You have no idea how hateful these people can be."

A Negro who served in part as a token leader, but who was also a person of considerable prestige in the Negro community and who had extensive contacts with influential white persons, was Robert Taylor. His background and his activities on a particular issue — public housing in Chicago — are examined in great detail elsewhere.[5] His reputation was high, particularly among Negro prestige leaders, many of whom were his colleagues in business ventures, and has grown since his death to the point that many Negroes speak of him in retrospect as a "great leader." In a sense, he was a more universal leader than any other person in this category. Successful in business and sought after by whites both as a private adviser and a public servant, he wielded great influence in certain areas. In part his success was due, of course, to ability, and in part it reflected his white sponsorship. As manager for over twenty years of an apartment project built by the philanthropist, Julius Rosenwald, he became personally close to Rosenwald and through him was brought to the attention of such influential whites as the chairman of the board of the First National Bank and the Mayor. No Negro leader today has the advantage of such a strongly defined pattern of white sponsorship in the city; no one is in the position of having almost all civic issues affecting the housing of Negroes referred to him for advice or direction — as Taylor did. Today no single Negro is preeminent in this field and a number of Negroes, none with Taylor's qualifications, now serve in this representative capacity.

Some mention should be made of the private channels of Negro representation. In addition to the "token leader," some Negroes can be described as "advisers." They are distinguished from the former by the fact that they are paid to provide information about the Negro community, anticipate its reactions, and in some cases attempt to influence Negroes on behalf of their employer. Although not, properly speaking, civic leaders when acting in this capacity, it is useful to note some of the attributes of Negroes who perform the adviser function as a means of highlighting the important differences between civic and business relationships and the constraints that operate on the former.

The relationship between adviser and advisee is private; the token leader, on the other hand, operates on the basis of a public relationship. Advisers are never militant leaders, but they can escape in good part the pressures that this can generate in more public cases. They are used by white businessmen, civic leaders, and even politicians who have market or civic problems with a racial element. One such adviser serves on a retainer fee to some white businesses with interests in the Negro market or in the Negro labor force. Another has organized a consulting service in the field of industrial relations. A third is a lawyer who is paid a fee by certain large white businesses for advice on problems involving Negroes, such as race violence in areas where the firm has plant investment. Taylor, mentioned above, often served in such a capacity. In one instance, he was hired to conduct a survey for the New York Life Insurance Company to assess the rental market among Negroes for its large Lake Meadows high-rise apartment project.

The value of Negro advisers rests, of course, on their service as discreet men induced to act through tangible rewards. The constraints on their action can be defined and maintained. The lay civic leader, or the voluntary association executive, makes a somewhat less satisfactory source of advice and guidance, for he may be, and usually is, seeking rewards beyond those the advisee can control — prestige, attention, or an issue upon which to base an appeal for funds or support. One adviser compares his function with that of the Urban League in just those terms:

> They can trust me. . . . I have no budget to raise. The League visits them and talks to them . . . [but] raising a big budget can just get in your way. Too tempting to make hay out of some break-through which should be kept quiet.

Since the adviser occupies a private, and often close, relationship with his client, he frequently displays the surest and most accurate knowledge about the organization, interests, and relative influence of the white civic leader — information superior to that at the disposal of most Negro civic leaders. At the same time, the adviser, with one exception, never serves in a civic leadership capacity in the city, and hence the information he possesses is rarely made a part of the mental equipment of those who attempt to exercise leadership for some race goal.

Within the Negro community itself, a few white-controlled businesses have begun to place Negroes in positions where they can simultaneously lend to the institution an "interracial" character (and thus improve the firm's public relations) and also advise on business matters in those cases where a race problem has been raised. Two small banks have added prestigious Negroes to their boards of directors in this manner, a third is considering it, and a department store long employed a Negro as public relations vice president whom the owner regarded, in his words, as "my liaison with the colored people." None of these people, as with the advisers discussed above, was active in any race problems or associations at the time of his appointment.

The Organizer

If one were to accept the definition of leadership implicitly held by many Negroes, the persons considered as "organizers" would be the only "true" leaders in the community. These are the leaders who raise issues and create, direct, and sustain organizations for the attainment of civic goals. These are the men and women who literally "lead" in the sense of directing action, standing in front and pointing the way, or leading into battle. It is maintained here, however, that there are many leadership functions, all of which serve — well or ill — the purposes of the group. One of these functions is that of initiating or stimulating activity by raising issues, setting goals, and sustaining organizations. That function — or that collection of functions — is performed by people who will be here called "organizers."

Not all of these people direct formal organizations. Some endeavor to create ad hoc groups which are little more than a collection of supporters that can act outside the established race relations organizations. Some attempt simply to goad other organizations into action. Most of them, however, are active in voluntary

associations of a wide variety, some of which are their own crea-
tions. Where other types of leaders contribute prestige or money
to these groups, the organizer contributes time and energy.

The fact that organizers contribute their activity rather than
their reputation or resources to civic enterprises suggests a possible explanation for their behavior. The organizers lack the
status or income or power which they desire and which others
have. Civic activity is a way of acquiring such status and power,
and perhaps eventually civic prominence will have monetary rewards because it enhances businesses or careers. These and other
private needs — the desire to belong to important groups, to be
"in the know," to meet important people — can perhaps account
for the public actions of the organizers. Such an hypothesis gains
some credence from the fact that prestige leaders — the men who
have conspicuously "arrived" — rarely nominate any organizers
when asked to name important Negro leaders. The organizers seem
to be separated from the top of the community by a gulf of income,
attainment, or status. The prestige leaders have "made it;" the
organizers have not.

Although this explanation has a certain plausibility and indeed
seems to account for the activity of several such leaders, it cannot account for the activity of all of them. Some organizers persist in their civic activity even though they are at the height of
their professions. Others not only do not seek entry into upper-
status groups or the esteem of members of these groups, but their
civic activity is of a character that virtually insures that they will
not gain such access or esteem. In any case, the data are not sufficient to permit either the acceptance or rejection of the hypothesis.
The motivation of Negro civic activity is an inadequately-explored
area.

Organizers tend to share attributes which distinguish them as
a type. Foremost among these is a high degree of commitment
to specific ends. Where the prestige leader is vague on specific
goals, the organizer is precise; and where the prestige leader is
superficial in his prescription of means, the organizer is actively
searching for and experimenting with techniques of influence. This
commitment to specific ends — redistricting schools, obtaining
conservation designation for a certain community area, blocking
the branch hospital plan — gives to all organizers certain militant

qualities, and tends to place them to some extent in competition with one another for the scarce resources of the community.

The organizer is most often restless, ambitious, eager to improve or gain more, and relatively imaginative. Most organizers are men who are obviously of secondary status in the community. But there are organizers of relatively high status — measured in terms of success in their profession, occupancy of high position in some formal organization such as a business, or apparent social acceptance. These men are at the same time notable as "lone wolves," men with "private crusades" or "pet interests" which they pursue in an individualistic fashion. This singularity usually has persisted since their earliest ventures, and seems to mark them as perpetual civic organizers, men who are congenitally enterprising.

The occupational background of these men is revealing. Of the ten persons considered in this category, two are doctors, one is a labor leader, one a teacher, one a housewife, and four are in the real estate and insurance business on a self-employed basis. The last four are the ones who most clearly have business stakes in the issues which concern them, while the first five do not. All of them are, except for the teacher and the labor leader, self-employed or in some other way the masters of their own time — they have the ability to set aside time for these activities with few corporate or institutional restraints. The availability of time is an important factor in determining the possibility of a man's becoming a civic leader.

Time may make civic enterprise possible, but it does not make it inevitable. The restlessness, the excess energy, of the organizer is observed and commented upon by other civic leaders. A prestigious Negro attempts to explain the vigor with which an insurance executive pursues his civic activities:

A man like [X] just has an obsession. . . . He wants to do these things, and I think quite unselfishly. . . . He wanted for a long time to have the local Tuskegee Alumni Association buy a building. . . . He felt so strongly about it that he manuevered to get himself elected President, and then things started happening. . . . [X] used to be the supervisor of the ———— shoe repair department, but he wanted to be successful on his own, so he quit and went into the insurance business. He gives a great deal of time.

It would be easy to assume that for the Negro, there are two goads to ambition: the normal goad for the economically and socially lower to rise, and the added goad for the Negro to rise in spite of his color. However, the comparative absence of Negro civic organizers suggests either that these goads are not mutually reinforcing, or that they do not take civic action as their outlet. It seems more likely that the latter is the case, and that for reasons which we can speculate about only at the conclusion to this study.

Gerald Bullock, a school teacher, is a civic organizer and leader who responds to intangible incentives. Born in North Dakota — one of the few Negro leaders not born in the South — and living in a predominately white apartment building, Bullock has been one of the most militant members of the local NAACP for several years. He is a member of a great variety of liberal associations, both white and Negro. Through volunteering his time and raising his voice, he has been able to serve in a large number of NAACP offices in a short length of time. Below the rank of branch president, there are few persistent volunteers for the work of that organization, and the sheer fact of volunteering is often sufficient qualification for appointment to many tasks. But Bullock is intelligent and articulate, and so becomes a major contender for the highest offices. He served as chairman of the legislative committee of the Illinois State Conference of the NAACP — a volunteer lobbyist for state legislation in Springfield — and then was elected president of the state NAACP. He became NAACP regional director for the northeastern region of Illinois. But the state organization is not the real corpus of the NAACP; the resources, in terms of funds and members, reside with the Chicago branch. He served as chairman of its legislative committee, conducting a series of public meetings on race issues, and then stepped forward as the presidential nominee of the liberal wing of the NAACP in the hotly-contested 1958 elections. His candidacy, supported by white liberals from the University of Chicago area and some locals of the United Auto Workers union, was energetic but doomed to failure. Throughout much of this period, he was a vice-chairman of the Independent Voters of Illinois, a local affiliate of the Americans for Democratic Action, and active in the Chicago Teachers Union.

In view of this record of race and civic activity, one might suppose Bullock would be a frequently cited leader in the Negro community. He is not. Almost no one, when asked to name leaders he admired, suggested Bullock. To prestigious Negroes, Bullock is a radical, connected with the labor wing of the NAACP, and not a member of their circles. Among many of his fellow militants, there are rivalries and mutual suspicions that are as intense as only differences among the ideologically devout can be.

Bullock laments the lack of Negro leadership — "there aren't any people willing to take up the cudgels" — and devotes what time remains after his NAACP duties to working to create new organizations of a racial character. In an open letter to Rep. Adam Clayton Powell, a man Bullock admires, he urged the Congressman to call a "People's Convention" to "solidify the efforts of Negro leaders."[6] The Convention would elect a "responsible, dedicated leadership" and would set up a "large and self-sustaining trust fund" to divorce this leadership "from the economic fears that hold most of our militant intellectuals in traumatic paralysis today." The leadership in turn would "galvanize the Negro citizen into active participation" in a program of "social protest and independent political action." Asked why he proposed such a plan, Bullock remarked:

> That was another part of the protest. . . . It was another threat to the status quo. I didn't have much hope, obviously, that it would get a warm reception from anyone but Adam Powell. . . . As a matter of fact . . . he seemed interested in the idea.

Nothing came of the "People's Convention," but when a scandal broke in the press involving allegations of police corruption in a Negro community, Bullock was a leader of the neighborhood meetings called to form a "Defense Committee."[7] His organizational efforts attract few beyond the faithful. The public "forums" held to discuss race issues, under NAACP sponsorship, drew only the smallest handful of people.

Dempsey J. Travis, a real estate broker, is a young and energetic businessman who has sought to organize Negro real estate and insurance men into a campaign to alter a policy of fire insurance companies that results in an inability to insure properties in Negro areas against fire losses. His energy had carried him to the presidency of the Dearborn Real Estate Board, a professional association of Negro real estate brokers, and to the vice-presidency of the Chicago Insurance Brokers Association, a group of Negro insurance men. Efforts by Negroes to halt and reverse the series of fire insurance cancellations on the South Side of the city brought Travis to the fore as an organizer and spokesman. The stake of the Negro businessmen in the issue was clearly a tangible one, since property and insurance sales are severely hampered by this inability to obtain fire coverage at a figure near the manual rates. "On this thing," he said, "I'm just a small boy crying in the wilderness. I'm just trying to make an honest buck."

Travis, with a few others, held a series of meetings among interested parties in the Negro community, and then met in conference with the Mayor and the state director of insurance, attended by insurance company representatives. The issue was quickly seen by Negro leaders such as Travis as a racial one, and he alleged in a newspaper interview that "290 [insurance] companies are practicing Jim Crow."[8] Although technically the insurance companies had only cancelled policies on properties in "slum" areas after a particularly bad winter of fire losses, Travis felt this was a "subterfuge" and that some companies "want to bleed us, that's all. . . . If you're a black man, you have to pay inflated rates." Whatever its merits, this charge was undoubtedly useful as a means of broadening support in the Negro community for the protest. One result of the agitation was the introduction of a bill into the state legislature by Negro representatives, many of whom themselves are property owners affected by the insurance cancellations, to forbid discrimination by insurance companies based on "race, creed, color, or locality."[9]

Travis laments the fact that many of his business contemporaries seem to lack his energy in pressing the issue which affects them all. "They have a self-interest . . . but they don't even act on that. It's incredible. . . . I get ideas and they can't even see how it affects them." Travis, the young organizer, is voluble and quick, moving from idea to idea in conversation and displaying a restive ambition:

My mother and my wife both wanted me to take a civil service job . . . which paid five or six thousand a year. I wouldn't take it. . . . I don't want a ceiling on what I can earn. I like to struggle. I like to fight and take chances. Six thousand a year is all right, but not when it means that you can only work up to eight thousand. . . . I want to take a chance on earning in one year what civil service might pay me in a lifetime of work. Maybe I won't get it, but I'll try.

Bullock and Travis are both organizers, displaying comparable energy and inevitably seeking opportunities for effort. Although on a given issue, their styles may be similar, fundamentally they display markedly different attitudes toward issues, ends, and means. There can be no doubt that Travis finds intangible rewards in his civic work — others, with the same objective stake in an issue, do far less — but the issues which attract him and the manner in which he speaks of his relationship to them reveal clearly the essential nature of the rewards he seeks, rewards significantly different from those sought by Bullock. As Travis develops in community and business activities, he will rise into a group of business-oriented, moderate-style Negro entrepreneurs and civic leaders who distribute prestige and status in a manner that does not consider militancy as an intrinsically desirable attribute. Bullock's style, commitments, and the rewards he seeks stem from other groups — protest leaders and the "dedicated volunteer workers," as he phrases it, who carry the burden of militancy on ideological issues. Neither Travis nor Bullock is nominated as a leader more than a few times by other Negroes, but in the future Travis probably will be named with increasing frequency, while Bullock probably will not. The distinction between business and non-business civic leadership is already clear in their minds. Bullock refers often to the businessmen as corrupted by "self-interest," while Travis names only businessmen as leaders and adds, "you don't want rabble rousers."[10]

It should be noted that often men are thrust into certain leadership roles, or asked to act as certain types of leaders, who are not strongly committed to the expectations that commonly surround or define such a role. An important example is the office of NAACP branch president. The moderate or conservative Negro civic leader who wins such a post cannot ignore entirely the expectations of the more militant elements of the community regarding the proper activities of such an officer. These elements provide, after all, the principal source of volunteer labor for protest actions, and one runs a risk in alienating them. But strains are created when a man who is a moderate in style occupies a position defined as one requiring militancy. When he attempts to meet these expectations he becomes a leader who cannot be conveniently labelled as some "type." One such leader discovered that by virtue of a public statement made at a Board of Education budget hearing which received press coverage, he was able to regain some ground lost when protest leaders had opposed him in NAACP politics. The statement, actually a rather mild one, was treated by the Negro press as a "blast" charging "racial discrimination of the highest order."[10] The *Chicago Tribune,* also misinterpreting the original statement, attacked the NAACP leader editorially. A Negro attorney then rallied to this leader's aid in a letter to the editor of the *Tribune.*[11] The next day, a columnist in a Negro newspaper could remark:

> The *Chicago Tribune* has inadvertently helped to heal the breach between the warring factions inside the Chicago branch of the NAACP. . . . Many members who have been criticizing [him] for being too soft on the arrogant, downtown dictators began to call and congratulate him. Leadership rests upon the kind of enemies you make. . . .[12]

The "New Negro"

Some logically possible leadership types appear to have no examples in the Chicago Negro community. For instance, the mass agitator is not only a possibility, but as Adam Clayton Powell has shown, a potentially successful leader. No counterpart to Powell is found in Chicago, nor, except perhaps for brief periods, has one ever been.

It is not easy to explain why there is no mass agitator, no Adam Clayton Powell with a large popular following, in Chicago. A complete answer would have to take into account the differences between the ethos of the Chicago Negro and his background and the ethos of the Harlem Negro and his background. Further, and perhaps equally important, there would have to be a close examination of the differences between the political structure of the two cities. Some observations on this latter point may illuminate the problem.

As has been suggested in earlier chapters, Chicago Negro political activity crystallized early in the history of the community into a pattern of organization or machine politics based on a geographically contiguous, densely-populated, all-Negro group of wards which the white political leadership of the city—the city machine—desired to control. Control was desirable for its electoral rewards, and it was made possible by the availability of material incentives—especially patronage—which could be used to construct the necessary organization. As political control of the city became centralized, so political control in the Negro areas became centralized into a "sub-machine." From the first, the area of Negro political leadership, and hence the area of possible Negro protest and agitation, was pre-empted by a well-disciplined and centrally-led organization. Politics as an avenue of agitation was closed. This closure was not, however, absolute, for a non-machine Negro political leader has been elected in the past to the City Council. His election was due partly to the efforts of a Republican organization which had been temporarily revivified by an unusually large injection of patronage from the party leader, the Governor, but in greater part to a popular appeal of an ideological and racial character. After having served for two terms, a total of eight years, the Negro "independent" —Archibald J. Carey, Jr.—was defeated by the Democratic party which had been reorganized for that purpose. Since that time, the Democratic organization has been particularly careful to prevent the rise to office of any Negro political leader who wished to gather to him a personal, rather than an organizational, following.

But politics is not the only avenue of popular leadership. The example of Rev. Martin Luther King in Montgomery, Alabama, is an oft-cited case in point. The possibility for the operation of his kind of leadership is obviously dependent on a number of factors, important among which are the character of the ends being sought by the leader, the situation in the community in which he seeks them, and the qualities of the leader himself. One point is worth discussing at this juncture, and that concerns the personal qualities of the leader. As indicated earlier, the leaders of the Negro community, for a variety of reasons, place a high value on "inspirational" or "exemplary" leaders, and they cite examples drawn from other areas or other times. It was also noted that no Negro leader thought such a person existed on the Chicago scene. But these same Negroes also express hope that such a person or persons will develop in Chicago or in the

North generally. The attributes such a leader presumably would have form a kind of standard by which present, inadequate leadership is judged. This hope for the future leadership of the community is expressed most commonly in terms of "the new Negro."

There is a widespread belief in, and hope for, the emergence of a "new" Negro leadership, and many Negroes point to signs that this development is already occurring. The "old" leadership, particularly what we have called the prestige leadership, is seen —most often by protest leaders—as beyond redemption, a group which must be replaced. One Negro says:

I don't believe you can change these people, you have to get rid of them. . . . A man at 60, or even 30, can't be changed on this. . . . They have their established patterns. Negro leadership has to await a new crop of men, young men, to come up.

The new Negro will have several attributes. He will respond to the intangible incentives for civic action, and contribute his time and money and energies selflessly or at least without hope of substantial gain. Indeed, he will be willing to perform these duties at some sacrifice to himself and his career. He will be immune to corruption. One leader described two young men whom he felt displayed these characteristics:

Who knows [X]? Nobody. But he is brilliant, trained, a willing worker. . . . Or a lawyer like [Y]? He is not a big, successful Negro lawyer like some, but unlike others, he will come and give time in meetings, time in committees, money. . . . He is willing to lose a few clients to work with us.

The new Negro will reject the advantages of segregation, and will resist acquiring a stake in the ghetto or letting such a stake interfere with his civic responsibilities. He will not "go along" with the status quo simply because it is easier than to wage a fight which might be costly. In his civic work, he will contribute organizing efforts, and not merely prestige or the luster of his name on a letterhead. He will be militant and outspoken on race issues, and at the same time prepared to co-operate with other Negroes in joint ventures. A columnist in a Negro newspaper attributed these qualities to a single factor in a description of the new Negro.:

If I were to ask what force or element triggered this change and led to the birth of the new Negro of today, I would say it lies basically in the loss of fear.[14]

The new Negro will work with the white man as an equal partner. A Negro politician, expanding on his hopes for a new political alliance between the traditionally hostile but mutually underrepresented Poles and Negroes, felt the new Negro could overcome past difficulties:

Not the *old* Poles or the *old* Negroes. But the *new* generation — the new Poles and the new, young Negroes would do it. In another twenty years, maybe, it will happen. . . . The Negroes and the Poles must form a coalition. . . . The new Negroes haven't the distrust of white people that those just up from the South have.

Young professional men are most commonly seen as the source of such leaders, and associations like the Urban League speak continually of their efforts to bring such new Negroes forward and to place them in leadership positions. A new leadership will be *created* out of civic enterprises, rather than merely co-opted from other areas of achievement. These new leaders will, in the hope of the professional staff members who endeavor to recruit and develop them, have a "clear" conception of the meaning of integration—i.e., a conception in accord with that of the staff men, which typically is a view that seeks status rather than welfare ends.

To be sure, young men with many of these attributes can be found already. The Urban League, for example, has brought onto its board and placed in positions of responsibility a doctor, a lawyer, a minister, and a school official who are almost never nominated by other Negro leaders as "leaders" (except, of course, by each other), but who are energetic volunteer workers.

The hope for the new Negro, heard principally among more militant leaders but not absent in any quarter, is one more indication of the extent and depth of the view that places such a high value on leadership and which so consistently laments its absence. The "new Negro" is supposed to do many different, and often conflicting, things, depending on who is speaking. Many wish to see him arise as a great popular leader; others hope to see him as an independent politician; and yet others hope to see him as a board member of a voluntary association who will invariably support the professional staff (who consider themselves, after all, to be the real new Negroes) in its organizational work. Similarly, he is to possess many, and often conflicting, attributes — militancy, for example, is not a common characteristic of those best able to work co-operatively with influential whites. Finally, the hopes for youthful selflessness may underestimate the power of economic success and increased status to reduce civic ambitions.

Nonetheless, important changes are occurring in the sources and character of Negro civic leadership in Chicago. The hope for the new Negro is not entirely misplaced. The types and styles of civic leadership which have been discussed here are undergoing certain transformations. These will be discussed in the last chapter, and the general themes of this discussion as a whole will be placed in an historical context.

Chapter XI

The Character of Negro Civic Action

T
HE NAACP has come to have a virtual monopoly of national Negro protest activity. Today it is the pre-eminent
race organization, almost unchallenged within its field of competence. This has not always been the case. In earlier years, the
NAACP was compelled to share its prestige with other, similar
organizations, such as the March on Washington Movement.
Doubts were expressed in the past as to the value of the NAACP's
legalistic approach to race problems. It was criticized for not
having a mass base, for ignoring economic and political problems in favor of legal problems, for having a "snobbish"
leadership, and for failing to form an effective alliance with liberal
forces in the American labor movement.[1] Membership in local
NAACP branches was generally small and the amounts of money
raised were not large.

These criticisms, while still heard in some quarters, have largely
been muted today. In part this has been due to the ability of
the NAACP to persist and to consolidate its reputation with
numerous victories. For the most part, however, the enhanced
prestige of the organization seems to be a direct result of its role
in the 1954 school desegregation decision of the United States
Supreme Court. The NAACP was hailed as the architect of the
greatest single Negro victory of this century. The legal approach
of the association was seen to have some merit. The NAACP
quickly became a symbol of Negro protest. Negroes who had
doubted its efficacy rushed to climb aboard the bandwagon. This

process was accelerated by the attack launched against the organization by whites in the South. By accusing it of radical and subversive tendencies, by elevating it to the position of the principal threat to white supremacy, the South immeasurably increased the standing of the NAACP among Negroes. For a Negro to criticize, much less oppose, the NAACP today is in effect to give aid and comfort to the enemy.

Although Southern opposition has made it difficult for the NAACP to recruit Negroes in the South, membership drives in the North have met with increasing success. In 1953, the year before the Supreme Court decision, the Chicago branch had about 4,000 members. In 1958, it had increased that figure to over 18,500. Since the bulk of the organization's money comes, at the local level, from membership dues (a minimum of $2 per person), this has meant a corresponding improvement in the NAACP's financial position.[2]

In the past, the local NAACP branches, such as the one in Chicago, have been regarded as a "tax base" which simply support the program of the national office by fund-raising campaigns. The national office firmly controls national policy for the organization. The association is not a federal structure, with power decentralized to local units; it is a unitary structure with support, but not policy-direction, coming from the base. Moreover, the national office has usually taken a "hands off" attitude toward factional quarrels in the local branches so long as fund-raising was not seriously impeded. The NAACP branches can be characterized as organizations with local memberships but a national constituency. The national program has been the overriding goal, and members are attracted, not on the basis of what the local branch is doing, but on the basis of what the national office has done.

The growing resources and prestige of the NAACP have, however, begun to alter this pattern somewhat. As the NAACP has come to monopolize the Negro protest, it has come to have greater significance for local leaders. It has risen in value as a source of status, and competition for its local control has become intense. In part because local leaders need to justify their tenure as officers of the organization, NAACP branches have attempted to develop a local program beyond simply dues-collecting. This programmatic emphasis has served to add fuel to the factional fires, for it causes principle as well as prestige to be at stake. Further, new groups in the Negro community have arisen which are demanding recognition and are asserting their claims to civic leadership. Foremost among these are certain Negro labor leaders. The Chicago branch has been gripped by a protracted controversy which has in part centered on the question of which segment of the Negro community will provide its leadership. On the one hand are the Negro lawyers and businessmen who, with certain ministers, have most often held the higher offices. On the other hand are some labor leaders and their allies who have in recent years been able to capture the executive committee and the presidency. Annual elections are typically a struggle between these groups in an organized form.

The intensity of this struggle seems, to the observer, to be completely out of proportion to what is actually at stake. No tangible rewards accrue to the victor. Neither group can usually attribute any significantly longer list of civic achievements to its tenure in office. Occasionally the NAACP becomes involved in an economic conflict between member groups, as it once did when certain labor leaders accused the lawyer-president of the association of supporting management in an all-Negro labor relations dispute. But typically Chicago remains the same no matter which Negro group controls the NAACP. These appearances are deceptive, however. Simply because the stakes are intangible does not make them insignificant. The NAACP is the most important and the best-known organization in the Negro community. Its president automatically becomes prominent. The values and goals of the race are intimately bound up with, if not actually embodied in, the association. The NAACP is not a mass organization in the sense that it organizes the Negro rank-and-file for any purpose; it is rather, an organization composed of and responsive to a relatively small but vocal and attentive group.[3] The game of NAACP control is played out almost entirely within this group and its component factions. When one faction gains control, it often alienates the volunteer support of another faction, but it almost never alienates the masses of Negroes. At the height of recent factional warfare, the NAACP was able to sell a record number of memberships in the community. The response of the community seems to depend, not on the achievements of the local NAACP, but on the state of race relations nationally. A brutal lynching or the closure of southern public schools will make donations easier to secure; a quiet year will make them harder to secure.

The game of civic leadership as a whole generally takes place in a relatively small group of persons. This group formulates its own rules of procedure, enforces its own penalties by manipulating reputations, and has its own rivalries. A Negro who was himself a member of this small universe described the elements of which it is composed and noted the consequences for each element of the incentives which attract it:

> There are three classes of people . . . active in it. . . . First, there are those who are quite common, the ones that are temperamentally joiners. . . . They want to believe in its purposes and they get all wrapped up in it. They are hard to deal with. They get all upset over little things. It is easy to insult them. . . . They get a satisfaction out of it. They get to be somebody and do something which is *good*. But you can't work with them. They won't compromise.
>
> Second, there are the professional groups — the lawyers, doctors, and all. I am one of these. They get a reputation out of work in the NAACP. Lawyers pick up a few cases and they get some publicity. . . . What the professional ethics prohibit you can accomplish indirectly by this sort of thing. They differ from the first group in that they have no emotional problems. . . . They aren't easily offended. You can work with them. They are in it for a crass reason, and they don't mind doing a little trading.
>
> The third group is the ordinary workers, the run-of-the-mill type, who do want to make a contribution and plug away at it. . . . The more serious Negroes think that supporting the NAACP is something they have to do; it is important; it is a duty. So they work at it.

Both the fact that the incentives for Negro civic action are largely intangible and the fact that the most important Negro civic organization—the NAACP—has come to be invested with moral and ideological significance contribute to an understanding of the character of Negro public life in Chicago. These two factors are important in explaining why there seem to be so few leaders and why the leaders that exist act as they do. Leaders are recruited and civic action occurs among white businessmen-civic leaders in a manner rather different from that in the Negro community, and one important reason for this difference is a frequent difference in incentives. White leaders, more than Negroes, act because for them or for the firms which they represent, something is at stake. Land holdings will be affected in value by urban renewal or railroad terminal consolidation or institutional construction. Tax rates will be affected by plans to subsidize public transportation systems. Private hospitals might have part of their more unremunerative patient load eased if a new branch of the county hospital is built. More customers may be induced to shop in the Loop department stores if high-density apartment projects are built near those stores. Membership on welfare and social service agency boards can, it is felt, help the firm by improving its public relations.

Fewer such incentives exist for Negro volunteer civic action. Negro leaders will rarely benefit as persons or as members of a business if an FEPC law is passed or if an open occupancy ordinance is adopted. Where tangible stakes are involved at all, they often dispose a person to act against the race end for fear of its implications for their own position. Few Negro businesses as yet have the resources to afford or the inclination to value the kind of public image that comes from civic service. Several Negro life insurance companies operate in Chicago, but only one is conspicuously active in encouraging its officers to take part in civic work. Where Negro businesses and professions do supply civic leaders, they are usually supplied for the less controversial forms of civic life where public relations will be enhanced at minimum cost. The most important race ends are hardly lacking in controversy, and correspondingly the incentives they contain for even those Negro businesses which are willing to act civically are considerably reduced. In an important sense, what is surprising is not that there are so few Negro civic leaders but that, given the situation, there are as many as there are.

The intangible incentives to civic action are many and varied, and no one can pretend to know in any given case which one attracts what civic leader. Men may act to seek personal prestige, to acquire power, to gain an audience, to pursue strongly-held convictions, to prevent others from acquiring a certain reputation, or simply because they feel they "ought to." The kinds of persons attracted by intangible incentives are not always the easiest to work with; indeed, it seems to be a general rule that no competition is fiercer or more bitter than competition for intangible stakes.* Negro civic life attracts ideologues; this can make compromises hard and dispassionate discussion difficult. The role of "interest-balancer"—the man who reconciles factions by arranging a solution in which everyone gains a little and no one loses a great deal—is a role which is almost impossible to play when the issue at stake is one of principle. Little can be offered a person motivated by an attachment to a moral cause that will induce him to alter his position to any great extent, and the man who attempts to make such an offer quickly becomes morally suspect. Organizations created to seek ends which reflect such principles, and which have acquired enough prestige in the community to permit them to confer status on those who actively lead the quest for these principled ends, often become the objects of hot competition. There is a competition for office and a competition for issues where desires for prestige and commitment to principle are inextricably linked in a manner that imparts an astonishing intensity to the annual elections and internal politics of the NAACP.

The character of Negro civic action cannot be accounted for simply on the basis of the nature of the incentives for such action, however. Civic activity even among white Chicago businessmen is often a result of inducements equally as intangible as those which exist for Negroes. Another equally important factor which conditions Negro public life is the problem of powerlessness—the inability, in the most critical issues, to influence markedly the course of public affairs. This absence of power and the sense of frustration and futility which often are its result not only reduce the attractiveness of civic action but also shape the conduct of such civic activity as is pursued.

Negro civic leaders stand on the periphery of power. They hope to prod or needle or anger or humiliate those who can direct the course of affairs into granting concessions to Negro demands. The Negroes themselves are remote from the centers of

---

*The struggle for intangible rewards—prestige or status, for example—makes the internal politics of university faculties, church hierarchies, and Negro organizations among the most bitter to be found. When one seeks money as a reward, it can be sought impersonally; when one seeks prestige, it only can be sought in the realm of personalities.

influence, and this distance gives a certain logic to their views of the public interest and appropriate strategies for action. But those whom they seek to influence are often powerless also, if by power we mean the ability to establish binding public policy. The white civic leaders and politicians are either complacent or caught up in their own conflicts of interest, and are severely constrained by their opinions and fears as to the consequences of any radical change in the racial patterns of the city. Real power seems to lie at the front lines, not at the command post; the whites who resist, often with violence and always with protest, the incursions of Negroes into their neighborhoods are the real influentials who seem to set the bounds of action for the civic leaders and politicians. Negroes are thus twice removed from power: they are not influential in the civic and political circles of the city, and these circles are in turn the willing or unwilling agents of their constituents in the racially-tense neighborhoods.

This clear lack of power has implications for Negro leaders that relate to their attitudes on civic issues. Lacking the kind of access and influence which seems—not always correctly—to characterize the white businessman-civic leader, the Negro leader is more easily persuaded of the plausibility of protest as the appropriate political style. It becomes hard to deny the logic of the frontal assault when efforts to negotiate fail. If one cannot "talk" to influential persons and induce them to make "decisions," then one is hard pressed to refute the claim of the militants that only an attack on these men with a mass campaign aimed at legislative remedies can hope to gain concessions. This appeal of protest leaders gains added plausibility when it is heard in the perspective of what is frequently an incorrect assessment of the position of the white businessman-civic leader. These men, the so-called "lords of the Loop," are seen by the Negroes to have almost palpable power which they concert to use against Negro interests out of either prejudice or desire for economic gain. Meeting obstacles with a call for new laws and legal action is a lure that can easily attract even Negroes who are not protest leaders, like a businessman who has hoped for a negotiated settlement of the housing problem:

I stood out against legislation for many years, feeling that it wasn't the best way to handle it. But I'm fast coming to believe that legislation is the only way it will ever be solved. . . . The industry could solve it because they cause the problem, but they won't. . . .

The absence of power has its consequences for the internal problems of Negro organizations which attempt to act in race relations. The NAACP, for example, is beset with internal conflicts. These conflicts are partly, but not wholly, a form of competition for status. They are also a response to the experienced powerlessness of the organization.[3] An atmosphere of uncertainty surrounds its activities. No one knows the details in full of the public issues with which the organization must deal. Past experience provides few reliable guides for action. The problems are complex and difficult, and only certain kinds of leaders are able to see simple answers for them. Plausible courses of action are scarce; there seems to be no "solution." The aspirations which most members hold for the organization are very high; possible levels of achievement are seen to be low. The environment of the organization is hostile and unyielding. In such conditions, conflict within the NAACP—or within any organization placed in a comparable situation—tends to be high. The resources for action are few—the organization seems to be powerless—and controversy begins with how best to simply exist as an organization. The disagreement and conflict over ends, which in one sense arises out of the powerless state of the organization, ends by denying that state. Factional lines harden, and soon accusations are heard that certain leaders are failing to exercise what power they have. Militant leaders charge that the organization is not really powerless, but only appears to be in that state because "soft" leaders have willed it by refusing to *be* powerful. Soon the controversy becomes cast in the form of a debate as to whether the strategic or limiting factor on effective civic action is to be found in the environment of the organization (the insuperable obstacles which make the organization powerless) or within the organization itself (the ineffectual character of the organization's leadership). The powerlessness of Negro leaders produces contradictory effects because it creates a sense of frustration to which people respond in different ways—some by resignation and hopelessness, others by anger and chagrin. Negro leaders vacillate between an awareness and a denial of their relatively powerless state.

The sense of powerlessness, and the concomitant imputation of power to another elite, produces a sense of defeatism among Negroes. Those who do not respond to this situation by becoming protest leaders often respond by acting simply for individual ends without reference to collective goals. If nothing one can do will aid the Negro community, then one is justified in trying to better himself. The argument is often heard that this self-improvement in the long run benefits the race as well, because a successful Negro businessman gains the respect of whites and reflects credit on his race.

The problem of powerlessness cannot be fully understood unless it is seen in the light of the character of the ends being sought. For some ends—particularly ends related to housing and real estate—the Negro can do nothing to remedy his powerlessness. At best he can hope for a crisis which will compel others to act in an area where they have, until now, been afraid or unwilling to act. The Negro has difficulty in acquiring the power to act in this area because, for the most part, the power to act simply does not exist anywhere. When seeking ends that elicit less irreconcilable passions, scraps of power can be collected and assembled. Certain things can be done: more police protection can be demanded; less discriminatory insurance rates can be pressed for; firms can be induced to hire Negroes. Here, when Negroes fail to act effectively, it is more often a case of failures internal to the Negro community than of constraints imposed by the larger community. Briefly stated, constraints exist and are enforced by the city on Negro action, but in many areas those constraints are not really tested by Negro action. The problem of power is not simply a function of one or the other. Many obstacles exist only because they have not been probed. Hiring Negroes in the Loop banks seemed for years to be an impossible goal; but when a picket line appeared, the banks began to give way with surprising suddenness. Similarly, no one can say in advance what style of political action will be the most efficacious; the appropriate type and style of leadership depends largely on the character of the end sought.

If there is, as has been argued here, a "Negro problem," it cannot be completely explained on the basis of end conflicts, disagreements over appropriate styles, an absence of incentives, influence relations, or the sense of powerlessness. In short, it cannot be satisfactorily explained by an inquiry into Negro leadership alone, but would have to include an investigation of non-leaders and followers as well.

With this limitation clearly understood, certain important relationships among the themes developed in this study can be brought together. First, leaders acting in situations where large formal organizations must be maintained by intangible inducements tend to employ the militant style; while leaders acting in situations where access or position must be maintained tend to employ the moderate or bargaining style. This distinction cannot be driven too far, for many leaders called upon to head formal organizations (such as the NAACP) are, for a variety of reasons, unable to act with the militancy that others expect of them. But the maintenance needs of the organization—the need to attract and hold members and fend off challenges from other factions — will inevitably serve to heighten the militancy of even temperamentally moderate civic leaders. Even militant leaders often do not go far enough to meet the expectations of their followers. One remarked, after failing to join a picket line around the City Hall some years earlier:

> I was criticized and still am for not joining that picket line. Some people said that they weren't going to support me for president this last year because I hadn't been in the picket line. You have got to toe the mark with these people.

Second, the distinction between welfare and status ends tends (with important exceptions) to correspond to the distinction between the militant and moderate styles. The broadest, most inclusive, most ideological, most "advanced" ends are typically sought by the militants; more tangible, specific, and immediate ends are sought by the moderates. This is related to the utility of broad, general programs as means to attract and hold followers, when *followers* (rather than access or personal influence or prestige) are the usual resource of the militant leader. A leader heading such an organization as the NAACP can set less venturesome goals and pursue them in a less militant manner only when he has established himself in a position where he can reasonably afford to dispense with the small group of active, attentive, volunteer workers who in most instances operate the organization. This has been the case when the leader could depend on organized forms of support apart from these activists, for normally the activists have opposed the moderate and favored the militant leader.

Third, many of the problems of civic leadership might be avoided by avoiding the constraints of formal organizations. Formal organizations make civic action possible by mobilizing resources and creating a corporate identity which can be used by those desiring to influence others. But these advantages are purchased at a cost. That cost includes the need to retain the support of members, the problem of earning funds to meet payrolls and rent bills, the limitations imposed by the requirement that one must always act as the "representative" of the organization, and the intensification of disagreement over ends and means when such disagreement is linked to a desire for office and power in the organization. The maintenance of the organization often supersedes or modifies the substantive ends which are being sought.

Fourth, the most consistent single set of distinctions that can be detected among Chicago Negro civic leaders are distinctions based on class and status. Militants are more often (but not always) of a lower economic class and of a different social stratum than moderates. So, too, are prestige leaders on the one hand and organizers on the other. The important fact to be noted here is that although the two groups are different in terms of status, they are not necessarily different within a common status system. Negro militant-organizers do not act as civic leaders in order to raise themselves to the status level of the moderate-prestige leaders. On the contrary, the very act of civic leadership of the former type and style precludes the possibility that they will be able to move into the latter category. To account for the different status systems in which different kinds of leaders move and in which they find their rewards, we must introduce the notion of "audience." Each leader plays to a different audience. Often that audience is a formal organization; sometimes it is simply a loose grouping of associates and friends. The audiences of various leaders are often mutually exclusive.

The audience to which the militant plays is frequently one which is not a part of the world of Negro mens' social clubs and fraternities. He seeks out and joins interracial activities, notably interracial social activities. Whites at these functions are often identified with liberal causes, but occasionally not. There are strong links with whites who act on behalf of Negroes and race ends. These Negroes have endeavored to leave the ghetto in either a psychological or a social sense or both. In Chicago, few have managed to leave it physically.

Moderate and prestige leaders move in an entirely different world. In Chicago, it is almost entirely a Negro world. There are social, professional and business links between almost all of them. Many of these people are uncomfortable in interracial social gatherings. Militant and organizer leaders outside this circle are acutely conscious of their exclusion and in turn are often the objects of suspicion because of that exclusion. As one militant remarked:

A strong current of nationalism runs through the Negro community. It is thinly disguised as racial patriotism and it looks with definite suspicion upon the Negro who speaks for the "race" but is not "one of us" in his personal associations. He is never harshly condemned but it is quite bruited about that he is not a "race man." Thus he is not to be fully trusted. [I encounter] this attitude in varying degrees in all strata of Negro society.

The militant-organizer in most cases will have far more regularized social contacts with whites than other kinds of Negro civic leaders. This has the interesting implication that those seeking status or integration goals most vigorously are those with the highest relative level of personal integration; while those who are more attracted to welfare ends have a lower level of personal integration. There are, of course, many exceptions to both tendencies—some militants are bound up with "black nationalist" movements and some moderates have a large number of routinized contacts with white businessmen. Again, the nature of the audience (conservative or liberal, social or business) as well as the character of the formal organization within which civic action occurs (business or labor, church or voluntary association) are important conditioners of leadership type and style.

Although we have no detailed data on the social background and position of Negro civic leaders in cities other than Chicago, interviews with such leaders offer at least some suggestions as to the relationship between personal position, race ends, and leadership style. In New York, for example, more Negro civic leaders are integrated as persons into much of the life of the city as a whole. Negro leaders, both in and out of public office, move in the active world of liberal voluntary associations and civic causes. They have, in a real degree, "left the ghetto" in a civic, social, and often physical sense. Many of them are members of or are associated with the national board of the NAACP and are bound up with the liberal civic movements—often, again, at the national board level—in the city as a whole. These individuals seek status or integration goals, resist efforts to concentrate on welfare goals, and are militant in their leadership style. One leader of considerable stature who had experience in civic life in both New York and Chicago noted much less "ghetto-mindedness" among Negro business and professional men in the former city than in the latter. He felt more civic, business and even social contacts between Negroes and whites take place in New York and that this in part accounted for some differences in attitude and behavior. In Chicago, more frequent cases of Negro "self-segregation" were to be found. Many Negro informants in both cities agreed that this was true.

Such contacts, such an audience, provide a kind of stimulus and reinforcement pattern that encourages more Negroes to take positions backing the most advanced race causes and to pursue them with vigor. One importance difference, then, between the quality of Negro leadership in Chicago and New York may be partially accounted for by the differing character and frequency of the contacts and audience which the more prestigious Negro leaders seek out.

Finally, many of the factors which have been discussed in this study—powerlessness, the lack of real progress, the cleavages which weaken the belief in race unity and race pride — have profound consequences for Negroes as persons, apart from their implications for civic action. Suggestions can be found in many interviews of a deep sense of personal inadequacy, perhaps even a feeling of inferiority, which is the product of so many frustrations and denials. This cannot here be illustrated, much less demonstrated, but it would be remarkable indeed if the forces which have been touched upon in this inquiry did not affect the lives of these people as individuals. For many Negroes, these doubts are heightened by an uneasiness over their economic position. The marginal nature of so many Negro business enterprises, the precarious state of the Negro in the economy, the awareness that so many of the gains of recent years could be wiped out by forces over which one has no control — all of these factors undoubtedly increase the sense of uncertainty and magnify the self-concern of many Negroes, leaders and led alike. An investigation into the ethos of the urban Negro might very well begin with this sense of limitation, of inadequacy, of an absent or uncertain future, as the central theme.

Chapter XII

Conclusions and Trends

IMPORTANT, although slow, changes are occurring in the Chicago Negro community. The old order of civic and political leadership is gradually passing, and a new order is emerging. Although this new order has not replaced its predecessor as yet, the tide is clearly running in its favor. The important points which this study has sought to make about Negro leaders in a northern city can be brought together and underscored by placing them in the perspective of this fundamental change.

The old order was led or represented by a group of "accepted leaders" who were usually persons of prestige and personal achievement in the community. This group was composed of men who were successful, who had "arrived" in terms of occupational and social position. They tended to be omnicompetent — that is, they were a fairly stable group which dealt with a wide range of issues. Of great importance in this group were the successful Negro ministers. They typified many of the attributes of what Negroes regarded as "leadership." They had a mass following, they possessed the dignity of their profession, and they were prepared to speak out on almost all those matters which were then sensed to be race issues. Upon almost any question on which it was safe to speak at all, these men could claim — with some justice — to be speaking "for" the Negro community. Ministers such as these were joined by a small number of prominent doctors, lawyers, businessmen, and politicians. All, with the exception of the politicians, were volunteer leaders. There was little or no professionalism in race leadership — the voluntary associations such as the NAACP were small in membership, weak in influence, and had no paid staff. Leadership in such associations was almost completely reserved for the middle- and upper-class Negro. The presidency of the NAACP was commonly rotated among a group of ministers and lawyers who served for short terms.

Such leaders sought typically welfare ends. The more manifest kinds of outrages against Negroes and Negro property were decried. The demand for jobs for Negroes was a never-ending source of civic action, as was the steady effort by Negroes to gain entry into public places such as restaurants, theaters, and hotels. Political recognition was sought by Negro politicians who were endeavoring to capitalize on the increasing concentration of Negroes in a few wards and districts. In this period, demographic concentration could still be publicly defended by leaders as a path to power and material gains. Some people, to be sure, hung back — Negroes who felt that it was unwise or imprudent to seek to gain entry into "white" places, that the Negro was "not ready," or that reliance should be placed on "education." But the general thrust of the period was unmistakable — the goals sought were largely tangible and direct, and they elicited a broad level of agreement as to their correctness.

Action on behalf of these goals tended to be sporadic and poorly organized, however. Only the politicians pursued their ends with any resolution or persistence, and for them, of course, the stakes were personal. Leadership was most often prestige leadership, at least in the ranks of the "accepted" leaders. Ends were typically sought by a deputation of leading Negroes paying a call on a public official, or by the formation of a committee which rarely proceeded beyond the stage of a newspaper announcement and a letterhead. Not much happened, and indeed, very little was attempted. Only from the ranks of the dispossessed did there come signs of more vigorous action. The economic plight of many Negroes was so desperate that direct protest movements arising from lower-income groups were not uncommon. The Negro Labor Relations League in 1937 began a series of campaigns to compel employers to hire Negroes or give Negroes equal treatment with whites in promotions and pay. Through picketing and boycott tactics, pressure was brought against a newspaper, a milk company, a bakery, motion picture theaters, a utility company, and a beer company. These efforts often erupted into violence, and Negroes were not infrequently arrested or manhandled. The Negro attacks on white firms were bitter and the resistance hard. Many "accepted" Negro leaders personally deplored such tactics but nevertheless contributed funds to the League. Other similar organizations would spring up from the midst of the unemployed and stage mass demonstrations from time to time.

The response of many of the "accepted" leaders was to band together to form respectable middle-class Negro organizations which could act with sufficient effectiveness to form an attractive alternative to what appeared to be an embryonic Negro radical movement. The times were tense and there were some excesses; nevertheless, limited gains were scored in such fields as jobs and public housing. The goals sought were mostly *things,* often things intended for the very men who were waging the struggle.

Contacts with the white community were very few and usually ritualized. "Spokesmen" for the Negro community were usually token leaders. The prevailing style of the Negro leaders was that of the moderate; the militant was largely excluded from the ranks of accepted leadership. The Negro politicians, however, were a vigorous and militant group; they were still caught up in the struggle to build a Negro political organization and to achieve recognition and rewards from the white political bosses. Race appeals were frequently used as a device to further these ends, particularly since the Negro political leader was often contesting against a white man for office and power.

The changes which have led to the decline of the old order and the advent of the new order have generally occurred since the end of World War II and most particularly during the 1950's. The new order is not by any means the diametrical opposite of its predecessor, but in order to show more clearly the direction and importance of the changes which have been occurring some exaggeration is of use. Those changes have taken place in the ends, the styles, and the types of Negro leaders in Chicago.

The accepted prestige leader has been challenged by a more vigorous group of organizers. The era of the omnicompetent leader has passed. The Negro middle class is now producing a collection of would-be leaders who are specialized by area of interest and competence. Housing, health, employment, and education are issues each of which elicits a different group of leaders. No one is or pretends to be a "representative" of the Negro community in all these fields. Leaders in each issue area by and large emerge from specialized organizations — professional associations and occupational groupings — which deal with those areas. The Negro voluntary associations — particularly the Urban League — have become more or less professionalized, having a sizeable paid staff that steadily works to create a Negro "public" which will agree on goals that can then be carried to influential whites. The League has sought to "create" Negro civic leaders where necessary for its purposes by selecting and elevating to positions of some prominence individuals who are prepared to contribute to the work of the organization. At the same time, it has endeavored to be the most "representative" Negro organization by bringing together on its board or committees key figures from business, labor, the ministry, and the professions. These new Negro civic leaders, particularly those associated with civic agencies, display skills which heretofore had not been found in abundance in the Negro community — education in the social sciences, administrative gifts, and a certain level of urbanity and sophistication in the ways of the world.

Nowhere is the change more evident than in the lessened role of the ministry. Whereas before the clergy had been universally conceded to be the principal source of Negro leadership, today it is rapidly becoming simply one group (albeit an important one) among many which the race relations professionals call upon for support, resources, and publicity. In the past, the ministers' contributions to civic life have often been more verbal than real, but the professionals are beginning to organize that civic life in such a way that the verbal — and occasionally monetary — support of the ministry is sufficient to enable these professionals to do the real work unhampered. The League has recognized that ministers, like other lay civic leaders, can be only part-time leaders; therefore, it has sought to use them in such ways as sending large delegations of ministers to pack the galleries at hearings on proposed state legislation in Springfield. The ministers are not called upon to speak, much less to lead; that is for the professionals and the titular heads of the civic associations.

The Negro minister is, of course, of greater significance in those northern cities where Negro politicians lack an independent base of power — i.e., where the politicians must rely on the support of other nonpolitical groups. Ministers seem to be more important in electoral and issue politics in the Negro communities of Los Angeles and Detroit than in Chicago. Nonpartisan city administrations must, in the typical case, be somewhat more responsive to citizens' groups than administrations which are based on professional political organizations into which the Negro politicians have been incorporated. In this situation, and given the general *imputation* of influence to the Negro ministers by many white leaders, it is not surprising that delegations of ministers in nonmachine cities are taken more seriously. A minister's civic group in Chicago, in contrast, often expresses frustration and anger at their seeming inability to influence the Mayor; one consequence of this is that the group frequently exaggerates the influence the Negro politician enjoys with the Mayor. The greater the degree of "professionalization" in any Negro community (in terms both of professional politicians and professional race relations experts), the less the activity and the narrower the role of lay leaders including ministers.[1]

The new Negro leadership is distinctly middle class. The direct action protest groups of the old order are no longer found for the most part, or they survive only in attenuated and sometimes discredited form. The middle-class leadership is not unchallenged, however. Negro labor leaders have risen since the end of the war, to be active competitors for the offices in the NAACP. In part, this competition has been due to the fact that the NAACP has come to have a near-monopoly on Negro protest action, and as such has been an association which can confer a considerable amount of prestige and status on its leaders; in part, it reflects real disagreement over local programs and policies; and in part, it springs from a fundamental class antagonism between the two groups. But this labor-business antipathy is only a comparatively small factor in the divisions which cut through the leadership of the Negro community of Chicago. The real split that has developed has occurred within the Negro middle class, not between the middle and lower classes.

Negro leaders drawn both from the ranks of the prestigious and the dispossessed are slowly being eclipsed. There is a heightened sense of militancy in the growing Negro middle class, and it is within this group that the most important differences occur. The associations which organize and sustain protest action are growing in size and influence and are steadily working toward an exclusive title to the mantle of civic leadership. The staff and budget of the Urban League have grown remarkably in only a few years. The NAACP is raising record budgets. More and more groups of leaders are being brought into these associations through elaborate committee systems. For the first time, a Negro protest organization was able to raise a fund to be spent on lobbying for an FEPC law. For almost the first time, a sizable delegation was organized and dispatched to the state capital to lend support to the campaign behind this bill. To a greater extent than ever before, the would-be Negro leader is being forced to make a choice of political style — the opportunities either for remaining silent on issues or for adopting a "moderate" line are decreasing. The tone and rhetoric of civic life in the Negro community are more and more being supplied by the voluntary associations, and particularly by their professional staffs.

At the same time, the issues confronting the Negro community — or, more accurately, the issues brought to its attention by the voluntary associations — are issues that involve status rather than welfare ends. These status ends are generally complex and often divisive. The campaign for FEPC is reaching a peak; it may be the last major issue upon which most Negroes can readily agree. Housing, almost universally proclaimed the next major target, is far more difficult and many more differences of opinion and reservations about both ends and means can be detected. The emergence of these new goals can be explained partly in terms of the natural movement of sentiment among Negroes to such areas of interest as housing. But to a great extent, these goals are conspicuously fostered by the voluntary associations. This "issue leadership" — the tendency to set the agenda of civic action — could be uncharitably explained as due to the need organizations have constantly to develop reasons for their existence. Somewhat more charitably, it can be explained in terms of the search by professionals for areas in which their skills and training will be most useful. The "agency" aproach to race relations springs from a conviction that the resources of the professional — the ability to carry on research, disseminate information, and engage in a constant public relations effort — are precisely those best suited to civic action. If these are the advantages of the agency approach, then their costs must not be overlooked.

These costs arise out of the constraints which the organizations place upon their leaders. The good of the community tends to become identified with the goals sought by the agency. It is not by any means self-evident, for example, that the pre-eminent goal of many race relations associations, i.e., the ending of those practices which exclude the Negro from white neighborhoods, is the goal must desired by or most relevant to many rank-and-file Negroes. Open occupancy is an end which may have some meaning to those aspirant members of the Negro middle class who either are prepared to take advantage of, or who find gratification in the symbolic character of, these opportunities. The large number of Negroes who choose to remain within Bronzeville may have other goals. They may seek, for example, better housing even if it is segregated or all-Negro; they may value the kind of Negro political representation which springs from Negro concentration in a few wards; they may value new schools even if they are placed in districts that render them all-Negro; they may, in short, value things over ideas or opportunities. These kinds of people may very easily not be represented on the boards of the leading voluntary associations, or indeed have any recognized leaders at all in the ranks of the middle class. The Negro church and the political machine pride themselves on speaking "for" those Negro masses, but this is true only in small degree. The churchmen who are recognized leaders tend to be those who have raised themselves and their congregations above their origins and who now speak with a mixture of surprise and disdain of the lower class people whom they "don't understand." The prominent ministers with recognizably lower-class congregations are usually not attracted by the incentives of civic leadership; they confine themselves to their own organizations which often involve large social service agencies created and maintained by the church itself. The political machine has won the major battles it set out to fight and, as a comfortably-situated organization, it has no further need for race appeals or race issues. Indeed, those appeals which once aided it in its formative years may now prove an embarrassment. Only a new struggle — either for control within the Negro machine or in its relations with the city organization — might provoke a renewed use of race appeals.

The Negro voluntary associations, insofar as they have become middle-class with a professional orientation, are ill-equipped to respond to issues which require mass protest tactics. The character of the ends being sought today — particularly in the fields of housing and employment — makes it difficult to rely on picketing, boycotting, and other protest tactics.[2] Nonetheless, there remain many areas in the North in which protest can be useful for certain goals. The NAACP, under a generally moderate, middle-class leadership, is not prepared to use those tactics vigorously. When in early 1960, Negro students in the South began their famous "sit-ins" in lunch counters, a wave of sympathy picketing movements began in the North. The NAACP in cities such as Chicago felt called upon to participate in this, but did so only on a sporadic and token basis. Picket lines were formed on Saturdays in front of certain chain stores in the city, but no attempt at a sustained campaign was made. The NAACP branch president was able to persuade a few business and professional men to walk the lines for one or two hours each; this, in itself, was a considerable accomplishment, but fell short of the kind of mass response such an issue seems to demand. The "distinctive competence" of such associations is foreign to the needs of certain situations. This is made clear when, paradoxically, northern sympathy boycotts in the lunch-counter dispute were often organized and led by white students.

It is argued that the ends of the race relations organizations must be sought as a necessary precondition for any radical improvement in the lot of the Negro; housing cannot be substantially improved until it is desegregated. There is some truth in this, to be sure, but given the limited resources for civic action in the Negro community, the matter becomes a question of priorities. In this state of affairs, it is not obvious that energies should be devoted to status rather than welfare ends.[3]

Another cost of organization leadership is that the natural and widespread disagreements on ends and means tend to be driven underground or at least concealed. Not all disagreements over policy reflect personal self-seeking or a stake in the status quo; some quite legitimate interests may be at odds with the interests of the race relations agencies. The deep differences and suspicions which separate many Negro political leaders from certain voluntary association leaders cannot all be automatically resolved in favor of the latter. The machine performs certain functions and provides certain services to Negroes who are not otherwise represented in the civic life of the community. The geographic dispersal of the Negro population in the city and county which might, in the long run, weaken the Negro machine may be desirable, but its desirability is not self-evident. In a Michigan city, for example, there is a deliberate move to *concentrate* Negroes in a single residential area in order that political representation can be secured on the city council. There is a tendency for organizations committed to social change as the principle which justifies their existence to force the pace of such change without a thorough examination of the consequences. The Negro machine commands the loyalties of many Negroes on a non-ideological or issue-free basis; in the absence of the machine, many of these same people could be organized by other forces on an entirely different basis, as the history of Negro politics in New York demonstrates. A careful assessment must be made of what an alternative to Dawson might entail in terms of ends and means.

Another area in which the change from the old to the new order is evident is found in the relations between Negroes and whites. Contacts are gradually becoming broader, more frequent, and less ritualized. Nowhere is this more evident than in the decline of the token leader. By virtue of intensive private efforts, the voluntary associations have been undermining the position of the innocuous token leaders in several city agencies. It is becoming increasingly difficult for the city officials to appoint a "good" Negro; the Urban League and the NAACP have attempted to influence such appointments more strongly than heretofore. Public criticism of Negro token leaders, of course, almost never occurs, but more such criticism is being heard today than in the past. These voluntary associations are becoming to a greater degree than before the "representatives" of the Negro community, taking the places of the older prestige leaders and politicians. It remains to be seen, of course, whether the constraints imposed by participation in city agencies will serve to convert the more militant Negroes now being recommended for appointment into less outspoken representatives or whether these constraints will serve to aggravate their militancy. In any case, the efforts being made to get "the right kind of person" on these boards may reflect an underemphasis on the structure of the situation in which such leaders will have to work.

In the civic life of the old order, not much happened and relatively little was attempted. In the emerging new order, much more is attempted. Still, in terms of substantive gains for the Negro, little in Chicago is changing. In part this is because in the critical issue areas, the quality of Negro leadership makes very little immediate difference. The value placed by Negroes themselves on leadership here may be exaggerated; there are many things that simple leadership — concerting activity toward some goal — cannot achieve. In these areas, change seems to occur at its own pace, a product partly of the broad and gradual shifts in mood among the community as a whole and partly of the needs of influential whites. As this was being written, the prospects for a state FEPC law seemed promising for the first time in recent Illinois history. These favorable prospects may have been due to the protracted propaganda on behalf of the law conducted over the past decade by various organizations, for the most part white-led. Much more relevant, however, were the political needs of the Republican Governor whose aspirations appeared to call for broadening his base of support among liberal elements in the community. The bill did not pass. The Governor gave it some support but could not give it all-out support without jeopardizing other measures in which he was interested.

A slight but detectable increase in responsiveness on the part of white civic leaders to the problems of residential segregation probably reflects as much a growing awareness of the *existence* and implications of the large and expanding Negro community as it does a reaction to the persuasiveness of Negro leaders.

At a level below that of the most critical and far-reaching issues, the increased level of Negro leadership and civic activity has probably had a much greater effect. Unmistakable signs indicate that Negroes now have better contacts among influential white civic and political leaders than formerly, and that these contacts can be utilized to gain concessions in certain areas. Progress of a limited sort has been made in advancing the cause of integration in private hospitals, reducing the harassment of Negroes by police officers, and securing the promotion of more Negroes in various city departments. These problems are essentially the same as those which faced the old order of Negro leadership, and increased success in recent years probably is a result of the increased ability of the new order of Negro leaders to organize and press for these ends. But improved organizational abilities have been achieved in an era in which the newer issues have become much more difficult and complex and in which the Negroes themselves have become far less certain as to what they want in concrete terms.

The differences and divisions in the Negro community today are deep and extensive. Many older leaders continue to place economic goals and self-improvement ahead of the housing and other integration goals of the newer leaders. The appropriateness of quotas as a solution to the problem of residential desegregation is not yet settled. The value of public housing remains an issue. Everyone is in favor of "better treatment" for Negroes in public schools, but whether this means redistricting or simply building better schools staffed with better personnel divides many leaders.

Differences in political style have not been reduced even though these differences no longer occur along class lines. The old order of leaders was composed of the dispossessed militants and the upper-class moderates. The new order may be more homogeneous in terms of class, but it is equally heterogeneous in terms of style. At the moment, the more extreme protesters are not in positions of influence in either the NAACP or the Urban League. Excluded from the former by electoral defeat and absent from the latter by choice, they have been active in or have formed ad hoc groups with which to carry on their civic work. A Chicago contingent for a youth march on Washington on behalf of a strong civil rights bill was organized, as was a Citizens' Housing Committee which attacked the Federal government for what were considered discriminatory practices in the administration of housing laws. That such leaders are a minority of the Negro civic leadership, that they must often wage their fights from outside the established organizations, and that publicity is virtually their only resource,

may all be factors which magnify — if they do not actually produce — the militancy of these leaders.

Similarly, the rise of a larger and more articulate Negro middle
class has not meant the elimination of other lines of division in
the Negro community. On the contrary, if anything these lines are
now more pronounced. The attempt to create and maintain middle-
and upper-class Negro neighborhoods has led to positions on
public housing and urban renewal which are often at variance
with the presumed goals of lower-income Negroes. The development of Negro businesses and professions has promoted differences, actual and potential, over the advisability of area conservation, redevelopment, enforcement of building and housing codes,
and reducing population densities. The prolonged existence of
segregated institutions in such fields as medicine and religion has
placed the beneficiaries in a position of having to protect these
organizations from the consequences of integration. In addition,
such Negro institutions tend to reduce the pressure for entry into
comparable white organizations.

Few of these divisions, of course, are allowed to become public
issues. There are important reasons why such differences are concealed or even reduced. These reasons form the basis for such
cohesiveness as exists in the Negro community. One such reason
is the fact that almost all Negroes of any stature are dependent
upon the Negro rank-and-file for power, income, and status. The
Negro publisher, insurance executive, doctor, lawyer, politician,
NAACP officer, and real estate broker all derive their position
or market from other Negroes. Only a tiny handful of Negroes
have managed to create enterprises which are fully nonracial —
for example, research or manufacturing in areas where the market
is not distinctively Negro. This dependence does not require the
Negro entrepreneur always to act as if the interests of the Negro
community were his goal. But it does require that the Negro
leader not allow himself to be conspicuously or dramatically
identified with a position or course of action at odds with the
consensual interests of the race.

The second factor which accounts for such cohesion as does
exist in the Negro community arises from the extent to which
the race values are widely shared. The desires for unity, leadership, and the elimination of the color line (however understood)

are all important elements of such solidarity as exists. All, of course, have their contrary elements as well: The desire for unity is in tension with the personal ambition to get ahead, to distinguish oneself somehow from the black masses; the desire for leadership is in tension with the suspicion with which any leader is viewed and the ritual condemnation of would-be leaders that proceeds at all levels in the community; the desire for the elimination of color barriers is often in tension with the desire to maintain the advantages of the status quo and the fear or discomfort which is experienced by some Negroes in interracial situations.

It was remarked at the outset of this study that a "Negro problem" exists together with the "white problem" as a factor in determining the course of race relations in northern American cities. This Negro problem has been the difficulty experienced by Negro leaders in concerting action toward collective or community goals. It has been suggested that, contrary to the common view that the Negro community has a high degree of unity and a strong sense of purpose at least in the area of race relations, there are here as much diversity and as many conflicts as one would expect to find in any large community. Further, it has been pointed out that few tangible incentives for civic action have existed in the Negro community, while there have been many such incentives for refraining from civic action. These problems — differences over ends and means and the absence of tangible incentives — account for much of the ineffectiveness of Negro attempts at civic action. A third factor, of significance in some but not all cases, is the sense of powerlessness and even futility which must inevitably blunt the enthusiasm for any venture undertaken in as hostile an environment for racial improvement as has existed in Chicago. But even when all of these explanations are taken fully into account, there remains a residuum for which other reasons must be sought. These reasons, at which a study of this kind can only hint, lie in the culture of the northern Negro ghetto itself.

The Negro in the North has the ability to create and sustain organizations of some kind. Bronzeville displays a plethora of organizations at almost all social levels. Like most organizations everywhere, their principal function is social. Civic or political purposes are typically secondary, if in fact they are not explicitly rejected. Whatever the exaggerations in Frazier's account of the "black bourgeoisie," there seems to be little doubt that the Negro's ability to organize has for the most part been confined to his social life. Only in a few areas are there signs that these social organizations can be made to serve more serious purposes. Some race relations associations are beginning to tap Negro societies for contributions and assistance. Social occasions are being turned to account for the benefit of race relations organizations. Some women's auxiliaries, fraternal orders, and social clubs are having their social functions invested with a civic purpose, or at least the proceeds are being diverted more and more to civic causes. These changes are slow and uneven, but the fact of change seems unmistakable.

The factors which have produced the rise of middle-class civic leadership and the renewed vitality of the voluntary associations have undoubtedly been connected with the general prosperity which has benefited both the Negro and the white communities, although unequally. The prospects for the future of both Negro civic activity and race relations in general are intimately bound up with the prospects for continued economic growth and full employment. The Negro middle class is now entering into its second and third generations. Young doctors, lawyers, and businessmen are increasingly the sons of business and professional men. The education these later generations receive probably equips them with attitudes and skills somewhat different from those acquired by the older generation. More and more, the Negro middle class is acquiring the attributes of any other middle class, and is losing the distinctively "Negro" forms of behavior. At the same time, increased prosperity has almost eliminated those direct-action movements led by the dispossessed and discontented. Apparently, sufficient regularized avenues are available for "getting ahead" to absorb the energies of the young and ambitious and divert them from organized protest.

The Negro has not been assimilated in America in the manner of earlier ethnic groups. His visibility remains an obstacle to that. Furthermore, no new wave of immigrants has arrived to push the Negro up one rung on the status ladder, as in the past succeeding waves of migration forced earlier ethnic groups up. Despite these great handicaps, however, postwar American prosperity has provided the northern Negro in America with an advantage which was enjoyed by few, if any, of the earlier ethnic groups — an advantage and, at the same time, a curse. The resources exist for the development of a large Negro middle class — a prerequisite for the improvement of the group as a whole — and simultaneously restrictions continue to be enforced against the Negro which frustrate the aspirations of many of those able to utilize these resources. The Negro cannot simply "buy" acceptance as others have purchased it; short of that, however, prosperity should enable him to overcome or evade many of the problems which have afflicted him in the past.

The arguments developed in this study may suggest to some readers both a doubt that real changes in race relations by human action are possible and a belief that many such changes would have very high costs in terms of the other ends of the community. This is not altogether the case. The entire study is based on the assumption that there are many areas in which Negro civic action can make a difference, although not perhaps as many areas as militant Negroes would like to believe. If these opportunities exist, there is a place for vigorous Negro leadership even if it serves no other purpose than to prompt whites into a clearer recognition of the existence of the race problem and its injustices. More and more, Negroes are getting that kind of leadership. Negro disgust with Negro leadership is in many areas greatly exaggerated; there is more leadership (in its various manifestations) than many Negroes are willing to admit. And this gradually improving leadership will inevitably be "unreasonable," "irresponsible," and "too radical" from the viewpoint of most whites and many conservative Negroes. Given the need for vigorous leadership, and given the magnitude of the problems and the relative lack of other forms of influence, it is difficult to see how Negroes can perform the protest function without utilizing tactics (such as racial appeals, extreme demands, an emotional rhetoric) that in different circumstances would be considered improper. It is inherently contradictory to look for "responsible" militants who will lead a "reasonable" protest movement.[4] Conflict is inherent in social change, and the disadvantages which rise in proportion to the intensity of such conflict must simply be weighed as a cost against the value of the ends being served. One implication of this study

is not that Negro leadership is irrelevant, but that it may be
decisively relevant only to a certain range of ends — principally
welfare ends.

The Negro in the North

The summary remarks made earlier in which the change in
Chicago from the old order to the new order was described take on
added force and relevancy when the city is seen in comparison
with others. The shift that is underway in so many areas in Chicago
can be seen elsewhere. The politicians and the civic leaders, formerly united, are drawing further and further apart in Chicago and
New York. The transfer of leadership from the old family elites
to the new business and professional groups is well along toward
realization. The change from personality leadership to functional
leadership, from the era of the "great spokesman" to the new
era of the professionally-staffed voluntary association is occurring,
at varying rates, everywhere.

New York has proceeded farther than Chicago, both in separat-
ing the political from the civic elites and in professionalizing race
relations. "Prestige" leaders in New York are, more commonly
than in Chicago, people who have been involved in the more
controversial aspects of human relations work. The access of these
men to the higher levels of influence in the city's political and
civic life is greater, in scope and frequency, than that enjoyed by
similar men in Chicago. The politician in New York exercises less
influence, controls fewer points of access to influential whites,
and intervenes less frequently (and with less effect) in the internal
politics of Negro voluntary associations. Chicago has set its foot
on the same path, but has taken fewer steps. But the forces that
will alter the present system are ineluctably at work.

New patterns are emerging in Detroit and Los Angeles. In
Detroit, a powerful ally of the Negro has had a profound impact.
The CIO has both championed Negro causes and provided an
alternative to Negro civic leadership. It has assisted in placing
Negroes in public office who are, ideologically and temperamentally, compatible with the civic leadership of the voluntary
associations. A similar interpenetration of political and civic elites
is seen in Los Angeles, but in a rudimentary state. There, the
combined impact on Negroes of an indifferent or hostile city leader-

ship, a weak labor movement, and a scarcity of valuable allies has been mitigated by the relatively low level of intensity with which race ends and causes are viewed.

Although this study offers little evidence that would support conclusions of such a high level of generality, it is nonetheless interesting to speculate on the relationships which may exist between civic and political leaders in various cities. The pattern in city politics, as Rossi observes,[5] has generally been for the political and civic elites to diverge and to form two relatively independent and often competing sources of civic influence. The complexity of the problems and issues facing cities and the increased specialization of interests has stimulated the development of the modern civic association with its board of lay civic leaders and professional staff. More and more, issues are raised and agitated and sentiment is mobilized by these organizations, particularly by their staffs. The felt importance of the volunteer civic leader drawn from the world of business or the professions has grown so enormously that corporate vice-presidencies are being created for that express purpose. Even if the lay leader does no more than act as an intermediary, communicator, or symbol of civic virtue on behalf of the professional staffs on the one hand and the professional politicians on the other, his role is becoming more and more significant. The Negro community has only begun to develop this "agency approach" to civic issues. In few northern cities is there a really vigorous, organized Negro civic life concerned with race or community goals. In no city are both the Urban League and the NAACP strong organizations.

In many major cities, white political leaders have been reduced more and more to simply seeking office and ratifying decisions which are welded together by outsiders. Some strong-mayor cities (such as Chicago, for example) have political leaders (like Mayor Richard Daley) who are real powers in their own right and who can both propose and dispose. But typically the civic groups propose and the political leaders acquiesce when they can do so without provoking excessive controversy. The Negro politician is now beginning to meet the challenge of these civic groups in the competition to speak "for" the community. The typical Negro political leader sees himself as the spokesman for the community. Within his own lifetime he was *both* civic leader and politician.

Breaking into the party organization meant the use of race issues and race appeals; this was the era of Negro political militancy. Only recently have groups, nonpolitical groups, arisen which are in competition with him for access to City Hall or other centers of influence. In most northern cities, the Negro political and civic elites are beginning to draw apart, just as they have already drawn apart in the total city. In some cases a new coalescence — a new merger of political and civic elites — is beginning to take place as middle-class "good government" groups find that politics may not be as disreputable as they once thought and that political leadership can be an instrument of social change rather than of stagnation.

Three different sets of relationships between Negro political and civic elites can be distinguished. In one sense, they may represent three stages in a single pattern of development. In other cities some stages may be skipped and no general trend can be discerned. But whatever the historical forces at work, these patterns can be discovered.

The first pattern we may call the period of *compatible elites*. Chicago Negro affairs were, in the 1920's, in this stage. This is the period of the early entrants into Negro political and civic life. The individuals active in these matters tend to be the same, or at least share common sets of values and motives, in both the political and civic sphere. Lawyers, ministers, and undertakers, for example, are often found working both in civic causes and political campaigns. Indeed, there seems to be, in the eyes of the Negro leaders, very little to distinguish the two areas. The rewards tend to be the same in both cases: prestige, access, and limited influence. The political leaders are trying to "break into" the established white organization. Race issues and race appeals become an asset in such campaigns. Civic organizations are mobilized to provide support for political leaders with whom they share a common stake in policy matters. The race issues, during this period, are typically concerned with welfare ends — goals which are relatively simple, direct, tangible, and unifying. There is no inherent or logical conflict of interest between the politician and the civic leader. The politician can argue that to advance race causes, political access is required; the civic leader can argue that race issues are a means of mobilizing Negro voters behind a politician who aspires to such access.

In Chicago, and probably also in New York, a second stage inevitably seems to emerge out of this early period of overlapping or coinciding elites. This we may call the pattern of *diverging elites*. Negro access to politics has been accomplished, and the Negro political organization has begun to coalesce and consolidate its gains. The problem of the Negro politician is no longer one of entry or access, but one of maintenance and stability. Race issues often become at best superfluous, at worst embarrassing. Meanwhile, new and younger men are entering the ranks of the civic leaders. To them, race goals are as far from attainment as ever. They see the Negro politician withdrawing from their causes and often becoming hostile to them. A natural conflict of interest arises between the two groups. One is desirous of changing the status quo, the other seeks to preserve it. Further, ambitious younger politicians, restless at the longevity of the older leadership, are maneuvering to advance their prospects and establish a claim to inherit the mantle of leadership. Some are tempted by the possibility of cultivating race issues and civic organizations as a source of political strength. The civic elite in the NAACP, the Urban League, or similar groups, seeks to compel the politicians to act by building up community pressure on them, or, failing that, to by-pass the political leaders by taking their cases directly to the city's white leaders. The political and civic elites enter a period of competition for the right to represent or speak "for" the Negro community. Deep antagonisms arise, which are often thinly concealed behind the general agreement not to expose deep divisions in the Negro community to the scrutiny of whites. In Chicago, the civic elite, confronted with a machine — Negro and white — which is very strong and cohesive, tends to despair of success and to make their attacks on it more and more open and direct. In New York, where the machine has already been weakened, the civic groups are often able to get around the organization and to influence the Mayor and other important leaders directly. The Negro politician is angered and resentful at the success of the civic groups, but is unable to acquire or rebuild his strength to the point where he can make an effective challenge. The appointment of Negroes to important and prestigious positions begins to be taken over by civic groups with good access and influential representatives.[6] The Mayor must deal with these groups, because the weakening of his political organization compels him to rely to a greater extent on issues and blue-ribbon appointments as a means of insuring his continued success at the polls. The patronage of the city becomes divided—the lesser posts of little prestige value (and hence of little political value in the new situation) are parceled out to the regular organization leaders, while the larger, more significant posts are distributed on the basis of recommendations from civic leaders and agencies.

A third pattern can be detected in one or two cities. Thus far, it is not the natural result of trends emerging out of older situations in cities such as New York and Chicago. But it can be seen in Los Angeles and Detroit. This is the period in which Negro politics becomes "reformed" in the eyes of the civic leaders. Certain factors, such as the emergence of strong, white, liberal political movements (for example the Democratic Clubs in Los Angeles or the CIO in Detroit) decide to challenge the existing, often weak, political leadership by creating a movement that will fuse civic action and politics. This we can call the *new merger*. "Good government" groups win political office or wage important political campaigns. A new interest in politics is born among the middle classes. Politics is no longer viewed as inevitably contaminated. Politics offers rewards which are suddenly discovered to be appealing to formerly disinterested groups — the possibility of altering public policy, the thrill of the game, or a desire to be "on the inside." Politics becomes characterized by the tea party, the kaffeklatsch, the block meeting, the spaghetti dinner with wine. New groups become part-time politicians — enthusiastic amateurs, university people, shop stewards, housewives, and ambitious young lawyers. For Negroes, politics once again becomes a possible avenue for raising and disposing of race issues. The belief arises that the natural hostility between the political and civic elites can be ended, and that the civic spirit can dominate the political leader. In this, they are probably overly optimistic. Although a change in incumbents may make some differences, the situational constraints on the politician in office will continue to be very much different from those on the board member of the NAACP. The civic elite has set out to repeal the iron law of oligarchy which it felt had made the political elite unresponsive to the needs of the masses, but in the end they may very well discover that they have only succeeded in amending it.

NOTES

Chapter I

1. St. Clair Drake, "Churches and Voluntary Associations in the Chicago Negro Community," unpublished paper, 1940 (mimeographed), p. 438.

2. Harry J. Walker, "Negro Benevolent Societies in New Orleans," Cited in Gunnar Myrdal, *An American Dilemma* (New York: Harper & Bros., 1944).

3. Myrdal offers some hypotheses to account for the high level of Negro membership in associations in *ibid.*, pp. 952-55.

4. (New York: Random House, 1947).

5. Claude McKay, *A Long Way From Home* (New York: L. Furman, Inc., 1937), p. 145.

6. Myrdal, *Op. Cit.* pp. i, ii, 26. Myrdal's statement is: "The Negro's entire life and, consequently, also his opinions on the Negro problem, are, in the main, to be considered as secondary reactions to more primary pressures from the side of the dominant white majority" (p. i); and further, "the thesis [is] that the Negro problem is predominantly a white man's problem" (p. ii).

7. Cf. E. Franklin Frazier, *The Negro in the United States* (2d ed. rev.; New York: Macmillan, 1957), pp. 292-300.

8. Peter B. Clark, *The Big Businessman as a Civic Leader*, (Glencoe, Ill.: The Free Press, forthcoming), chaps. iii, vii.

Chapter II

1. See bottom of page 21.

2. William L. Dawson of Chicago, first elected in 1942; Charles Diggs, Jr., of Detroit, first elected in 1954; and Adam Clayton Powell, Jr., of New York, first elected in 1944. Before Dawson, there were two Negro Congressmen from Chicago: Oscar de Priest (1928-34), and Arthur W. Mitchell (1934-42).

3. For example, in St. Louis in 1959, six wards returned Negro aldermen but only two of these had Negro ward leaders (wards 18 and 19).

4. Negro voters were strongly opposed to Mayor Cobo and always voted heavily for his opponent. Many Negro leaders, and some liberal whites, believe that part of Cobo's appeal, especially to middle-class whites who felt threatened by Negro residential expansion, was what they considered to be Cobo's anti-Negro policies in public housing, real estate, and other areas.

5. See Walter F. White, *A Man Called White* (New York: Viking Press, 1948), pp. 212-19.

6. In 1952, Negroes were 19 per cent of a random sample of Detroit UAW members. Cf. Arthur Korn-

hauser, *et al., When Labor Votes* (New York: University Books, 1956), p. 24. At the time, there were about 290,000 UAW members in Detroit or about 30 per cent of both the labor force and the eligible voters (p. 22).

7. Polish and German UAW members expressed more hostility towards Negroes in a sample survey than did native Americans. Cf. *ibid,* p. 180.

8. The CIO partially reimburses some union political workers for time lost on the job. Further, some members combine political work with the position of shop steward, and thus in a sense have a "job" with political overtones. But by and large, precinct politics is a volunteer operation.

9. For a complete account of the impact of the Cincinnati electoral system on Negro politics, see Ralph A. Straetz, *PR Politics in Cincinnati* (New York: New York University Press, 1958), esp. chap. viii.

10. I am indebted to the researches of Ralph Ottwell, former Nieman Fellow at Harvard, for most of my facts on Boston.

11. The four districts are the 11th, 12th, 13th, and 14th Assembly Districts in Harlem. The difference between the Democratic and Republican totals in the four districts is divided by the difference between the Democratic and Republican vote for Manhattan as a whole. The results are: 1954 — 32.46 per cent; 1956 — 55.57 per cent; 1958 — 49.05 per cent.

12. On Jewish tendencies to vote split tickets, see Lawrence H. Fuchs, *The Political Behavior of American Jews* (Glencoe, Ill.: The Free Press, 1956), pp. 131-49.

13. See bottom of page 33.

14. Cf. Chester Barnard, *The Functions of the Executive* (Cambridge: Harvard University Press,

1938), and his notions of "effectiveness" and "efficiency," esp. chap. iii.

15. La Guardia was elected Mayor in 1933. His election, and the revelations of the Seabury investigation, led to the adoption of a new city charter in 1937 which centralized power in the hands of the Mayor and the Board of Estimate.

16. Negro judges in Detroit were first *appointed,* to fill vacancies, by party leaders. High-calibre men were deliberately selected in each case. They then stood for election as incumbents.

17. John Morsell, "The Political Behavior of Negroes in New York City" (PhD dissertation, Columbia University, 1950). See also Harold Gosnell, *Negro Politicians* (Chicago: University of Chicago Press, 1935); St. Clair Drake and Horace R. Cayton, *Black Metropolis* (New York: Harper & Bros., 1945); and Henry L. Moon, *Balance of Power: The Negro Vote* (Garden City, N. Y.; Doubleday & Co., 1948). On Negroes in New York, see Oscar Handlin, *The Newcomers* (Cambridge: Harvard University Press, 1959).

18. The Chicago *Daily Defender,* August 18, 1959, carried an editorial on this subject, written on behalf of Chicago Negro lawyers who were anxious to gain greater representation on the bench. The editorial, in a manner characteristic of much Negro thought on the subject of the political goals of the race, spoke of the need for "recognition" of the race in proportion to its numbers. It provided a table with the Chicago population of several major ethnic and nationality groups together with the number of judges drawn from each group. To this I have added another column, showing judges per 100,000 population:

Group	Population	Judges	Judges per 100,000 population
Irish	400,000	33	8.25
Jews	285,000	20	7.02
Poles	500,000	10	2.00
Italians	175,000	6	3.43
Negroes	900,000	3	0.33

The editorial was based on a report of the all-Negro Cook County Bar Association, prepared by its Committee on Public Affairs (June 29, 1959). The report also listed 38 Negro lawyers who held adminis-trative posts in city, state, and federal agencies in Illinois, including about 16 Democrats and 19 Republicans. (The population figures here should not be considered accurate.)

Chapter III

1. Norton Long, "The Local Community as an Ecology of Games," *American Journal of Sociology,* LXIV (November, 1958), 251-61. Compare this view to that in Ernest A. Barth and Baha Abu-Laban, "Power Structure and the Negro Sub-Community," *American Sociological Review,* XXIV (February, 1959), 69-76.

2. The literature on machine politics includes Frank R. Kent, *The Great Game of Politics* (rev. ed.; Garden City, N. Y.: Doubleday & Co., 1923) and David H. Kurtzman, *Methods of Controlling Votes in Philadelphia* (Philadelphia: University of Pennsylvania Press, 1935). On Chicago in particular, consult Harold F. Gosnell, *Machine Politics, Chicago Model* (Chicago: University of Chicago Press, 1937); Sonya Forthal, *Cogwheels of Democracy: A Study of the Precinct Captain* (New York: William-Frederick Press, 1946); and Martin Meyerson and Edward C. Banfield, *Politics, Planning, and the Public Interest* (Glencoe, Ill.: The Free Press, 1955), pp. 61-88 and 285-302.

3. The Republican vote in the Negro wards appears to be based on an irreducible core of traditional Republicans, ranging in number (in the First Congressional District) from about 23,000 to about 36,000 votes.

4. In another study conducted ten years ago, it was revealed that of a sample which included half the Negro lawyers in Chicago (112 of the approximately 225), fifty-eight had been active in politics to some extent — holding office, running as a candidate, receiving clients from the organization with a "kick-back" fee, etc. William Henri Hale, "The Career Development of the Negro Lawyer in Chicago," (PhD. dissertation, University of Chicago, 1949), p. 74.

5. Cf. Charles W. Smith, Jr., "Campaign Communications Media," *Annals,* CCLIX (September, 1948), 90-97.

6. See bottom of page 65.

7. Precinct 78, second ward, cast 101 Democratic votes, or 63.92 per cent of the total votes in the precinct. This should be compared to the median precinct in the ward, which cast 90.90 per cent Democratic votes, and to the highest precinct, which cast 98.41 per cent Democratic votes.

8. See R. Gene Geisler, "Chicago Democratic Voting, 1947-57" (Ph.D. dissertation, University of

Chicago, 1958), pp. 11, 100, 109, and 130.

9. Data from a chart published by the Chicago Plan Commission, "Chicago Population, 1900-1950, By Square Mile for Each Decade."

10. Geisler (*op. cit.*) argues that between 1948 and 1956, the "potential vote" in Chicago increased by 4 per cent, while voter registration decreased by 10 per cent (p. 75) and that this decline was greatest in those areas where the Democratic machine has traditionally been the strongest (p. 63). The Republicans did not gain these Democratic losses — rather, it was an absolute loss in votes unaccounted for by either population losses or a switch to Republicanism (p. 65).

Chapter IV

1. See bottom of page 78.

2. Negro politicians are keenly, and often bitterly, aware of the power of the Mayor. "Daley is the czar in this town. . . . He's got all the power, and I mean all. There aren't any men any more on that Council, only mice." Another politician referred to the Chicago City Council as "fifty sheep and a shepherd." Nevertheless, the Negro aldermen are kept steadily busy dealing with constituent's problems. Records maintained by four Negro aldermen show that in 1958, a total of 22,569 constituents were interviewed on personal problems.

3. It is interesting that Negro wards persistently approve most "good government" and spending measures that appear on the ballot for voter ratification. Just why this should be so is a matter for speculation. The result, however, is often that the Negro (and other "machine" wards) supply the majorities necessary to approve measures which later result in civic projects Negro leaders deem hostile to Negro interests (e.g., land clearance), while the "newspaper" wards that are politically independent often disapprove these same measures that eventually result in the expenditure of public funds for their benefit.

4. An intensive analysis of this issue can be found in Peter Rossi and Robert A. Dentler, *Rebuilding the City* (Glencoe, Ill.: The Free Press, forthcoming).

5. Chicago, *Municipal Code,* chap. 137, sec. 137-13.1. Passed March 14, 1956.

Chapter V

1. It is likely that a crucial variable in northern race relations is the *perceived* size of the Negro community. In Boston, for example, many whites (*and Negroes*) tend to underestimate the size of the Negro population. In Chicago, on the other hand, both Negroes and whites persistently over-estimate its size. I gathered no systematic data on this point, but the general pattern seems to be unmistakable.

The first four states to pass open occupancy legislation were Colorado, Connecticut, Massachusetts, and Oregon. In each, the Negro population is small. Cf. Donald S. Frey, "Open Occupancy for American Cities," *Municipal Law Service Letter, IX* (September, 1959).

2. This is simply a hypothesis. Much more research on race politics in state legislatures would be required for conclusive answers.

3. The distinction made here between "community-involving" and

"Negro-involving goals should be borne in mind throughout the study, but particularly in Chapter VIII on the goals of Negro leaders.

4. Estimate made by the Real Estate Research Corporation of Chicago and contained in *Chicago Tribune* "Market Data Report," 1955. In mid 1959, the rate of expansion slowed somewhat. In July, 1959, about two city blocks were becoming 25 per cent non-white each week. In the period 1956-57, the rate had been 3¾ blocks per week. Part of the decrease is likely due to a drop in the rate of in-migration. See *Chicago Market Letter of Real Estate Research Corporation,* October, 1959 (Chicago).

5. For studies of Negro population patterns in Chicago, see Otis D. and Beverly Duncan, *The Negro Population of Chicago* (Chicago: University of Chicago Press, 1957). Social and political implications of the Negro population growth in northern cities are discussed in Morton Grodzins, "Metropolitan Segregation," *Scientific American,* October, 1957, pp. 33-41; "The New Shame of the Cities," *Confluence,* VII (Spring, 1958), 29-46; and *The Metropolitan Area as a Racial Problem* (Pittsburgh: University of Pittsburgh Press, 1958). The data on race violence are from the *Report of the United States Commission on Civil Rights,* (Washington, D. C.: U. S. Government Printing Office, 1959), p. 431.

6. Cf. Scott Greer, *Last Man In: Racial Access to Union Power* (Glencoe, Ill.: The Free Press, 1959).

7. I share Kurt Lewin's view that increased interaction between members of formerly segregated groups, increases conflict in many cases. Cf. Gertrude Lewin (ed.) *Kurt Lewin, Resolving Social Conflicts* (New York: Harper & Bros., 1948), p. 167. I do not agree with Homan's

thesis that increased interaction necessarily promotes shared values and sentiments. Cf. G. C. Homan, *The Human Group* (New York: Harcourt, Brace & Co., 1950), pp. 113ff.

8. A related factor which may be of considerable importance in distinguishing one northern Negro community from another (although not directly at the level of leadership) is the source and pattern of in-migration. Each large northern city is served by a distinctive set of major transportation lines along which move Negroes (and other migrants). The route of those lines works to draw migrants from different backgrounds. Thus, Chicago is linked to rural Mississippi, Louisiana, and Alabama by the Illinois Central railroad. New York is tied, by the Pennsylvania and other lines, to the tidewater states of the southeast and, by ship, to the West Indies. Los Angeles is linked, by the Southern Pacific and other lines, to the southwestern states. These southern areas vary considerably in the level of education, income, urbanization, and previous integration experienced by Negroes. Mississippi is one of the largest sources of Negro in-migrants to Chicago, and it also is one of the most disadvantaged states. On the other hand, New York has received many West Indian Negroes who have no experience in the American South. Indeed, a perennial bone of political contention in New York is "American" Negro resentment at what is felt to be the inordinate proportion of "West Indian" Negroes in important political offices in Tammany. A remarkable number of Harlem district leaders, for example, have been of Caribbean origin — Hulan Jack, Lloyd Dickens, Antonio Rasmus, and others. No simple explanation can be given here that would account for the success of West

Indians in rising faster than others in Harlem politics.

Many Negroes are convinced that these differences in origin are of considerable importance in the civic life of the Negro in the north. This possibility is intriguing, but the basic research on the source and pattern of Negro migration in the United States has yet to be done. One project bearing on this is now underway at the University of Chicago.

Chapter VI

1. Gerald Bullock quoted in *Chicago Defender*, July 5, 1956.

2. Quoted in *Chicago Defender*, September 4, 1956.

3. Estimated in Roi Ottley, *The Lonely Warrior: The Life and Times of Robert S. Abbott* (Chicago: Henry Regnery Co., 1955), pp. 364-65.

4. From Audit Bureau of Circulation (ABC) statements for national and local circulation of the weekly *Chicago Defender* in *Ayer's Directory* (Philadelphia: N. W. Ayer & Son, Inc., 1958). By comparison, the Negro magazines had far greater circulation: *Ebony*, 427,-444; *Jet*, 405,861; and *Tan*, 168,297.

5. In 1934, the *Chicago Defender* derived about 80 per cent of its revenue from circulation, with the balance from advertising. Today, the proportions are almost reversed (Interview document). *Chicago Defender* circulation figures, based on June and March Audit Bureau of Circulation Statements (sworn by publishers) since World War II, reveal a largely static or declining position.

Year	Chicago Edition (Weekly)	National Edition (Weekly)	Daily Edition‡
1945	56,534	81,701	
1946	73,475	129,156	
1947	68,009	126,917	
1948	59,301	133,758	
1949	60,668	128,466	
1950	62,474	98,534	
1951	62,907	82,759	
1952	61,717	79,726	
1953	57,841	54,145	
1954	54,145	65,730	
1955	53,598	54,243	
1956	49,386	37,242	
1957	91,470	47,128	25,672†
1958	63,111*		15,606

*Figures for local and national editions in 1958 were apparently combined in one report.

†Not an ABC statement.

‡Begun in 1957.

6. *Daily Defender*, January 29, 1959.

7. Lucile Edley, "Strategies and Techniques of Politics: A Study of Ten Selected Precinct Captains from Chicago's Third Ward," (Master's Thesis, University of Chicago, 1955), p. 55.

8. Cf. Gunnar Myrdal, *An American Dilemma* (New York: Harper & Bros., 1944), p. 911.

9. Quoted in *Chicago Tribune,* Sept. 26, 1959.

10. See Scott Greer, *Last Man In: Racial Access to Union Power* (Glencoe: The Free Press, 1959), for a study of unions and Negroes in Los Angeles. Cf. also Paul Jacobs, "The Negro Worker Asserts His Rights," *Reporter,* July 23, 1959, pp. 16-21, on the conflict between the NAACP and the AFL-CIO on integration within organized labor.

11. This account follows that in Fay Calkins, *The CIO and the Democratic Party* (Chicago: University of Chicago Press, 1952), pp. 83-84.

12. St. Clair Drake and Horace R. Cayton, *Black Metropolis* (New York: Harper & Bros., 1945), pp. 412-29.

13. *Chicago Defender,* April 18, 1959.

14. When maintenance needs are more nearly alike, the differences in viewpoint are proportionally less. This is true in Detroit, for example. Cf. Chapter II.

Chapter VII

1. For a description of the kinds of white civic leaders who become active in Chicago race relations, and for material on the world of white business-civic leadership generally, see Peter B. Clark, *The Big Businessman as a Civic Leader,* (Glencoe, Ill.: The Free Press, forthcoming), Chap. II.

2. This quotation was kindly supplied by Peter B. Clark from one of his series of interviews with white civic leaders in Chicago.

3. Interview document from Peter B. Clark.

4. Interview document from Peter B. Clark.

5. *Hansberry* v. *Lee,* 311 U. S. 32 (1940).

6. Martin Myerson and Edward C. Banfield, *Politics, Planning and The Public Interest* (Glencoe, Ill.: The Free Press, 1955), pp. 218-19. The Negro newspaper observed that "powerful colored political leaders" as well as important middle and upper class Negroes "have remained mute and silent on this housing tragedy." *Chicago Defender,* December 17, 1949.

7. A suggestive comparison can be drawn between the levels of philanthropy prevailing in the Chicago Negro community today with the Chicago Jewish community of thirty-five years ago. Total Negro contributions, drawn from a population of over three-quarters of a million, to the NAACP and the Urban League did not exceed $50,000 in 1954-55. Louis Wirth reports the Chicago Jewish community in 1922 totalled an estimated 285,000 people. In 1923 this community raised $2,500,000 and in 1925 over-subscribed a drive for $4,000,000. *The Ghetto* (Chicago: University of Chicago Press, 1928), pp. 275-78.

8. See H. L. Sheppard, "The Negro Merchant: A Study of Negro Anti-Semitism," *American Journal of Sociology,* LIII (September, 1947), 96-99, and Wolf, Loving, and Marsh, *Negro-Jewish Relationships* (Detroit: Wayne University Press, 1944). Sheppard quotes one Chicago businessman as follows:

"There's no doubt about it. They [the Jews] get together and put into business anybody they want. And most of the time it's another Jew. . . . They get together to throw out of business

anybody they don't want —
Negroes, of course. That's what
happened to me. I opened a
laundry . . . and was doing O.K.
for about a month, and then the
Board of Health forced me out.
. . . I know the Board was urged
on by Jews who don't want
colored business, even in our own
community. They control all the
businesses here."

9. See Arnold M. Rose, *The
Negro's Morale* (Minneapolis: University of Minnesota Press, 1949),
pp. 133-34. A columnist in the
Negro *Pittsburgh-Courier* wrote, in
the editions of May 24, 1947, and
March 27, 1948, that Jews in Palestine were pursuing "Hitler-like"
tactics to obtain Palestine as a base
for "world power." Zionism was described as a "racket" and "im-
perialistic."

10. A respected editor of the
Negro newspaper wrote recently in
his column that "the number of
those among us who are anti-Semitic
is far fewer than a decade ago" but
that there are still "a few of our
leaders [who] are anti-Semitic." He
added: "To me this is absolutely un-
pardonable. No other minority in
American life including ourselves,
has fought more vigorously nor
more effectively against prejudice
and bigotry than the Jews. . . . If
we were to subtract somehow the
dynamic liberalizing influence of the
Jewish culture from American
society, we would be a lost ball in
high grass." Louis Martin in *Chicago Defender,* April 5, 1958.

11. Herbert Garfinkel, *When
Negroes March* (Glencoe, Ill.: The
Free Press, 1959), pp. iii-iv, 254.

12. When the Negro March on

Washington Movement was pressing
for the creation of a federal FEPC,
the *Pittsburgh-Courier* editorialized
on August 22, 1942: Although
FEPC helps Jews, the "Jews did
not help to force the creation of
this agency. And, as a matter of
fact, they stood off on the sidelines
to see how it was going before they
began to avail themselves of its
power and authority. . . . There are
some foxy Jews. We believe that
they should not be so foxy, that
they should FIGHT with us if they
hope to share the benefits of our
fighting." Then, a few sentences
further, the editorial went on to
"deplore" anti-Semitism among the
Negro masses.

12. White allies of the Negro are
not, of course, always *liberal* allies.
Occasionally anti-Negro whites can
make common cause with Negroes.
The Lake Meadows housing project
was opposed both by Negroes (who
did not want to lose their homes or
who were concerned over problems
of relocation) and by whites who
feared that the displaced Negroes
would attempt to enter their all-
white neighborhoods. Both the
Negro aldermen who represented
the areas from which Negroes were
being moved and the white aldermen who represented the far south
areas to which the Negroes might
go voted against the project in the
City Council. One of the leading
white opponents of the plan admitted that his organization had
helped Negroes finance court fights
against condemnation proceedings.
David Wallace, "Residential Concentration of Negroes in Chicago,"
Ph.D. thesis, Harvard University,
1953, pp. 258-61.

Chapter VIII

1. St. Clair Drake and Horace R.
Cayton, *Black Metropolis,* (New

York: Harper & Bros., 1945), pp.
728.

2. *Ibid.,* pp. 718ff.

3. David Riesman, *Faces in the Crowd: Individual Studies in Character and Politics* (New Haven: Yale University Press, 1952), p. 89. Riesman observes: "Indeed, it may be doubted whether any group in the county on the same socioeconomic level would be capable of demonstrating the activism, the concern, the knowledge about some political issue that almost all of our Harlem Negro respondents display on the race question" (p. 91).

4. Drake and Cayton, *op. cit.,* p. 723.

5. See bottom of page 171.

6. At least four Negro civic leaders who are examined in this study had married white women.

7. See column by Louis Martin, "Dope and Data," *Chicago Defender,* May 17, 1958.

8. Drake and Cayton, *op. cit.* pp. 723ff. Cf. also Gunnar Myrdal, *An American Dilemma,* (New York: Harper & Bros., 1944), pp. 766-67.

9. Drake and Cayton, *op. cit.,* pp. 725-26. Cf. also Myrdal, *op. cit.,* pp. 774-75, 857.

10. A thoughtful and well-informed Negro civic leader from Alabama, on the other hand, criticized Martin Luther King. He said, "I can't understand how these people up here [in Chicago] admire him so. Most people where I come from think he is just a front-man who has lost interest in his people and gotten carried away by all that national publicity." Inspirational leadership requires some form of distance—geographical or temporal. For a comparison of northern and southern Negro leaders that praises the latter and condemns the former, see an editorial in *Daily Defender,* March 8, 1960, entitled "Bankrupt Leadership."

11. Cf. the remarks of Ralph Bunche in his manuscript, "A Brief and Tentative Analysis of Negro Leadership," September, 1940, an unpublished document prepared for the Myrdal study on the American Negro. Bunche observes that "there is an almost universal tendency among Negroes to declare that Negro leadership is 'bad.' It is common practice to ascribe many of the ills of the race to the lack of competent leadership. . . . Hope for the future is often predicated upon the possibility of developing a 'new and better leadership' " (p. 50). At the same time, Bunche himself adds: "There is no real leadership in the sense of powerful personalities who can command enthusiastic followings" (p. 196). Many of Bunche's remarks are then devoted to a prescription for a "new and better leadership."

12. Samuel Strong distinguishes between a "race leader" and a "race man" on the basis of motive. The *race leader* acts selflessly, is sincere, and benefits the race without personal gain. The *race man* has questionable sincerity and uses race in order to further his own ends. Strong finds these "social types" widely recognized among Chicago Negroes, and provides many quotations illustrating the suspicion with which any trace of self-interest in a leader is viewed. Samuel Strong, "Social Types in the Negro Community of Chicago: An Example of the Social Type Method," Ph.D. dissertation, University of Chicago, 1940, pp. 67ff.

13. *Daily Defender,* June 11, 1959.

14. In a study of Negro precinct captains, Lucile Edley found no clear indication of a "race appeal" effectively used by Negroes to attract Negro votes. In middle-class precincts, the captains felt "that racial stuff is *passe.*" It had been used so much as a "football" that it was not appealing. Nor do

Negroes vote for Negro candidates simply because they are Negroes. In the 1959 aldermanic elections, heavy majorities were scored by white candidates running with regular Democratic organization backing in wards with large numbers of Negro voters despite the fact that they were opposed by Negroes who also claimed to be Democrats. But the race appeal is still used, particularly by those who face an uphill fight. In his campaign for the Congressional seat of Negro leader William L. Dawson in 1950, Archibald Carey, a Negro Republican, took full-page advertisements in the Negro press accusing Dawson of having supported whites for office in Negro districts. Cf. *Chicago Defender,* November 4, 1950, p. 29, and Lucile Edley, "Strategies and Techniques of Politics: A Study of Ten Selected Precinct Captains from Chicago's Third Ward," Master's thesis, University of Chicago, 1955, pp. 51-52.

15. An officer of the Negro insurance company remarked: "Negroes tend to look at it [the Negro company] on the basis of creating opportunities for Negroes to hold jobs. . . . Most Negroes deep down inside will want to help Negro business, but not enough will help. . . . The trouble is, today Metropolitan and New York Life are hiring Negro girls, too. . . . So it's kind of a dilemma. I guess what sustains us is pride or clannishness."

16. Quoted in Alfred de Grazia, "The Limits of External Leadership Over a Minority Electorate," *Public Opinion Quarterly,* XX (Spring, 1956), 125.

17. Reported in the *New York Times,* January 10, 1960, p. E5.

18. When Dr. J. H. Jackson, a leading Chicago Negro Baptist minister, opposed certain NAACP actions against the Little Rock, Arkansas school board and spoke out against Negroes seeking to force an entry into all-white churches, he was sharply attacked in the Negro press. *Daily Defender,* August 20 and October 1, 1959. The attack was couched in terms of a flat rejection of a bargaining approach to the issues.

19. Quoted in David Wallace, "Residential Concentration of Negroes in Chicago," Ph.D. dissertation, Harvard University, 1953, p. 261.

20. The distinction between "welfare" and "status" ends can also be viewed, in part, as a distinction between "Negro-involving" and "community-involving" ends. The latter are, of course, a much greater source of conflict.

21. Louis Martin, in *Chicago Defender,* February 11, 1956. A case in which a group of Negro leaders petitioned the Governor of Missouri to veto an appropriation bill for a new law school building for the all-Negro Lincoln University in St. Louis on the grounds that such a building would "solidify segregation" is reported in Arnold M. Rose, *The Negro's Morale* (Minneapolis: University of Minnesota Press, 1949), pp. 79-80.

22. *Daily Defender,* November 10, 1958.

23. *Chicago Defender,* November 15, 1958.

24. *Chicago Defender,* January 17, 1959.

25. *Daily Defender,* October 29, 1958, column by L. A. H. Caldwell.

26. *Chicago Defender,* November 1, 1958.

27. *Chicago Defender,* January 2, 1959.

28. *Chicago Defender,* November 1, 1958. In February, 1960, the Negro doctor who had been leading the opposition to the branch hospital plan announced that he was withdrawing his opposition because private hospitals "have continued to

discriminate." *Chicago Sun-Times,* February 25, 1960.

29. *Chicago Defender,* April 5, 1958.

30. Chicago Home Rule Commission, *Chicago's Government — Its Structural Modernization and Home Rule Problems* (Chicago: University of Chicago Press, 1954), p. 320.

31. *Ibid.,* pp. 63ff.

32. *Ibid.,* pp. 74-75.

33. *Daily Defender,* September 29, 1958. See also *Chicago Defender,* April 25, 1958; *Daily Defender,* May 26, 1958; and *Daily Defender,* July 23, 1958.

34. Concord Park, a Philadelphia suburban development, contains 139 moderately-priced homes built for sale as an interracial project. The sales program was geared to an announced ratio of 55 per cent white and 45 per cent Negro buyers. Over half the whites said, in a survey, that "they would *not* have bought without assurance that Negroes would not be in a clear majority." Chester Rapkin, "Market Experience and Occupancy Patterns in Interracial Housing Development" (Institute for Urban Land Studies, University of Pennsylvania, July, 1957). (Mimeographed.) A similar project was announced for Chicago. *Chicago Daily News,* June 6, 1958, p. 42. By late 1959 this group had moved to obtain land in Deerfield, a Chicago suburb. It promptly encountered strong white protest. Cf. Chicago *Sun-Times,* Nov. 15, 1959.

Subsequently, the move to build was blocked by an organized group of Deerfield's white citizens. They used a variety of tactics including the designation of the proposed project area as the site for a new public park and the beginning of condemnation proceedings to acquire the land. Legal moves to prevent acquisition by the city failed; a federal district judge

held that Deerfield was acting within its powers. A general survey of private, integrated housing developments and the efforts of some white communities to block them is contained in Eunice and George Grier, *Privately Developed Interracial Housing* (Berkeley: University of California Press, 1960).

35. In the spring of 1959, a white executive of a voluntary association, the Industrial Areas Foundation, suggested in public testimony before the Federal Civil Rights Commission in Chicago that a quota system be considered as a means of achieving integrated neighborhoods. The public reaction of most Negro leaders was prompt and negative. In letters to a daily newspaper, the executive secretary of the (Negro) Cosmopolitan Chamber of Commerce rejected the idea. To accept the quota system "smacks too much of paternalism, a condition which intelligent Negroes object to." While campaigns to get acceptance of Negro neighbors are good, "it must be understood that . . . [certain] powerful organizations entered into a conspiracy to completely segregate Negroes . . . and are entirely responsible for the present segregation pattern." *Chicago Sun-Times,* May 15, 1959. The Negro executive director of the Chicago Urban League also opposed quotas in testimony before the Federal Civil Rights Commission. See U. S. Commission on Civil Rights, "Housing" in *Hearings,* (Washington, D. C.: U. S. Government Printing Office, May 6, 1959), pp. 844ff.

36. Of the civic issues traced in the course of this study, nine involved conflicts of ends among Negro leaders at some level.

37. Martin Meyerson and Edward C. Banfield, *Politics, Planning, and the Public Interest* (Glencoe, Ill.: The Free Press, 1955) pp. 100, 101, 198.

38. Myrdal, *op. cit.*, p. 305: "The entire Negro middle and upper class becomes caught in an ideological dilemma. On the one hand, they find that the caste wall blocks their economic and social opportunities. On the other hand, they have, at the same time, vested interest in racial segregation since it gives them what opportunity they have."

39. E. Franklin Frazier, *Black Bourgeoisie* (Glencoe, Ill.: The Free Press, 1957), pp. 216ff.

40. Stone, in a study of Negro businessmen in Chicago, denies that there is any "recognizable dilemma" in the consciousness of his subjects. Negro businessmen, he argues, are class, not race, conscious, and act almost exclusively in terms of personal and business interest. This is an overstatement, but it is a valuable corrective to Myrdal's hypothesized "dilemma." Charles Sumner Stone, Jr., "The Negro Business Man and Organized Labor," Master's thesis, University of Chicago, 1951, pp. 75-76.

41. Dietrich C. Reitzes, *Negroes in Medicine,* (Report prepared for the Commonwealth Fund [Cambridge: Harvard University Press, 1958]), pp. 114-15.

42. Chicago Urban League, "Integration in Hospital Appointments and in Hospital Care," Staff Paper prepared for the Second Imhotep National Conference on Hospital Integration, May 23-24, 1958, p. 18. (Mimeographed.)

43. *Ibid.,* p. 17.

44. Cf. Meyerson and Banfield, *op. cit.,* p. 102.

45. On the entire issue, see Marya Mannes, "School Trouble in Harlem," *Reporter,* February 5, 1959, pp. 13-19.

46. On this problem in another context, see David E. Apter, "Political Modernization in Ghana and Uganda — An Essay in Political Anthropology," 1959 (unpublished). Cf. also Georg Simmel, *Conflict and the Web of Group-Affiliations,* trans. K. Wolff and R. Bendix (Glencoe, Ill.: The Free Press, 1955), pp. 39-40, on the consequences of "supraindividual goals."

Chapter IX

1. Cf. the distinction between the "ethic of ultimate ends" and the "ethic of conscience" in Max Weber, "Politics as a Vocation," *From Max Weber,* trans. H. Gerth and C. W. Mills (London: Routledge & Kegan Paul Ltd., 1948), pp. 120ff.

2. Mannheim describes what he calls "utopian thinking" in these terms: "Certain oppressed groups are intellectually so strongly interested in the destruction and transformation of a given condition of society that they unwittingly see only those elements in the situation which tend to negate it. Their thinking is incapable of correctly diagnosing an existing condition of society. . . . Their thought is never

a diagnosis of the situation; it can be used only as a direction for action." Karl Mannheim, *Ideology and Utopia,* trans. Louis Wirth and Edward Shils (New York: Harcourt, Brace and Co., 1936), p. 40.

3. Eric Hoffer compares what is "practical" for the leader with what is "practical" for the man of affairs: Eric Hoffer, *The True Believer* (New York: Harper & Bros., 1951), p. 76.

4. *Chicago Defender,* October 15, 1955.

5. A Negro author describes Adam Clayton Powell's justification for his rather unprogrammatic protest action when he was a member of the New York City Council: "He

frankly says he has no program . . . [but] he insists that his *presence* there is sufficient. For, to the young leader, a public office is a platform and he sounds off regularly in behalf of the Negro." Roi Ottley, *New World A'Coming* (Boston: Houghton Mifflin Co., 1943), p. 234. But protest tactics can sometimes place even a militant leader in a difficult position. Garfinkel, in his study of the March on Washington Movement, notes that the Negro leader, A. Philip Randolph, had to "postpone" rather than cancel the actual March in part to reassure those Negroes who felt let down that there was no "sell-out." Randolph met constraints some of his more ardent followers did not feel, and he wrote to them in words which illuminate the problems of protest action and the valuation placed in the effort itself: Quoted in Herbert Garfinkel, *When Negroes March*, (Glencoe, Ill.: The Free Press, 1959), p. 85.

6. Nelson C. Jackson (Director of Community Services, National Urban League), "An Evaluation of the Chicago Urban League," unpublished typescript, Urban League files, May, 1955.

7. *Chicago Defender,* May 29, 1958.

8. An interesting source of illum-inating comment on this point is contained in the letters to the editor column of the Negro newspaper. The absence of "real" leadership is probably the single most common theme of these correspondents. "Our NAACP here seems too busy giving teas to investigate gross instances of economic discrimination. It seems that we need a more militant organization. We have no leadership in the community." *Daily Defender,* August 21, 1958. "Most of our so-called leaders have integrated and slammed the door and left us outside, yet they call themselves leaders. . . . Our so-called leaders . . . are protecting their investment in their education and their social standing." *Daily Defender,* September 1, 1958.

9. See Wilson Record, *The Negro and the Communist Party* (Chapel Hill: University of North Carolina Press, 1951).

10. One should not underestimate the important and often brilliant role played by Negro lawyers in race litigation. For an excellent discussion of NAACP legal strategy, see Clement E. Vose, "NAACP Strategy in the Covenant Cases," *Western Reserve Law Review,* VI (Winter, 1955), 101-45.

11. See James Coleman, *Community Conflict* (Glencoe, Ill.: The Free Press, 1957).

Chapter X

1. Cf., E. C. Banfield, "The Concept 'Leadership' in Community Research," unpublished paper read at the September, 1958, convention of the American Political Science Association.

2. See editorials in the daily and weekly editions of the *Chicago Defender* on April 25, 1958, May 4, 1958, July 23, 1958, July 26, 1958, September 29, 1958, October 4, 1958, October 21, 1958, and January 31, 1959.

3. *Daily Defender,* January 20, 1959.

4. *Chicago Defender,* January 24, 1959.

5. Martin Meyerson and Edward C. Banfield, *Politics, Planning and The Public Interest* (Glencoe, Ill.: The Free Press, 1955), pp. 42-43 and entries under "Taylor" in the index.

6. Letter printed in the *New Crusader,* July 5, 1958, p. 10.

7. *Daily Defender,* January 26, 1959.

8. *Chicago Sun-Times,* April 22, 1958.

9. *Chicago Defender,* February 8, 1959.

10. It is interesting to note that in December, 1959, Travis defeated Bullock for the presidency of the Chicago NAACP. Travis had busi- ness and political support; Bullock, the backing of white and Negro liberals.

11. *Daily Defender,* December 18, 1958.

12. *Daily Defender,* December 14, 1958.

13. *Daily Defender,* December 25, 1958.

14. *Chicago Defender,* October 11, 1958.

Chapter XI

1. Cf. Gunnar Myrdal, *An American Dilemma* (New York: Harper & Bros., 1944), pp. 831ff.

2. The income for the Chicago branch of the NAACP during the year 1958-59 was approximately as follows: From the sale of memberships, $40,000; Freedom Fund Dinner, $20,000; Tag Day, $4,000; Annual Tea, $7,000. Of the $71,000 total, over half was sent to the national office. This total was an all-time high.

3. In Philip Selznick, *Leadership in Administration* (Evanston, Ill.: Row, Peterson & Co., 1957), pp. 52-53, there is an interesting discussion of the "distinctive competence" of the NAACP as an organization which fits it for legal action but not for mass action. The inability of the NAACP to lead mass action is suggested in Martin Luther King, *Stride Toward Freedom: The Montgomery Story* (New York; Harper & Bros., 1958), pp. 34-35, and brought out explicitly in a discussion of the conflict between the NAACP and Rev. King contained in Paul Jacobs, "The NAACP's New Direction," *New Republic,* July 16, 1956, pp. 9-11. All these sources note the fact that local NAACP organizations are largely "dues-collecting stations" for the national headquarters, are supported mostly by middle-class Negroes, and have lost most of their initially heavy white membership. The Chicago branch of the NAACP has been struggling to solve its internal difficulties and at the same time define a role for itself in community civic action, but it has been unsuccessful so far in both areas. Meanwhile, the initiative has passed to the staff of the Chicago Urban League which, of course, has a different "distinctive competence" — one which fits it for research, persuasion, community liaison, and public relations work.

3. March and Simon make this point explicitly in a discussion of the sources of intraorganizational conflict. I have used several of their phrases here, although they state the proposition much more formally than I: "We can predict directly that organizational conflict of the intraindividual type is most likely to occur when the conditions surrounding the organizational decision involve widespread uncertainty or a scarcity of acceptable alternatives of action." James G. March and Herbert A. Simon, *Organizations* (New York: John Wiley & Sons, 1958), p. 119.

Chapter XII

1. On this see my article, "Two Negro Politicians: An Interpretation," *Midwest Journal of Political Science* (forthcoming) and the discussion in H. D. Price, "The Negro and Florida Politics, 1944-1954," *Journal of Politics,* XVII (May, 1955), pp. 198-220, and H. D. Price, *The Negro and Southern Politics* (New York: New York University Press, 1957). On white tendencies to impute influence to Negro ministers, see Floyd Hunter, *Community Power Structure* (Chapel Hill: University of North Carolina Press, 1953).

2. I have developed some aspects of this problem more fully in "The Strategy of Protest" (mimeographed, March, 1960).

3. The ability of the "new" Negro leaders to sustain professionally-staffed voluntary associations is, of course, limited by the resources of the community. The recent sharp rise in the budgets of the local NAACP and Urban League suggest that these resources were underused in the past. In 1950, the U. S. Census reported the number of males in each state with incomes of $10,000 per year or more, distinguished by race. (The figures are based on a 20 per cent sample of the population.)

Between 1950 and 1956, a marked rise in Negro income occurred. The National Housing Inventory of 1956 (U. S. Bureau of the Census, *National Housing Inventory: Chicago*

| | $10,000 a year or more | | Median income males | |
State	White males	Negro males	White males	Negro males
California ..	92,415	335	$2,966	$2,121
Illinois	71,590	365	3,030	2,260
Massachusetts	28,435	25	2,630	1,944
Michigan	37,230	250	3,039	2,659
New York ...	138,865	410	2,929	2,097

Supplement, Bulletin No. 4), based on a sample of households, estimated that there were 5,897 Negro families in Chicago with an income of $10,000 per year or more. Even though the reporting units are different (households rather than males) and the areas are dissimilar (Chicago rather than Illinois), the differences in higher incomes between 1950 and 1956 are undoubtedly significant.

4. Cf. Herbert Garfinkel, *When Negroes March* (Glencoe, Ill.: The Free Press, 1959), pp. 181-82 on

this same point.

5. Peter Rossi, "The Study of Decision-Making in the Local Community," August, 1957 (mimeographed), pp. 3-4.

6. In New York, for example, many Harlem politicians complain of the apparently greater access and influence enjoyed by the Negro executive director of the Urban League to the Mayor and the large number of attractive positions given to Negroes on League recommendations.

INDEX

335